Blockchain Applications in IoT Security

Harshita Patel
Vellore Institute of Technology, India

Ghanshyam Singh Thakur
Maulana Azad National Institute of Technology, India

A volume in the Advances in
Information Security, Privacy, and
Ethics (AISPE) Book Series

Published in the United States of America by
IGI Global
Information Science Reference (an imprint of IGI Global)
701 E. Chocolate Avenue
Hershey PA, USA 17033
Tel: 717-533-8845
Fax: 717-533-8661
E-mail: cust@igi-global.com
Web site: http://www.igi-global.com

Library of Congress Cataloging-in-Publication Data

Names: Patel, Harshita, 1985- editor. I Thakur, Ghanshyam Singh, 1976-
    editor.
Title: Blockchain applications in IoT security / Harshita Patel and
    Ghanshyam Singh Thakur, editors.
Description: Hershey, PA : Information Science Reference, an imprint of IGI
    Global, 2020. I Includes bibliographical references and index. I
    Summary: "This book examines the role of blockchain technology in IoT
    generated data security issues"-- Provided by publisher.
Identifiers: LCCN 2019039207 (print) I LCCN 2019039208 (ebook) I ISBN
    9781799824145 (hardcover) I ISBN 9781799824152 (paperback) I ISBN
    9781799824169 (ebook)
Subjects: LCSH: Internet of things--Security measures. I Blockchains
    (Databases)
Classification: LCC TK5105.8857 .B58 2020 (print) I LCC TK5105.8857
    (ebook) I DDC 005.8/2--dc23
LC record available at https://lccn.loc.gov/2019039207
LC ebook record available at https://lccn.loc.gov/2019039208

This book is published in the IGI Global book series Advances in Information Security, Privacy,
and Ethics (AISPE) (ISSN: 1948-9730; eISSN: 1948-9749)

British Cataloguing in Publication Data
A Cataloguing in Publication record for this book is available from the British Library.

All work contributed to this book is new, previously-unpublished material.
The views expressed in this book are those of the authors, but not necessarily of the publisher.

For electronic access to this publication, please contact: eresources@igi-global.com.

Advances in Information Security, Privacy, and Ethics (AISPE) Book Series

ISSN:1948-9730
EISSN:1948-9749

Editor-in-Chief: Manish Gupta, State University of New York, USA

MISSION

As digital technologies become more pervasive in everyday life and the Internet is utilized in ever increasing ways by both private and public entities, concern over digital threats becomes more prevalent.

The **Advances in Information Security, Privacy, & Ethics (AISPE) Book Series** provides cutting-edge research on the protection and misuse of information and technology across various industries and settings. Comprised of scholarly research on topics such as identity management, cryptography, system security, authentication, and data protection, this book series is ideal for reference by IT professionals, academicians, and upper-level students.

COVERAGE

- Internet Governance
- Security Information Management
- Privacy-Enhancing Technologies
- Electronic Mail Security
- Technoethics
- Risk Management
- Network Security Services
- Computer ethics
- Device Fingerprinting
- Information Security Standards

IGI Global is currently accepting manuscripts for publication within this series. To submit a proposal for a volume in this series, please contact our Acquisition Editors at Acquisitions@igi-global.com or visit: http://www.igi-global.com/publish/.

Titles in this Series

For a list of additional titles in this series, please visit:
https://www.igi-global.com/book-series/advances-information-security-privacy-ethics/37157

Large-Scale Data Streaming, Processing, and Blockchain Security
Hemraj Saini (Jaypee University of Information Technology, India) Geetanjali Rathee (Jaypee University of Information Technology, India) and Dinesh Kumar Saini (Sohar University, Oman)
Information Science Reference • © 2021 • 285pp • H/C (ISBN: 9781799834441) • US $225.00

Privacy Concerns Surrounding Personal Information Sharing on Health and Fitness Mobile Apps
Devjani Sen (Algonquin College, Canada) and Rukhsana Ahmed (University at Albany, SUNY, USA)
Information Science Reference • © 2021 • 300pp • H/C (ISBN: 9781799834878) • US $215.00

Establishing Cyber Security Programs Through the Community Cyber Security Maturity Model (CCSMM)
Gregory B. White (CIAS, The University of Texas at San Antonio, USA) and Natalie Sjelin (CIAS, The University of Texas at San Antonio, USA)
Information Science Reference • © 2021 • 221pp • H/C (ISBN: 9781799844716) • US $195.00

Applied Approach to Privacy and Security for the Internet of Things
Parag Chatterjee (National Technological University, Argentina & University of the Republic, Uruguay) Emmanuel Benoist (Bern University of Applied Sciences, Switzerland) and Asoke Nath (St. Xavier's College, Kolkata, India)
Information Science Reference • © 2020 • 295pp • H/C (ISBN: 9781799824442) • US $235.00

Advanced Localization Algorithms for Wireless Sensor Networks
M. Vasim Babu (Institute of Technology and Sciences, India)
Information Science Reference • © 2020 • 300pp • H/C (ISBN: 9781799837336) • US $195.00

701 East Chocolate Avenue, Hershey, PA 17033, USA
Tel: 717-533-8845 x100 • Fax: 717-533-8661
E-Mail: cust@igi-global.com • www.igi-global.com

Table of Contents

Detailed Table of Contents

Chapter 1

Padmavathi U., National Institute of Technology, Puducherry, India
Narendran Rajagopalan, National Institute of Technology, Puducherry, India

Blockchain refers to a distributed ledger technology that helps people to regulate and manage their information without any intermediaries. This technology emerges as a promising panacea for authentication and authorization with potential for use in every possible domain including financial, manufacturing, educational institutions, etc. Blockchain has its birth through the concept of Bitcoin, a digital cryptocurrency by Satoshi Nakamoto, called as Blockchain 1.0. Blockchain 2.0 came into existence in 2014 with Ethereum and smart contracts. The challenges such as scalability, interoperability, sustainability, and governance led to the next generation of Blockchain also called as IOTA, a blockchainless cryptocurrency for the internet of things runs on the top of their own ledger called Tangle, which is immune towards quantum computers. This disruptive technology evolved to provide cross chain support and more security through Blockchain 4.0. Finally, the chapter concludes by discussing the various applications of this technology and its advantages and security issues.

Chapter 2

Mohd Azeem Faizi Noor, Jamia Millia Islamia, India
Saba Khanum, Jamia Millia Islamia, India
Taushif Anwar, Pondicherry University, India
Manzoor Ansari, Jamia Millia Islamia, India

Blockchain, the technology behind most popular cryptocurrency Bitcoin and Ethereum, has attracted wide attention recently. It is the most emerging technology that has changed the financial and non-financial transaction system. It is omnipresent.

Currently, this technology is enforcing banks, industries, and countries to adopt it in their financial, industrial, and government section. Earlier, it solved the centralize and double-spending problems successfully. In this chapter, the authors present a study of blockchain security issues and its challenges as well. They divided the whole chapter into two parts. The primer part covers a holistic overview of blockchain followed by the later section that argues about basic operations, 51% attack, scalability issue, Fork, Sharding, Lightening, etc. Finally, they mention an intro about its adaptation (financial or non-financial) in our 24/7 life and collaboration with fields like IoT.

Chapter 3

Vinod Kumar, Madanapalle Institute of Technology and Science, India
Gotam Singh Lalotra, Government Degree College for Women, Kathua, India

This century is the time of ubiquitous, smart, and intelligent devices. These devices have a wide variety of applications in different fields like business, manufacturing, healthcare, retail, education, security, transportation, etc. Internet of things is now becoming the inexorable part of the all these fields. But security has always been a major concern in embracing these technologies. The blockchain technology is the next frontier for securing the internet of things. It will play a pivotal role to secure the communication in internet of things ecosystem. This chapter discusses the blockchain-enabled secure internet of things (IoT).

Chapter 4

Sreelakshmi K. K., Department of Computer Science and Information Systems, Birla Institute of Technology and Science, Pilani, India
Ashutosh Bhatia, Department of Computer Science and Information Systems, Birla Institute of Technology and Science, Pilani, India
Ankit Agrawal, Department of Computer Science and Information Systems, Birla Institute of Technology and Science, Pilani, India

The internet of things (IoT) has become a guiding technology behind automation and smart computing. One of the major concerns with the IoT systems is the lack of privacy and security preserving schemes for controlling access and ensuring the security of the data. A majority of security issues arise because of the centralized architecture of IoT systems. Another concern is the lack of proper authentication and access control schemes to moderate access to information generated by the IoT devices. So the question that arises is how to ensure the identity of the equipment or the communicating node. The answer to secure operations in a trustless environment brings us to the decentralized solution of Blockchain. A lot of research has been going on in the area of convergence of IoT and Blockchain, and it has resulted in some remarkable progress in addressing some of the significant issues in the IoT arena. This work reviews the challenges and threats in the IoT environment and how integration with Blockchain can resolve some of them.

Chapter 5

Dharmendra Singh Rajput, Vellore Institute of Technology, India
Pankaj Shukla, Vellore Institute of Technology, India
Thippa Reddy G., Vellore Institute of Technology, India
Rajesh Kaluri, Vellore Institute of Technology, India
Kuruva Lakshmanna, Vellore Institute of Technology, India
Praveen Kumar Reddy Kumar Maddikunta, Vellore Institute of
    Technology, India
Harshita Patel, Vellore Institute of Technology, India

In today's world, security has become a major issue in our lives, and in this era, one cannot trust the government for handling their lifetime savings. That's where the bitcoin comes to our lives. In this chapter, the authors try to understand one of the famous innovative payment methods (Bitcoin), how it is used and the data structure (Merkle tree) that is used in it. Also, they discuss one of the most recent attacks that involved the use of bitcoin (Wanacry). Further, they try to understand how this hack succeeded in stealing 10,800 euros that is 8,74,290 rs from the hospital with the help of bitcoin. They also discuss the various bitcoin companies now emerging with their own security measures against such hacks.

Chapter 6

Neha Gupta, Symbiosis University of Applied Sciences, Indore, India

Wireless communication networks are highly prone to security threats. The major applications of wireless communication networks are in military, business, healthcare, retail, and transportations. These systems use wired, cellular, or adhoc networks. Wireless sensor networks, actuator networks, and vehicular networks have received a great attention in society and industry. In recent years, the internet of things (IoT) has received considerable research attention. The IoT is considered as future of the internet. In the future, IoT will play a vital role and will change our living styles, standards, as well as business models. The usage of IoT in different applications is expected to rise rapidly in the coming years. The IoT allows billions of devices, peoples, and services to connect with others and exchange information. Due to the increased usage of IoT devices, the IoT networks are prone to various security attacks.

Chapter 7

Manjula Josephine Bollarapu, Koneru Lakshmaiah Education
Foundation, India
Ruth Ramya Kalangi, Koneru Lakshmaiah Education Foundation, India
K. V. S. N. Rama Rao, Koneru Lakshmaiah Education Foundation, India

In recent years, blockchain technology has attracted considerable attention. As blockchain is one of the revolutionary technologies that is impacting various industries in the market now with its unique features of decentralization, transparency, and incredible security. Blockchain technology can be used for anything which requires their transactions to be recorded in a secure manner. In this chapter, the authors survey the importance of the blockchain technology and the applications that are being developed on the basis of blockchain technology in area of IoT and security.

Chapter 8

Harsha Kundan Patil, Ashoka Center for Business and Computer
Studies, Nashik, India

"Blockchain" as the name suggests is the chain of blocks. It is the chunk of digital information (blocks) that are connected through the public databases (Chain). It is nothing but the newer version of file organisation. Blocks store digital information like actual record of any transaction, details of involve entities in the transaction, time stamps, and other metadata of the transactions. Blocks also have unique ids, which are known as hash. Blockchain technology is built using peer-to-peer networking. Anyone who is on network can access the blocks. There is no centralised community to control the blockchain. It is operated by miners, the peoples who lend their computing power to the network to solve the complex computation algorithm problems. These blocks are stored in multiple computers. Due to its distribution and decentralisation, the validation process is broadcast in nature, which provides it "the trusted approach". Blockchain enables security and tamperproof capabilities for storing data and smart contracts. Any tampering of data attempted by a node or user in a block changes the hash of the block. The blockchain technology has the capability to face and provides the solution to fight with the problem of risk and security concern online. In 2008, a mysterious white paper titled "Bitcoin: A Peer to Peer Electronic Cash System", by visionary Satoshi Nakamoto gave birth to the concept of blockchain. The chapter explains the structure of blockchain technology in detail and enlighten the aspects that make blockchain technology the secure concept of today's world.

Blockchain, as the name suggests, is a linear chain of blocks. It is a digital ledger that holds information on transactions taking place over the web. So every block contains data in the form of coding that is organized in a chronological manner. In 2004, a concept called "reusable proofs of work" was introduced by Hal Finney. In 2009, a mysterious white paper titled "Bitcoin: A Peer to Peer Electronic Cash System," by visionary Satoshi Nakamoto gave birth to the concept of blockchain. This is a survey of blockchain technology that first provides a short introduction of the blockchain, discussing its advantages and followed by possible limitations and their possibilities for the future.

Chapter 10

Adoption of the internet of things (IoT) and blockchain technology opens new opportunities of business process automation in apparel supply chain management. The IoT technology helps to capture real-time information from different aspects of garment manufacturing activities by using radio frequency identification (RFID) tags and sensors. Blockchain technology is an emerging concept of computing that enable the decentralized and immutable storage of business transactions. In combination with IoT, blockchain technology can enable a broad range of application scenarios to enhance business value and trust. This chapter presents some of the blockchain-based IoT technology applications in apparel business processes. Moreover, the chapter provides a classification of threat models, which are considered by blockchain protocols in IoT networks. Finally, the chapter provides a taxonomy and a side-by-side comparison of the state-of-the-art methods towards secure and privacy-preserving blockchain technologies concerning the blockchain model, specific security goals, performance, and limitations.

Internet of things (IoT) is a collection of smart equipment that creates a smart world. It has not just changed the way we interact with important devices but has also enhanced the potential of these devices. A major limitation of IoT is that it relies on centralized communication models. Traditional IoT solutions require high infrastructure and maintenance costs, which result in scalability problems. Moreover, the vulnerability of cloud servers and their failure can affect the IoT system. There is still no one platform that connects all devices. The peer-to-peer communication model instead of the standard server/client one can be the sustainable solution the IoT industry is looking for. The major challenge with the peer-to-peer networks is security. This is where the use of blockchain in IoT can help the IoT industry scale up in a sustainable way. Indeed, blockchain and IoT together can handle a portion of IoT's greatest difficulties. The main objective of this chapter is to provide an overview of IoT and Blockchain in Indian perspectives.

Chapter 12
Integrate Hybrid Cloud Computing Server With Automated Remote
Rohit Sansiya, Maulana Azad National Institute of Technology, India
Pushpendra Kumar, Central University of Jharkhand, India
Ramjeevan Singh Thakur, Maulana Azad National Institute of
Technology, India
Abdulhai Mohammadi, Maulana Azad National Institute of Technology,
India

Blockchain is also used for bitcoin transactions as a technology for accumulating data files in the cloud for key distribution and file manipulation in distributed fashion. It is a service of cloud that manages elasticity of compute cloud, storage, and technology of network security (i.e., secure solution to store and share information by offering a distributed ledger service). In distributed systems, abandoned events are much more frequent than centralized system. This concept causes a number of issues including data reliability, high economical cost, and information system security. In this chapter, the authors present a new framework in blockchain to supervise the cloud server for administration of blockchain, which is verified the transaction reliability in peer-to-peer networks for sharing of data files in centralized manner. Each transaction can be generated keys for server authentication to verify all the connected members for monitoring the web server.

Preface

Blockchain and internet of things are two very popular and powerful technological names which have proven their significance already in various fields. Blockchain came into existence for the security of a magical cryptocurrency 'Bitcoin' while internet of things is justifying its name itself. Internet of Things is a rapidly growing, easy to use technology and also had achieved the popularity in remarkably short period; it has covered almost every arena of life. Internet of things is now involved from day to day life to high end technical scenarios, so security becomes a crucial issue. This security issue is an expanded term, as security and privacy of all stakeholders, device security, prevention from hacking and malfunctioning etc. No technology could be assumed without data now, so obviously data security is one important issue to take care about. This book is designed to discuss the blockchain application for securing Internet of things. For reading convenience we will use the commonly known substitution 'IoT' for Internet of Things. We have received good contribution from the community. Authors of chapter of this book are from research and academia and their work shows the soundness of knowledge. Chapters consisted in this book are well written, easy to grasp and technically rich. They exhibit knowledge about these two technologies, explaining them in different aspects. Overview of the chapters is given here.

Chapter 1: Blockchain Concept and Emergence

Authors of this chapter have shown their keen observation on the knowledge available around about the blockchain technology. They have shown the emergence of blockchain chronologically followed by the systematic theoretical discussion. After detailed description of the types and versions of blockchain, authors have shown various applications of blockchain too such as finance, healthcare etc. Also they discussed the advantages and security issues of blockchain.

Chapter 2: A Holistic View on Blockchain and Its Issues

As the name suggests, the chapter provides a holistic view on block chain technology. Authors have thoroughly discussed the technology, from emergence to compatibility in present scenario. They described characteristics, types and different consensus of blockchain in detail. After making a better understating on working of blockchain authors have shown the various challenges too in a very descriptive way. Beauty of this chapter is its proper writing flow and informative figures. Study of this chapter itself is a gateway to go deeper into the technology.

Chapter 3: Blockchain-Enabled Secure Internet of Things

The chapter is exact detailing of its title, started with the discussion on Internet of Things, authors have moved one by one to the all essential aspects. After settling the better understanding on IoT concept, devices and its application deployment they have given a much needed overview of blockchain technology and argued that how blockchain can help to solve security issues of IoT.

Chapter 4: Securing IoT Applications Using Blockchain

Authors have deeply evaluated the security issue of IoT and deployment of blockchain for such purpose. In a descriptive review of IoT and blockchain they have included imperative chunks of work of researchers. They concluded that for every IoT application, blockchain may not be needed so careful assessment is required before applying blockchain. It can save resources and reduce complexity.

Chapter 5: A Review on Bitcoin and Currency Encryption

Bitcoin is a very popular and game changing cryptocurrency of modern electronic -financial world. With the concept of removal of intermediaries or third parties and enabling peer-topeer transactions endorsed this popularity of bicoin. Authors of this chapter have provided systematic description of bitcoin concept, pros, cons and other technical details. They explained, when security issue came into picture and how it affected organizations and individuals involved in bitcoin transactions. This need of security brought Blockchain into existence.

Chapter 6: Security Issues of IoT

Security requirements of IoT are deliberated here in this chapter such as data authentication, access control, client privacy, threat etc. After taking IoT challenges into account cyber security and privacy related information is shared. Smart home is taken as the primary example of IoT application and its security is discussed in detail. Chapter is concluded with IoT identity protection.

Chapter 7: A Review on Importance of Blockchain and Its Current Applications in IoT Security

This chapter is providing a detailed literature review on blockchain technology and its applications in IoT security. Authors began their study from blockchain based decentralized framework for IoT forensics investigations followed by various other IoT applications to be secured. Chapter is basically intended to exhibit the important role of blockchain in securing different IoT applications.

Chapter 8: Blockchain Technology-Security Booster

The chapter is another beautiful description of blockchain technology as a security booster. Author has arranged all the key points very systematically and used decent flow charts and figurers to show the technology astutely. Blockchain is discussed from its beginning to recent usage nicely. This step wise study is giving opportunities to readers for getting better understating on how blockchain is not limited to cryptocurrency but helping to maintain IoT security, now in wider way.

Chapter 9: Blockchain Technology Limitations and Future Possibilities

In continuation with the previous chapters on blockchain, this chapter is talking about limitations and future possibilities of blockchain technology. Authors have discussed limitations preceded by advantages of blockchain. In limitations they have mentioned Weak performance, Signature verification, Redundancy, Energy and resource consumption, Security Pitfall, System failures, Attaining consensus etc. At the end they provided future possibilities of blockchain in different fields.

Chapter 10: Blockchain Technology for the Internet of Things Applications in Apparel Supply Chain Management

This chapter is a perfect exhibition of supply chain management in apparel industry. It is mentioned wisely that how this industry embracing the new and advanced technologies, IoT is one of them. Chapter is meticulously showing the various aspects of IoT in apparel supply chain. Then authors has stated the various challenges of using

IoT and emphasized on security and privacy of all stakeholders. They have shown how blockchain is helping this industry to keep security and privacy up to the mark.

Chapter 11: IoT and Blockchain in Indian Perspective

The chapter is chattering about IoT and Blockchain in Indian Perspective. India is one of the leading countries in technology, well known for its IT products and services, also a big market for IoT. In this chapter authors have shown how IT industry affects Indian economy, when comes to IoT, they are comparing global scenario with Indian market and argued that how India is consuming a big portion of total of world's economy for IoT. After this various industry wise technology usage explained in analytical way.

Chapter 12: Integrate Hybrid Cloud Computing Server With Automated Remote Monitoring for Blockchain as a Service

The chapter talks about integrated hybrid cloud computing server with automated remote monitoring for blockchain as a service. Though it is about cloud-based systems, blockchain is playing a vital role in maintaining security, thus the chapter is opening a gateway for more study in such direction. Authors have mentioned that blockchain as a service is a third-party modelling of cloud-based networks management for organizations in blockchain applications.

Chapter 1
Concept of Blockchain Technology and Its Emergence

Padmavathi U.
National Institute of Technology, Puducherry, India

Narendran Rajagopalan
National Institute of Technology, Puducherry, India

ABSTRACT

Blockchain refers to a distributed ledger technology that helps people to regulate and manage their information without any intermediaries. This technology emerges as a promising panacea for authentication and authorization with potential for use in every possible domain including financial, manufacturing, educational institutions, etc. Blockchain has its birth through the concept of Bitcoin, a digital cryptocurrency by Satoshi Nakamoto, called as Blockchain 1.0. Blockchain 2.0 came into existence in 2014 with Ethereum and smart contracts. The challenges such as scalability, interoperability, sustainability, and governance led to the next generation of Blockchain also called as IOTA, a blockchainless cryptocurrency for the internet of things runs on the top of their own ledger called Tangle, which is immune towards quantum computers. This disruptive technology evolved to provide cross chain support and more security through Blockchain 4.0. Finally, the chapter concludes by discussing the various applications of this technology and its advantages and security issues.

DOI: 10.4018/978-1-7998-2414-5.ch001

EMERGENCE OF BLOCKCHAIN

Blockchain, the underlying technology behind cryptocurrencies has its origin that stem from a problem of verifying timestamp digitally in the late 1980s and early 1990s. In 1990, Haber & Stornetta published a paper titled 'How to Timestamp a digital Document'. In this paper, they proposed to create a hash chain by linking the issued timestamps together so that the documents get prevented from being either forward dated or back dated. Later in 1992, the concept of Merkle Trees was added to this design by Haber, Stornetta and Dave Bayer. Merkle trees helped to improve the efficiency of the system by collecting several time-stamped documents into a cryptographically secured chain of blocks. Each record in this chain is connected to the one before it. This helps the newest record to know the history of entire chain. Then, Wei Dai one of the noted researchers, introduced the concept of b-money which is used to create money through solving computational puzzles and decentralized consensus. But this proposal lacks implementation details. (Blockchain, an emerging technology for the future - Data Driven Investor - Medium n.d.)(The Exponential Guide to Blockchain - Singularity University n.d.)(History of blockchain I Technology I ICAEW n.d.)

(A brief history in the evolution of blockchain technology platforms - By n.d.)In 2005, a concept called "Reusable Proof of Work" (RPoW) was introduced by Hal Finney, a cryptographic activist. This concept combined the ideas of both b-money and computationally difficult Hashcash puzzle by Adam Back for the creation of cryptocurrency. RPoW registers the ownership of tokens on a trusted server. These servers allow the users to check the correctness and integrity of users which in turn helps to solve double spending problem. (History of Blockchain I Binance Academy n.d.)

In 2008, a mysterious white paper titled "Bitcoin: A peer to peer Electronic Cash system", by visionary Satoshi Nakamoto gives birth to the concept of Blockchain. In this paper, Nakamoto combined cryptography, computer science and game theory to describe the digital cash "Bitcoin". This helps the participant to transact from one account to another account without the help of intermediaries such as central authority or bank. (A Brief History of Blockchain: Blockchain Basics Book from ConsenSys Academy n.d.) The following timeline table gives a brief explanation on the emergence of blockchain.

Concept of Blockchain

As the world needs more modernization and digitization, everyone is ready to accept and adapt new technologies(Blockchain Technology Explained: Introduction, Meaning, and Applications - By n.d.). Blockchain, a new disruptive technology was

Table 1. Timeline for the Emergence of Blockchain

Year	Emergence of Blockchain
1990	Stuart Haber & Stornetta introduced timestamping a digital document so that they could not be tampered.
1992	The concept of Merkle trees was proposed to collect several documents in one block.
2000	The theory and idea of cryptographic secured chains was proposed by Stefen Konst
2005	Hal Finney introduced "Reusable Proof of Work" (RPoW) that helps users to solve double spending problem in the creation of cryptocurrencies.
2008	Satoshi Nakamoto Proposed Bitcoin, a digital currency which makes use of Blockchain as the underlying concept.

introduced with its very first modern application termed Bitcoin. The term Blockchain is simply defined as the chain of blocks containing encrypted information stored on a decentralized distributed network. This blossoming technology impacts various industries miraculously and its application grows numerously.

Blockchain, a shared ledger in which all the data are recorded digitally has a common history and is available to all the participants in the network. This eliminates any fraudulent activity or duplication of transactions(Blockchain Technology for the Transportation Industry: Where the Future Starts n.d.).

A blockchain is a chain of blocks. Each block contains encrypted information and hashed pointers to previous block, making it difficult to retroactively alter without modifying the entire chain (What's inside a Block on the Blockchain? n.d.). The first block is called genesis block. Every block contains two components. They are

Block Header
Block Body

Block Header

It is a bunch of metadata about the block. The various components present in the block header is

Version: The Block version number
Hash of the previous block: Used to make connection between the blocks
Merkle root: The hash of all the transactions inside the block
Time: Timestamp of the block
Target or difficulty: A value used to regulate blocks
Nonce: An arbitrary number used once to solve cryptographic puzzle.

Figure 1. Block Header in Blockchain(What Is Hashing? [Step-by-Step Guide-Under Hood Of Blockchain] n.d.)

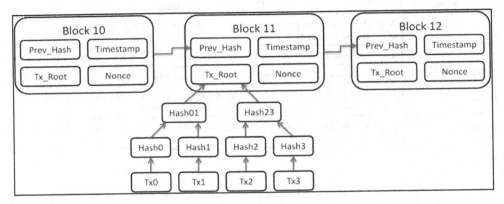

The Block header looks as follows

Block Body

It contains all the transactions the are confirmed in the block. Each transaction contains a set of entries and one transaction header which references to other entries in the transaction. Every entry in transaction is identified by its unique ID.

How Does Blockchain Work?

1. A transaction must occur.
2. The transaction must be verified.
3. The transaction must be stored in a block.
4. The block must be given a hash. After hashing, the block can be added to the blockchain.

For example, suppose if we want to add a purchase transaction to the blockchain, then it could be done as follows. Initially a purchase has to be made. After the purchase is made, the transaction details such as transaction time, amount and participants has to be verified. The verified transaction is now stored in the block. Then, the block is given is a unique hash and is added to the blockchain(Blockchain: Everything You Need to Know n.d.).

Types and Versions of Blockchain

More types of Blockchains are required in order to solve problems such as reliability on huge servers, need for trusted parties, cost effective transaction processing and so on. In General, there are three different types of Blockchain(6 Essential Blockchain Technology Concepts You Need To Know n.d.). They are

1. Public Blockchain
2. Private Blockchain
3. Federated or Consortium Blockchain

Public Blockchain

It is a fully decentralized network in which only the transaction information is completely viewable to the public. In this type of Blockchain, any user can join the network at any time and they can store, send and receive data at any time and anywhere. This feature of Public Blockchain network makes it call as Permissionless network. The participants in this network gets incentivized and rewarded using the token associated with them. Various decentralized consensus mechanisms such as PoW, PoS are used to make decisions(What are the Different Types of Blockchain? n.d.).

Public Blockchain networks provide self-governance and higher level of security since all the transaction information are present in all the nodes in the network which makes hacking a particular node impossible.

Example: Bitcoin, Litecoin.

Private Blockchain

Private Blockchain usually called Permissioned Blockchain are used within an organization in which the participants need consent in order to join the network. Private Blockchains are more centralized and the transactions are private. The enterprises that want to collaborate and share data can make use of private blockchains since it provides more efficiency and faster transactions. The code in this type of blockchain is precisely private and hidden which results in eliminating decentralization and disintermediation(3 Types of Blockchain Explained - HedgeTrade Blog n.d.). Here, the central-in-charge helps to achieve consensus by giving the mining rights to anyone in the network.

Example: Bankchain.

Consortium or Federated Blockchain

A hybrid model between public and private Blockchain in which a number of approved users have control over the network. The term consortium is defined as the group of companies or the group of representative individuals who come together to make decisions for the best benefit of the whole network. The consortium blockchain allows only a few selected predetermined parties to verify transactions and to participate in the consensus process instead of allowing any user in the network in case of public blockchain and a single organization in case of private blockchain(The Different Types of Blockchains - ALTCOIN MAGAZINE - Medium n.d.).

Example: r3, EWF

In a nutshell, we can conclude that Public Blockchain is a good option where openness and censorship resistance is needed and Private and Consortium Blockchain fits where privacy and control is required.

Blockchain Version

Figure 2. Versions of Blockchain(ICO InterValue - World's First Practical Blockchain 4.0 Project — Steemit n.d.)

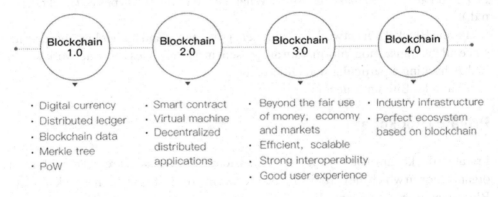

Blockchain 1.0

Blockchain born with the concept of Bitcoin(Blockchain Version - Javatpoint n.d.). Blockchain 1.0 represents the application of Distributed Ledger Technology over cryptocurrencies for transfer of values and to confirm transactions. Bitcoin, developed as a decentralized, peer-to-peer digital cash system comes as a result of 20 years of research in cryptocurrency and 40 years of research in cryptography. A core breakthrough in computer science comes as a long-standing solution to the issues associated with digital cash. With bitcoin, users are able to receive funds in digital wallets immediately without waiting for days for transfers. Blockchain currencies assures that any transaction can be sourced and completed directly without the involvement of any third parties intermediary.

Blockchain 2.0

In order to overcome the issues such as wasteful mining, lack of network scalability that come with the concept of Bitcoin, one visionary named Vitalik Buterin extends this concept beyond currency and proposed a platform called 'smart contracts' where the developer's community can build distributed applications (DApps) for the Blockchain network. Smart Contracts are small computer programs that are deployed on the Blockchain are usually triggered by events. These smart contracts can perform tasks automatically which in turn eliminates the need to manage time consuming and costly manual business processes. A most prominent example is the Ethereum Blockchain network. It is impossible to tamper or hack smart contracts. It reduces the cost of verification, execution and allows transparent definition overcoming moral hazard problems. This version of Blockchain successfully processes a high number of transactions than version 1.0.

Blockchain 3.0

Many new technologies such as NEO, IOTA and EOS want to improve the capabilities of Blockchain 1.0 and Blockchain 2.0. This gives birth to Blockchain 3.0 which focuses to address the issues associated with the previous versions. For this, Blockchain 3.0 makes use of different protocols, techniques and frameworks. It avoids centralized architecture and employs decentralized storage and communication. The scalability problem that persisted from the first generation to second generation of blockchain is resolved in this version using the concept called Tangle. Various features that distinguishes Blockchain 3.0 from previous versions are high scalability, interoperability, adaptability and sustainability(Blockchain: 1.0, 2.0, 3.0 and Future n.d.)(The Future is Here – The Evolution of Blockchain - Toshi Times n.d.).

Blockchain 3.0 mainly focuses on integrating IoT devices with the Blockchain technology. IOTA generally called the Blockless chain was designed for the demanding IoT ecosystem. The following table 2 shows the comparison of blockchain version 1.0, 2.0 and 3.0

Table 2. A comparison on various attributes of Blockchain 1.0, 2.0, 3.0(Padmavathi and Rajagopalan 2019)

Attributes\Blockchain version	Version 1.0 (Bitcoin)	Version 2.0 (Ethereum)	Version 3.0 (IOTA)
Mining	Miners	Miners	Each node
Speed	7 TPS	15 to 20 TPS	Increases as the number of nodes increases.
Language	Stack based	Turing Complete	Turing Complete
Hashing Technique	SHA-256	Ethash	Curl
Reason	Created as an alternative to regular money	Is developed as a platform which facilitiates peer-to-peer contract applications	Is designed as a communication protocolfor IoT
Data Structure	Linked List	Linked list	DAG
Block validation time	10 minutes	14 to 15 seconds	No blocks
Vulnerability	Vulnerable to brute force attacks and quantum computers	Vulnerable to quantum computers	Quantum resistant

Blockchain 4.0

In addition to scalability and safety issues, Blockchain 3.0 lacks business level infrastructure. So, it could not be used for real world business. Moreover, the DApp developers have to work a lot in designing and programming, since everything has to be started from the scratch and there is no service-oriented framework on the base-layer ledger. The next generation of Blockchain is designed in such a way that it tries to solve the problems associated with Blockchain 3.0(What is blockchain 4.0? - Quora n.d.)(TOP Network: The Harbinger of Blockchain 4.0 Era - TOP Network - Medium n.d.).

Blockchain 4.0, a nascent technology brings about lower costs and shorter development cycles, encouraging companies to make use of this technology. In the history of blockchain evolution, Blockchain 4.0 will be the business-accommodating superior public chain that can execute various use cases and applications.

Here are some of the highlights of various Blockchain 4,0 projects

Seele
- Aims to provide unity in the Blockchain platform.
- It enables users to perform cross chain communication.
- Matrix Proof-of-Work Consensus Algorithm.
- On-chain and off-chain sharing.

- Heterogeneous Forest Network.
- Value Internet.
- 2000+ TPS.

Top Network
- Completely Permissionless
- 2-layer sharding, 2-layer lattice DAG, 3-layer network.
- PBFT-DPoS consensus algorithm
- Upto 300,000 TPS

Multiversum
- SQL-based phrase structure
- Proof-of-Integrity consensus algorithm
- Upto 6400 TPS

Metahash
- Provides reliable and quick transactions of any assets
- Multiple Proof-of-Stack consensus algorithm
- 100,000 TPS

InterValue
- Creates infrastructure for Blockchain 4.0
- HashNet Datastructure
- Counterattack to quantum attacks
- Both turing and non-turing language
- 2-layer consensus based on interaction of HashNet and BA-VRF acknowledgement mechanism.
- Upto 1 M TPS

Integrating IoT devices with Blockchain

According to various research reports, there are about 5 billion IoT connected devices today which is predicted to increase up to 50 billion devices by 2022. The IoT devices plays an important role in changing the current world to smart world. As the number of IoT devices continues to proliferate, data verification, transaction verification, access control all become vital. Further, the security breaches of IoT increases due to the gathering of data from different devices at one place, remote control of devices by hackers, managing the devices, lack of ability to find compromised nodes, leakage of sensitive data and other activities. It is an arduous task to overcome the security issues faced by IoT devices(Leading Blockchain Integration With IoT Devices for

Enhanced Security n.d.)(Blockchain IoT: How Will Blockchain Be Integrated Into the Growing Internet-of-Things? n.d.). The problems and security issues with IoT devices could be unlocked if IoT devices becomes decentralized.

Many security experts believe that Blockchain could be the silver bullet needed by the IoT devices to solve its issues. Blockchain when integrated with IoT could improve security and distributed processing power of IoT devices and also solves the problem of cloud-based data monopoly(Blockchain Applications in Internet of Things (IoT) Explained n.d.). Further, the blockchain is able to track and process the massive flow of data that pours from myriad of IoT devices. Blockchain and IoT is viewed as a perfect match since blockchain could solve many of the issues associated with IoT devices.

Even though many of the issues of IoT devices are solved by rapidly accelerating Blockchain technology, the convergence of these two blossoming technologies suffer from certain problems. Since the IoT devices are designed to be light weight and have low processing power, the integration of Blockchain in these devices poses a problem. Also, associated with Blockchain is the scalability issue and sky rocketing fees. So, many companies took convergence of these technologies on their many agenda and starts working on it.

(Elsts, Mitskas, and Oikonomou 2018)IOTA, the Blockchainless cryptocurrency for the Internet of Things is especially being designed for the integration of IoT devices with Blockchain technology. It is a quantum resistant Directed Acyclic Graph (DAG) which works on the top of their own ledger called Tangle. In this graph, nodes are the IOTA transactions and the validation corresponds to edges. Each transaction must validate two other transactions before joining the network. For validation, Proof-of-Work mechanism is used. IOTA is designed to provide zero fee transactions and unique verification process which is able to solve the scalability issues of Blockchain.

DAG differs from other blockchain in such a way that DAG works on 'horizontal' scheme and blockchain is based on 'vertical' scheme and also there are no miners and blocks in DAG, hence the name blocklesschain(Blockchain 3.0 and COTI - Next Generation Technology Without Mining? n.d.). The nature of graph is acyclic and also flows in a specific direction. The transactions in IOTA is not duplicated and there is no wait time for the blocks to be confirmed which in turns reduces the sky rocketing transaction fees. Even though, IOTA tries to be a perfect solution, there exists communication overhead of integrating IoT devices with IOTA blockchain.

Applications of Blockchain

It has become apparent the Blockchain technology has broken shackles and its application stack grows continuously from cryptocurrency to digital identity in the

Internet-of-Things and entered mainstream business operations across industries(Top 10 Blockchain Technology Applications Explained In-Depth n.d.)(20 Real-World Uses for Blockchain Technology | The Motley Fool n.d.)(Blockchain Applications That Are Changing The World | Edureka n.d.).

The following are some of the real-world applications of Blockchain.

1. Finance
2. HealthCare
3. Land Registry
4. Insurance
5. Digital Voting
6. Global Trade
7. Copyright and royalty protection
8. Inheritance
9. Drug traceability
10. Government
11. Supply chain monitoring

Banking

The banking sector is prone to errors and frauds, since it involves handling of money and highly dependent manual networks. More than 40 percent of the financial bodies suffer from heavy economic crimes annually. In order to keep money safe and secure, the financial institutes require mediators in large amount. The involvement of mediators lead to an increase in expenses and an increase in manual processes which in turn increase errors and frauds. Blockchain technology comes as a solution to these issues and helps improve banking services by allowing only authorized participants to access the data. It keeps a log of all the logging transactions thus preventing errors and frauds. The major areas in which Blockchain helps the banking sector is in making faster cross border payments, cheaper KYC and trade finance(Blockchain and Finance: Two Peas in a Pod - Blockgeeks n.d.)(How is Blockchain Revolutionizing Banking and Financial Markets - By n.d.).

Healthcare

Patient data which plays a critical role in Healthcare sector is scattered across different departments in the Hospital. Because of this, the data is not easily accessible at the time of need. In addition, the patient has to waste some time in collecting these data. In order to resolve these issues, Healthcare could be equipped with Blockchain Technology. When Health data is stored on Blockchain technology, it becomes available and accessible to the health care providers as well as patients at any time and at any place.

Land Registry

Land registry involves the transfer of ownership of a land from seller to buyer. Since this process is handled on paper, it leads to many frauds and confusion. Blockchain aims to give crystal clear view of legal ownership by providing 100% computer-based solution instead of paper-based titles.

Insurance

Existing insurance claim processes have high complexity and are more fraudulent. It takes a long time period for the customers to claim their insurance. Blockchain could help solve these issues and also make the process easier. Using this technology, the payers are able to collect the required information automatically and the customers are able to get their claims without any delays.

Digital Voting

Even a single vote can change the fate of a country. Voting plays a critical role in the future of a country. Blockchain technology, if combined with voting could make the voting process transparent and its immutability property make to truly count the votes.

Global Trade

Global trade refers to Exchange of goods, capital and services across different countries. About one-fifth of the cost of transportation is mainly spent on trade documentation. This is because different systems are involved for processing different transactions between various supply chain participants. This cost could be reduced with the help of Blockchain technology, because all the information that needs to documented are stored on blockchain and is shared by everyone in the network.

Wills or Inheritance

The wills documented on a paper may sometimes go into wrong hands and could be used illegally. This could be avoided by storing the wills digitally on a Blockchain network. With the help of smart contracts, the wills become crystal-clear and legally binding without leaving any space for frauds.

Copyright and Royalty Protection

In this growing world of internet access, it is mandatory to have copyright and ownership laws on our digital contents. Real time and transparent royalty protection could be provided with the help of blockchain technology. It ensures the artists and the creator of the content to get their fair share on purchase of their content by others.

Drug Traceability

The problem of counterfeit drugs leads to millions of deaths every year all over the world. Blockchain technology proves itself as a solution to this problem by tracing the drugs from the point of their origin as raw products till it reaches consumers as end-product. The tracking of drugs is done based on their serial and/or batch numbers which in turns ensures that the process is transparent and the consumers get the right deal.

Monitor Supply Chain

It is the process of viewing the performance of the product from the place of its origin till it reaches the retailer. Blockchain helps doing this process in a secure and shared manner. If anybody wants to alter the product on its way to the customer, Blockchain easily identifies and reports it to the producer before the product reaches the customer.

Government

Government sector which work in siloes faces a lot of data transactional challenges. Blockchain technology boasts the power to transform these challenges and enable management of data in an easier and better way. Because of the use of Blockchain technology, the data becomes transparent and monitoring and auditing the transactions become an easier job.

Advantages of Blockchain

The various advantages that are associated with blockchain are as follows: (The Top Advantages Of Blockchain For Businesses n.d.)(5 Big Advantages of Blockchain, and 1 Reason to Be Very Worried | The Motley Fool n.d.)(Top five blockchain benefits transforming your industry - Blockchain Pulse: IBM Blockchain Blog n.d.)(Advantages and Disadvantages Of Blockchain Technology - DataFlair n.d.) (Blockchain Applications and Its Future - By Roger James n.d.)

1. Decentralization

    The lack of central data storage in Blockchain is an exciting feature of this technology that avoids running massive data centers for verifying transactions. It also ensures that, the entire network could not get compromised even if it falls into the hands of wrong persons.

2. Reduced Transaction Costs

    The business-to-business transactions and peer-to-peer transactions that take place in Blockchain network allows for verification and completion without the involvement of middleman. This reduces cost to both users as well as to the businesses over time.

3. Efficiency

    Completing a transaction using traditional paper work processes is exhausting and consumes a large amount of time and man power. Moreover, there are chances for human errors. Blockchain technology helps us to complete the process faster by streamlining and automating transactions. Further, the participants in the network need not maintain multiple documents. Instead, the same single digital ledger is shared by everyone in the network making establishment of trust easier.

4. Traceability

    Monitoring and tracing supply chain of a product from its origin is a complex and tedious process. But, with Blockchain, the tracking of ledger along the chain from its point of origin is made easier. This helps us to learn where a product come from and also helps to locate and correct any problems that come in the path of the product.

5. Security

    Blockchain technology offers high level of security, since all the transactions are added to the blockchain only after maximum trust verification and also every participant in the network is given a unique identity key linked with their account. In addition, the data ledgers are protected using cryptography and the ledgers are dependent on the adjacent block to complete this cryptography process. Further, the transactions are recorded in the chronological order making the blockchain timestamped. This makes tougher for the hacker to hack or disturb the chain.

6.   Faster Processing

In case of traditional banks, it takes lot of time even days to months to initiate and process transactions. This is because the financial institutions across the world are open at different time zones and are functional only during week days. But, after the invention of Blockchain technology, which works 24 hours a day, seven days a week, the processing of transactions is done more quickly. That is, the process gets completed within few minutes or few seconds.

Security Issues in Blockchain Technology

1.   Majority Attack (51% Attack)
2.   Social Engineering Attacks
3.   Software flaws
4.   Malware
5.   Eclipse attacks

51 Percent Attacks

If more than 50 percent of a blockchain's computing power is produced by a hacker, then it is called as 51 percent attack. In this attack, a lie could become a truth if it is said by more than half of the nodes present in the network. Here, the hackers assume control of the entire network and double-spend coins preventing others from creating blocks and transactions. This type of attack was first highlighted by Satoshi Nakamoto in Bitcoin. Smaller Blockchains have high level of risk suffering from this attack(What are Blockchain's Issues and Limitations? - CoinDesk n.d.) (5 Blockchain Problems: Security, Privacy, Legal, Regulatory, and Ethical Issues - Blocks Decoded n.d.).

Social Engineering Attacks

This type of attack is almost very common in all fields. Its main goal is to fetch the private key or login information of the user. Phishing is one of the most popular social engineering attacks. In phishing, a malicious actor sends the victim a mail or a message or sets up a website or social media and asks you to send your credentials immediately. If we give all our credentials to them, then it would be highly impossible to stop them from clearing our account.

Social engineering attacks could be prevented by not sending our credentials or private leys to any malicious actors and by making the participants of the blockchain network to be aware of such kind of attacks.

Software Flaws

Blockchains have proven themselves to be resilient to almost all types of attacks, but it is inevitable that Decentralized Applications (DApps) built on top of them suffer from bugs. A report said that, over $24 million was lost in the blockchain network because of software bugs. To prevent such types of flaws, the software used by the blockchain network must undergo rigorous testing and review.

Malware

There are many types of malware that could cause security issues to the blockchain network. It could range from any malicious crypto mining software to code that could shut down a company's server. The most popular malware associated with blockchain network is cryptojacking. It mainly deals with cryptocurrency. In this, the computer's resources are taken over by unauthorized persons referred as cryptojackers. It leads to performance issues and increased electricity usage. It paves way for other hostile codes and a loss of multi million dollars to victims. Through vigilance, we could stop malware from its performance.

Eclipse Attacks

This attack happens in decentralized network in which the aim of the attacker is to eclipse a specific node or a specific set of nodes from the entire network. It could simply be defined as monopolizing a node's connection from others so that the victim node does not receive any information from any nodes other than the attacking nodes. The malicious actors exploit the victim nodes in such a way that the victim nodes receive information only from the malicious nodes believing the incorrect state of the blockchain. Eclipse attack could also be used to attack the whole blockchain network by hijacking the mining powers of eclipsed nodes. The attacker by this way can easily gain enough support from the victim nodes and establish a fork to the true ledger. The occurrence of eclipse attacks depends on factors such as data structure of the network, number of connections per user and the unique IP addresses assigned per node.(What is an Eclipse Attack? I Radix DLT - Decentralized Ledger Technology n.d.)

CONCLUSION

This chapter concludes that, Blockchain a hotly debated topic could be the probable solution for many of the problems and loopholes faced by the current technologies.

This ground breaking technology bridges the gap in current technology and ensures safety of our personal information. The various types and versions of blockchain are discussed. The chapter also concludes that, if IoT and Blockchain are integrated, they could be called as a perfect match made in heaven that would help the users in handling large amounts of data, allocate and distribute processing power, improve connectivity globally and efficiently. A few of the interesting real-world applications of Blockchain are discussed. But still, there exists a lot more applications like immutable data back-up, distributed cloud storage, equity trading and so on. Even though blockchain inherent several advantages and security features, that makes the Blockchain records resistant to attacks, there still do exists some security risks that must be recognized and mitigated in order to make the future of Blockchain bright.

REFERENCES

20. Real-World Uses for Blockchain Technology. (n.d.). https://www.fool.com/investing/2018/04/11/20-real-world-uses-for-blockchain-technology.aspx

3. Types of Blockchain Explained. (n.d.). https://hedgetrade.com/3-types-of-blockchain-explained/

5. Big Advantages of Blockchain, and 1 Reason to Be Very Worried. (n.d.). https://www.fool.com/investing/2017/12/11/5-big-advantages-of-blockchain-and-1-reason-to-be.aspx

5. Problems, B. Security, Privacy, Legal, Regulatory, and Ethical Issues - Blocks Decoded. (n.d.). https://blocksdecoded.com/blockchain-issues-security-privacy-legal-regulatory-ethical/

6. EssentialB. T. C. Y. N. T. K. (n.d.). https://tradeix.com/essential-blockchain-technology-concepts/

A Brief History in the Evolution of Blockchain Technology Platforms. (n.d.). https://hackernoon.com/a-brief-history-in-the-evolution-of-blockchain-technology-platforms-1bb2bad8960a

A Brief History of Blockchain: Blockchain Basics Book from ConsenSys Academy. (n.d.). https://consensys.net/academy/blockchain-basics-book/brief-history-of-blockchain/

Advantages and Disadvantages Of Blockchain Technology. (n.d.). https://data-flair.training/blogs/advantages-and-disadvantages-of-blockchain/

Blockchain: 1.0, 2.0, 3.0 and Future. (n.d.). https://www.linkedin.com/pulse/blockchain-10-20-30-future-marian-marik-danko

Blockchain 3.0 and COTI - Next Generation Technology Without Mining? (n.d.). https://www.forbes.com/sites/geraldfenech/2018/11/23/blockchain-3-0-and-coti-next-generation-technology-without-mining/#7719151f4ce4

Blockchain, an Emerging Technology for the Future - Data Driven Investor. (n.d.). https://medium.com/datadriveninvestor/blockchain-an-emerging-technology-for-the-future-b7856af83175

Blockchain and Finance: Two Peas in a Pod. (n.d.). https://blockgeeks.com/guides/blockchain-and-finance/

ApplicationsB.FutureI. (n.d.). https://hackernoon.com/blockchain-applications-and-its-future-f42fee305873

Blockchain Applications in Internet of Things (IoT) Explained. (n.d.). https://www.blockchaintechnologies.com/applications/internet-of-things-iot/

Changing, B. A. T. A. The World. (n.d.). https://www.edureka.co/blog/blockchain-applications/

Blockchain: Everything You Need to Know. (n.d.). https://www.investopedia.com/terms/b/blockchain.asp

Blockchain IoT: How Will Blockchain Be Integrated Into the Growing Internet-of-Things? (n.d.). https://businesstown.com/blockchain-iot-be-integrated-into-the-growing-internet-of-things/

Explained, B. T. Introduction, Meaning, and Applications. (n.d.). https://hackernoon.com/blockchain-technology-explained-introduction-meaning-and-applications-edbd6759a2b2

Technology, B., & the Transportation Industry. Where the Future Starts. (n.d.). https://enterprise-info.trimble.com/blockchain-technology#applications

VersionB. (n.d.). https://www.javatpoint.com/blockchain-version

Elsts, Mitskas, & Oikonomou. (2018). Distributed Ledger Technology and the Internet of Things: A Feasibility Study. doi:10.1145/nnnnnnn.nnnnnnn

History of Blockchain. (n.d.). https://academy.binance.com/blockchain/history-of-blockchain

History of Blockchain. (n.d.). https://www.icaew.com/technical/technology/blockchain/blockchain-articles/what-is-blockchain/history

BankingH. I. B. R.MarketsF. (n.d.). https://hackernoon.com/how-is-blockchain-revolutionizing-banking-and-financial-markets-9241df07c18b

ICO InterValue - World's First Practical Blockchain 4.0 Project. (n.d.). https://steemit.com/blockchain/@sergeyklimenok/ico-intervalue-world-s-first-practical-blockchain-4-0-project

Leading Blockchain Integration With IoT Devices for Enhanced Security. (n.d.). https://www.forbes.com/sites/geraldfenech/2019/01/22/leading-blockchain-integration-with-iot-devices-for-enhanced-security/#52f4d0a031bf

Padmavathi, U., & Rajagopalan, N. (2019). A Research on Impact of Blockchain in Healthcare. *International Journal of Innovative Technology and Exploring Engineering*, 8(9), 35–40.

The Different Types of Blockchains. (n.d.). https://medium.com/altcoin-magazine/the-different-types-of-blockchains-456968398559

The Exponential Guide to Blockchain. (n.d.). https://su.org/resources/exponential-guides/the-exponential-guide-to-blockchain/

The Future Is Here – The Evolution of Blockchain. (n.d.). https://toshitimes.com/the-future-is-here-the-evolution-of-blockchain/

The Top Advantages Of Blockchain For Businesses. (n.d.). https://www.smartdatacollective.com/top-advantages-blockchain-for-businesses/

Top 10 Blockchain Technology Applications Explained In-Depth. (n.d.). https://www.blockchaintechnologies.com/applications/

Top Five Blockchain Benefits Transforming Your Industry. (n.d.). https://www.ibm.com/blogs/blockchain/2018/02/top-five-blockchain-benefits-transforming-your-industry/

Network, T. O. P. The Harbinger of Blockchain 4.0 Era. (n.d.). https://medium.com/top-network/top-network-the-harbinger-of-blockchain-4-0-era-84137d572f60

What Are Blockchain's Issues and Limitations? (n.d.). https://www.coindesk.com/information/blockchains-issues-limitations

What Are the Different Types of Blockchain? (n.d.). https://dragonchain.com/blog/differences-between-public-private-blockchains

What Is an Eclipse Attack? (n.d.). https://www.radixdlt.com/post/what-is-an-eclipse-attack/

BlockchainW. I. 4.0? (n.d.). https://www.quora.com/What-is-blockchain-4-0

HashingW. I. (n.d.). https://blockgeeks.com/guides/what-is-hashing/

What's inside a Block on the Blockchain? (n.d.). https://learnmeabitcoin.com/guide/blocks

Chapter 2
A Holistic View on Blockchain and Its Issues

Mohd Azeem Faizi Noor
ⓘ https://orcid.org/0000-0002-8257-4985
Jamia Millia Islamia, India

Saba Khanum
Jamia Millia Islamia, India

Taushif Anwar
ⓘ https://orcid.org/0000-0002-6937-7258
Pondicherry University, India

Manzoor Ansari
Jamia Millia Islamia, India

ABSTRACT

Blockchain, the technology behind most popular cryptocurrency Bitcoin and Ethereum, has attracted wide attention recently. It is the most emerging technology that has changed the financial and non-financial transaction system. It is omnipresent. Currently, this technology is enforcing banks, industries, and countries to adopt it in their financial, industrial, and government section. Earlier, it solved the centralize and double-spending problems successfully. In this chapter, the authors present a study of blockchain security issues and its challenges as well. They divided the whole chapter into two parts. The primer part covers a holistic overview of blockchain followed by the later section that argues about basic operations, 51% attack, scalability issue, Fork, Sharding, Lightening, etc. Finally, they mention an intro about its adaptation (financial or non-financial) in our 24/7 life and collaboration with fields like IoT.

DOI: 10.4018/978-1-7998-2414-5.ch002

INTRODUCTION

Blockchain is a neoteric technology that promises to shift routine activities from central parties to the actual users (decentral parties). It is seen as significantly for making systems more transparent and decentralised, an innovation through peer-to-peer architecture and cryptographic methods that should make middle intermediaries unnecessary and empowered individuals. All entries in the ledger are immutable. Blockchain advantages force businesses, banks, and various other fields towards decentralization. Also, the potential of blockchain is far beyond and higher than any buzz and it will change society by enabling trust among them.

Decentralization has various positive aspects over centralized and distributed systems. The centralized system has central dependency which affects the overall system if the central hub fails. To get rid of the dependency on single-point failure different nodes are empowered and made self-dependent. These participants or nodes of the system participate and work collectively to share, verify and build trust in the overall system (Yli-Huumo,Ko,Choi, Park, & Scotlander, 2016).

The objective of the research to explore various aspects of blockchain. We have tried to cover holistic view by encompassing vital sections of blockchain like different consensus mechanism, issues, and challenges in detail.

The Chapter is divided into four major sections. first section introduces the basic characters along with the difference with relative terms. Second sections shed light on working, types, and consensus mechanism. Third section issues and challenges in detail. And lastly, issues are mentioned specific to blockchain applications.

1.1. Characteristics of Blockchain

a). **Trust:** One of the main characteristics of blockchain, which is mainly invoked by decentralization architecture of the system. The trust factor means not trusting anyone in the system. It eradicates the role of the third party from the system and only the involved user has the power to move their asset and makes the system transparent. The evolution of the internet has failed to solve the trust factor but blockchain does successfully.

b). **Shared and Public:** In order to ensure transparency, the ledger is kept public. Every stakeholder has a copy of the ledger. Manipulation in the ledger transaction can be easily identified. A change in the single entry will change the hash of not only the current block but also changes the hash of the previous block. For example, in the Banking system, the complete ledger is maintained by banks or government bodies and kept privately. Now due to blockchain this ledger does not involve any bank or government authorities. All entries are kept public and any peer can directly connect to the ledger and check the validity of transactions.

c). **Peer verification:** Firstly, the new user's identity is verified using an authenticated process. Once the node becomes part of the system, it has access to viewing the blockchain. Any transaction initiated is checked and verified by another peer node in the transaction and then only added to the ledger. After all, the participants have been empowered to check the verification of the transaction as the distributed ledger of the system is shared among all.

d). **Immutability:** The transactions or data saved in blockchain remains unaltered and indelible. This feature of blockchain makes the system incredible. Blockchain, instead of relying on the central authority ensures the transaction with the help of peer nodes. The process of verification includes the mining process and the validity of the transaction is done by every peer node. If the transaction is not approved by the majority of peer users, the transaction is not added to the ledger. Once the transaction is added in the block, no one has the authority to manipulate, alter, delete or update the transaction.

e). **Decentralization and democratic:** The concept of decentralization is to make the system independent. It means the whole network is not controlled by any governing authority. The group of nodes itself regulates the network. So, blockchain users can directly access relevant data from the web and store their assets. This asset can be anything viz. cryptocurrency, important documents, contracts, or any other digital asset. Decentralization gives power to the common person on their assets. Moreover, no need to worry about single-point failure and data security. Data is not maintained by a single hub, every node in the network is having the ledger copy. This deficit the system from total breakdown. Lastly, the system runs on the specific algorithms which control scams and fraud in the system.

f). **Redundancy:** The ledger is with everyone who is authorized to use the system. This characteristic of blockchain has increased the availability and trust among all unknown participants. As a result, no single point failure can exist.

g). **Enhanced Security:** In blockchain there is no third-party control. So, no one can change the information stored on the ledger. This feature enhances the security power which is achieved through "cryptography". Cryptography includes encryption through complex mathematics algorithms like SHA256, HMAC etc. that helps to secure the network from attacks. Every information in the block is first hashed and then saved into the ledger. Every block data is hashed and linked with data in the previous block. This makes all blocks in the chain and hence named "Blockchain". A change in the current block will change the hash of the previous blocks. It is very difficult for an attacker to change the hashes of all the blocks of the blockchain. So, Changing or tampering in data using Hash IDs become quiets impossible

h). **Consensus:** This feature is extremely important for the smooth functioning of the blockchain. It is the core part of any blockchain architecture. Every blockchain is having a consensus mechanism viz. PoW (Proof of Work), PoS (Proof of Stake), DPoS (Delegated Proof of Security) etc.

1.2 How Blockchain is Different From Various Terms

As with any new technology, there is an enormous amount of hype and misinformation. The same incident happens with blockchain and various misinformation and misunderstanding lead to confusion among users and they fail to differentiate the terminology related to blockchain. Figure 2 shows how various terms are related to blockchain.

1.2.1. Bitcoin

Word Bitcoin got popularity before the word blockchain and most people are not able to differentiate between both terms. Bitcoin is the first application implemented over the blockchain framework. Cryptocurrencies are created on the top of blockchain and Bitcoin is one of the cryptocurrency (Vujičić, Jagodić, & Ranđić, 2018). Bitcoin cannot work without blockchain. Ethereum is another example of cryptocurrency that works on the top of the blockchain.

1.2.2. Cryptocurrency

S. Nakamoto proposed a framework for peer-to-peer exchanges of currency (Nakamoto, 2008). His goal was to invent a decentralised digital cash system. The by-product of this system was Cryptocurrency. Even Nakamoto missed this term significantly.

Jan Lansky (2018), defines six conditions for a system that will be considered as cryptocurrency:

1. It does not need a middle authority such as a bank or state.
2. It keeps track of cryptocurrency units with respective owners.
3. The system should define the process of creating new cryptocurrency and ownership of these created units.
4. One can prove exclusively cryptographically ownership of cryptocurrency units.

5.   The cryptographic unit will be changed after performing transactions. Such transaction records can be proved by an entity by declaring the current ownership of these units.
6.   If two apart transactions are instructed for the same cryptographic units at the same time then at most one of them will take place.

Thus, cryptocurrency is the token based on the idea of Distributed Ledger and this facility is provided through blockchain. Cryptocurrency is referred to as a digital currency platform whereas blockchain is applied to store the transactions record. So, both are interrelated but have different roles.

1.2.3. Cryptography

Bitcoin transactions are backed by Cryptography and blockchain record cryptography-based Bitcoin transactions (Crosby, Nachiappan, Pattanayak, Verma, & Kalyanaraman, 2016). The Bitcoin protocol uses public-key cryptography for cryptographic hash functions and digital signatures (Gaurav, Kumar, Kumar, & Thakur 2020). The elliptic curve cryptography, which is asymmetric in nature, is a cryptographic algorithm used in Bitcoin (Lu, 2018). Compared to the RSA algorithm, it requires less computation with a smaller key size and provides more protection.

So, the cryptography algorithm is used for the transaction in financial blockchain and it is not blockchain rather it is a more security mechanism.

1.2.4. Linked List

Blockchain is like the linked list with some differences. Blockchain is the chain of blocks. These blocks are interconnected like nodes are connected in the linked list. Every block has a link with the previous block with a hash function whereas Linked list uses pointers for the same. Linked List is a linear way of arranging and storing records or data whereas blockchain follows Merkle Tree to store all the info related to the transaction. Data manipulation and tampering are nearly impossible in blockchain whereas linked lists permit such activities. Blockchain follows the only structure of Linked list which is accompanied by the hash function, mining, and consensus protocols (Gupta & Sadoghi, 2018).

1.2.5. Distributed Ledger Technology

DLT is an automated system that records the transactions with their details in a distributed fashion across several sites. DLT has no central authorities, unlike traditional databases (Alketbi, Nasir, & Talib, 2018). DLT has different types based on usability. Some of them are DAG, Tempo, Holochain etc. blockchain is one of them which is most popular. Some of the well-known cryptocurrencies that use blockchain DLT are Ethereum, Bitcoin, Dash, Dogecoin etc.

Conclusively, blockchain is a subset and type of DLT. All blockchains are DLT but all the DLTs are not blockchain.

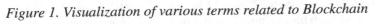

Figure 1. Visualization of various terms related to Blockchain

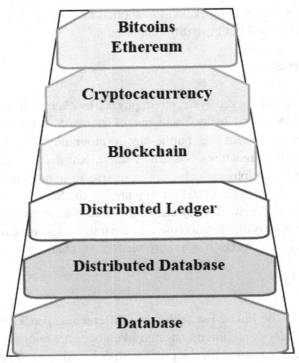

1.3. Current Trends and Practices

Now blockchain has worldwide recognition and a lot of research work has been done in recent years and it is still a hot topic for researchers throughout the world. This is only possible because blockchain is currently being used in different fields with great success. HealthCare, e-voting, Land- registration, Assets- registrations, securing supply chains of goods etc are some real-life examples of using blockchain. These applications encompass decentralization, immunity and transparency that makes it unparallel from other technologies.

The United Kingdom, Denmark, Honduras, Australia, Saudi Arabia, Switzerland, and many others have taken footstep to unleash the hidden capabilities of blockchain technology. Estonia is the first country that implements blockchain-based e-voting. Dubai, the city of future, aims to adopt blockchain in all their transactions in a paperless manner by 2020. Swiss global project Health bank is a milestone in this field. Similarly, the U.S. has Gem and Estonia has Guard time as a healthcare project based on blockchain platform (Mettler, 2016). Experts relate Malta as 'Mecca of blockchain' due to their unrestricted and open regulations for blockchain and cryptocurrencies. Many other countries have invested a huge amount of money for their economy, data management security, transparency and to build trust within the people of their country.

2. BLOCKCHAIN WORKING, ITS TYPES & CONSENSUS

This section explores the in-depth knowledge of blockchain technology by discussing it's working in detail. Highlighting its types with advantages and disadvantages in each type. Moreover, the core of the blockchain "consensus" mechanism types are elaborated with pros and cons.

2.1 Working of Blockchain

The blockchain contains a chain of blocks where each block encompasses many details like data, hash of the block, hash of the previous block it chained with and transactions logs. A node that has no parent block is known as genesis block which is considered as the first block in the chain of blocks. The node stores the basic data about the block like sender, receiver, timestamp, and the electronic cash. The blockchain acts as a database which records and shares information between the communities. Each member of the group has a true copy of all transactions and all members participate in the validation and updation process collectively. There is no central authority or moderator in the case of blockchain.

Suppose Alice wants to send some coins to Bob. She will broadcast this message to the network. Now Miner (one who mines the block) will select the transaction and check its validity. If the transaction is valid then miners will solve a complex mathematical puzzle and broadcast the solution. After validating the solution, the block will be added to the chain. Figure 1 depicts the working of blockchain.

Figure 2. Working of Blockchain technology (Nadeem, Rizwan, Ahmad, & Manzoor,2019).

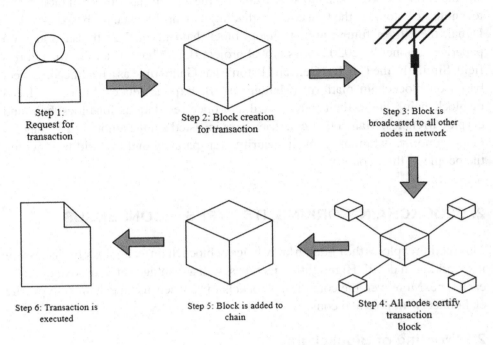

2.2. Types of Blockchain

Blockchain can be categorized based on the application type (financial or non-financial), evolution type (1.0 Bitcoin, 2.0 Ethereum, 3.0 EOS). There are three kinds of blockchain (Table 1) on Usability basis:

a.) *Public Blockchain*: Anyone can join the network after the verification and validation process. Everyone has access to the whole ledger. Every peer has equal rights, nobody can empower other peers. The first blockchain, Bitcoin, introduced by Satoshi Nakamoto was public and open for all. The direct transfer of cryptocurrency takes place between the peer nodes. Having empowered nodes, this public blockchain has many benefits but at the same time, if any way any theft occurs in the system the peer node can-not claim anywhere.

b.) *Consortium Blockchain*: In this type of blockchain the peers are empowered with equal rights but there are some regulators which help in making the decision. This is the most talked and promising blockchain according to researchers.

Table 1. Blockchain Types

Characteristics	Public Blockchain	Consortium Blockchain	Private Blockchain
Read Permission	Anyone	Known users	Known users
Write Access	Anyone	Multi-selected organisation	Single organisation
Consensus	PoW (Proof of Work), PoS (Proof of Stake)	PoW (Proof of Work), PoS (Proof of Stake)	PoA (Proof of Authority)
Immutability	Almost impossible	Could be altered	Could be tampered
Transaction Speed	Slow	Lighter and faster	Lighter and faster
Energy Consumption	High	Comparatively low	Quiet low
Examples	Bitcoin, Ethereum	Ripple, R3	Multichain, Blockstack

c.) *Private Blockchain*: This blockchain is more like a centralized system. Certain stakeholders have all the access. Not everyone can become the part of the blockchain and hence only involved stakeholders have the right to access the ledger. The consensus is different as used in the public and consortium blockchain. Decision-making power is with certain owners like previously with banks.

With public blockchain any person can download the data, participate, and read the data. Public blockchains are open source and with high security using cryptography and consensus protocol. Consortium blockchain is run by a group of members. The Private blockchain is centralised in nature where a user needs permission to join or leave the group. Companies who wanted to create their own currencies started using this type of blockchain. Additionally, these blockchains differ in transfer rate, node rights and usage range. Examples of public blockchain include Bitcoin, Ethereum, private types include Multichain and Blockstack and consortium blockchain include Ripple and R3.

2.3. Different Consensus Mechanism

Consensus Mechanism is the protocol for legitimate transactions which is added to the blockchain. Through this protocol, the blockchain network agrees on a transaction globally. Different consensus mechanism is used by the different types of cryptocurrencies. For example, Proof of Work (PoS) used by Bitcoin, Ethereum, Proof of Stake (PoS) used by Peercoin, Ethereum (maybe in future), Delegated

Proof Of Stake (DPOS) used by EOS, Bitshares, Practical Byzantine Fault Tolerance (PBFT) by Hyperledger etc. Table 2 highlights the comparison among them.

a)   Proof of Work (PoW)

PoW is suggested by Satoshi Nakamoto which is considered as a first blockchain consensus mechanism. The consensus process is recognised as mining and the involved nodes are recognised as a miner. Miners mine the block. Miners bundle the transaction from mempool as Block and check the accuracy of all transactions within the block. Now they try to solve a difficult mathematical puzzle that needs huge computational power. This puzzle is difficult to solve but easy to verify. It can be solved through the 'trial and error' method. Random value of nonce is adjusted to get the required hash value. The first one to solve this puzzle will publish the hash value of the block and will get block rewards along with fee reward for it. This block will be appended in the chain.

PoW requires a lot of resources which is unsustainable and not feasible in the future. So many blockchains are moving to new or different consensus algorithms.

b)   Proof of Stake (PoS)

It is an environmental friendly approach as it does not solve a highly complex puzzle like PoW. Therefore, it consumes very less electricity to verify the transactions. It is a randomized process that selects validators for verifying the transactions. The validators are like miners who produce the blocks. The validators have to deposit their tokens for a certain amount of time to become eligible for producing blocks. The validators who deposited higher stake had the highest chance to validate a block. On completing the process Validators will get rewarded for their work.

It has a major disadvantage. As the rich validators will have more chance to validate the block so rich validators will become richer and rest validators don't get enough chance to validate the block and win rewards.

c)   Delegate Proof of Stake (DPOS)

This is a very fast consensus and implemented in EOS popularly. This process introduces a new word 'Delegate' or 'witness'. Delegate can be a person or organisation who will produce blocks. The user stake their coin to vote for particular delegates. Higher the stake, higher will be the weight of the vote. Several delegates are selected based on the percentage of their votes. Now, they will get a chance to produce new blocks in a round-robin manner and get rewarded for their work. This reward will be distributed among their respective electors proportional to their tokens as a vote.

d) Practical Byzantine Fault Tolerance (PBFT)

This consensus mechanism is designed as a 'fault-tolerance' algorithm that works in the asynchronous and distributed system. This network reaches consensus even when some of the malicious components propagate wrong information or fail to respond. This algorithm ensures correct information to flow among the nodes and mitigating malicious nodes' effects. It can tolerate malicious nodes if their number is less than one-third of the total nodes.

All nodes in this network are ordered in sequence. One of them is selected as leader or primary node and the rest are referred to as backup nodes. The primary node gets a message from the client and broadcasts it to the backup nodes. Now, backup nodes will send a message to each other including the primary node. Each node ensures that they get 2F+1 (F = max no of the faulty nodes) valid 'Prepare messages' including themselves. Finally, Primary and backup nodes reach on an agreement and reply back to the client. If the client receives F+1 replies from different nodes with the same results then it is considered a successful reply.

Table 2. A comparison among Consensus Algorithm

Property	PoW	PoS	DPoS	PBFT
Resource Consumption	High	Low	Very Low	Very Low
Nature	Decentralize	Decentralize	Centralize	Decentralize
Type	Permission-less	Permission-less	Permission-less	Permissioned
Throughput	Low <10 tps	Average <20 tps	High >5000tps	High >1000 tps
Tolerated Power	<50% Computing Power	< 50% Stake	<50% Validators	<33.33% Malicious replica
Transaction Fee	High	Low	Low	Very Low
Example	Bitcoin	DoS	EOS	Hyperledger

3. CHALLENGES AND ISSUES OF BLOCKCHAIN

3.1. 51% Attack

51% attack refers to an attack on a blockchain in which a group of miners controls more than 50% of the network's mining hash rate or computing power (Chanti, Anwar, Chithralekha, & Uma 2020). This will prevent any new transaction to occur and to reverse the transaction. 51% attack can further cause double spending problems. The attackers surely were not able to create new coins but would compromise the security of the blockchain (Apostolaki, 2017).

The Dangers of a Mining Monopoly

The objective of Bitcoin (underline technology -- Blockchain) is to run a distributed ledger that powers permission-less peer-to-peer transactions. A 51% attack is not dangerous only that it can create a double-spend which causes a merchant to lose money, but rather it can finish the entire system. With a majority of sustained hash power, an invader can continuously (or periodically) invoke a blockchain reorganization which disturbs the reliability of the network. At the extreme, they can mine empty blocks forever and only lengthen the chain on their own blocks, shutting all others out and causing the chain to be totally impractical.

3.1.1 Previous Approaches to the Problem

- Invalidating blocks: This logical approach is used by miners to invalidate fishy looking blocks. The process of invalidation invokes a clean break and the chain extends to null or void block.
- The Threshold Paradox: Now, the vital part is to decide which block behaviour is suspicious and when to invalidate? Setting time limit (threshold) could be one option, but soon the time limit theory is discarded as due to network and propagation issues half of the block could be considered in invalidating zone. The paradoxical aspect is no matter how the big-time limit is set; the fault line does not withhold with the time limit.
- Block re-org depth ("automatic checkpoints"): Keep in check using block height and forbidden beyond re-orgs. This method also not able to fulfil the expectation. As any block deeper than blocks could be valid or invalid because of the threshold timing problem.
- Nakamoto Consensus and the Byzantine General's Problem: "Nakamoto Consensus" is the original consensus used in the first application (Bitcoin) of blockchain. The beauty of the original proof-of-work lies in identifying the correct version of the ledger.

Byzantine general's problem describes a group of generals who want to attack a city but is not able to coordinate their attack. In Bitcoin, each solved block as a "general" that the rest of the army can follow. Doing the work thus designates a miner as having a turn to play the role of general. It is been realized that the genius of using proof of work as a distributed time-stamping mechanism is very difficult to tamper with.

3.1.2. Some Solution to - The Problem

i) *Non-fully distributed solutions*: - If we consider a simple solution not to allow reorgs > 6 blocks, then a 6-block reorganisation, that comes at the same time as a new block could divide the chain. Though, it would be simple for attentive miners to sense the split and reset it. But, this action can't be fully automated and it requires human intervention and coordination among honest miners. This can work as a practical matter, but this is not a wholly distributed solution.

ii) *Non-distributed solution:* - It allows a group of reliable pools (3 out of 5 signatures) to invalidate a block. This could be completed in a way where nodes must observe the re-org taking place; the pools can't arbitrarily direct the chain.

iii) *Middle Ground*: - It would be possible to get some penalty in the middle, 20, 30, 50%... and this could create a race condition, but only at a shallow reorg depth. The race would soon be over, and just as important, an attacker could not fool honest nodes into battling each other because they would each see a similar penalty.

3.2. Finality

It is an affirmation, that all the committed blocks in the blockchain will not be revoked again if wrong data is input in the blockchain. As the transaction once added to the blockchain could not be altered. Finality falls back to Nakamoto Consensus. When the race ends and the longest chain proof of work overtakes the attacker chain eventually (no matter how long), it is finalized in the purest sense. The 51% attack is discussed by satoshi in his first white paper, elaborates that blockchain characteristics can be overtaken by attaining 51% of the computation power. To ensure the proper functioning of blockchain finality become vital. There are three types of finality in the blockchain

1). Probabilistic Finality
2). Absolute Finality
3). Economic finality

In the *probabilistic finality*, chained-based protocols are used. Bitcoin's Nakamoto consensus is an example of probabilistic finality, where it is recommended to wait for at least 6 blocks to confirm a transaction. This ensures the less likelihood of revert of transaction. In the case of *absolute finality*, a transaction is confirmed by PBFT-based protocols viz. Tendermint. A list of validators approves the transaction.

Economic finality applies monetarily cost for a block to be reverted. This type of finality is opted by Casper FFG.

According to Eric Brewer's CAP theorem, in case of partition, a distributed system can preserve either consistency or availability. Consistency ensures the correct state of the system which can be attained through probabilistic finality and availability is favoured by absolute finality.

3.3. Scalability

Scalability is one of the main rooted issue related to blockchain. The researchers are trying to solve the scalability issue from its initial stage. The scalability defines the number of transactions per second. The very first application of blockchain is Bitcoin that offers maximum 6-7 transactions per second (tps) and 2nd application is Ethereum that offers 20 tps which is very low as compared to other application's transactions. For example, Visa handles 1667 tps, PayPal process 170 tps etc (Conti, Kumar, Lal, & Ruj, 2018).

Scalability depends on many factors such as block size, network latency, Consensus algorithm, complex calculations etc. With the advancement of these factors, we have to compromise with security and tend more towards centralisation. Each factor has its own cons and pros. Scalability depends on many factors such as block size, network latency, Consensus algorithm, complex calculations etc. With the advancement of these factors, we have to compromise with security and it tends more towards centralisation. Now, we will discuss block size and median confirmation time that play a big role for scalability issue.

3.3.1 Block Size

Nakamoto suggested 1 MB Block size for Bitcoin. These Blocks contain numerous transactions. Generally, a Block contains approximately 1500-3500 transactions, given the 1 MB limit. It varies with the size of transaction details. Miners take 10 minutes to generate a new block (Conti et al, 2018). Let's consider some cases with block size to increase the scalability.

First one is to increase block size upto tolerable limit that will acquire more number of transactions. In this case, all nodes need to perform all the required calculations. Due to increase in size, it will be harder for the node to process all transactions. To verify the transactions, miners need more advanced resources and it will filter the less equipped miners and will empower the more equipped miners. Thus, it will lead to more centralisation. Also, it results, threat over security like 51% attack.

The second case is to increase the block size up to infinity. This case is the worst situation. For miners, it will be very difficult to process the transactions and resources can't be enough for it. The final case is to increase block size narrowly. It will amass a bit more transactions but it is not an optimal and feasible solution.

Another case is that we have several blockchain and run the different applications on different blockchain, i.e. no need to run all computation on a single blockchain rather distributes it. This approach distributed the load of single blockchain into many of them. So, it increases the performance but will do bargaining with Security. This approach will distribute the hash power in different blockchain and to avoid from 51% attack we need a large chain that should have all hashing power with it. So, scattering the hash may lead to security.

3.3.1.2 Median Confirmation Time: Another Reason for Scalability

This is one more reason that delays the transaction and generating the block. Median Confirmation Time is the duration of time that the user must wait as the transaction accepted into a mined block. It happens due to the lower transaction fee. The more transaction fee, the more chance to be accepted for the mining. Currently (on 19-05-2020) 71,141,960 bytes is the aggregate size of transactions that are waiting to be confirmed and this is known as Mempool size.

To solve the scalability issue many approaches had been done and some new techniques and methods are introduced. Sharding and Lightning Network are the methods that tried to solve the scalability issue. Now, we will have a look over it.

3.3.2 Sharding

Sharding is a database concept to make it more efficient. In blockchain, Sharding splits the overhead of computation among multiple groups of shards/nodes. These shards keep a part of blockchain and not complete blockchain information. These shards work in parallel to increase efficiency that allows the network to enhance the scalability. Sharding based projects are Ethereum, Zilliqa, and Carding to get scalability solution. However, Sharding is still unproven technology in term of blockchain (Moubarak, Filiol, & Chamoun,2018).

3.3.2.2. Lightning Network

This technique is also called off-chain approach. In this network, no need to keep each record on blockchain rather it adds another layer on the top of blockchain and creates a payment channel between any two parties on that extra layer.

These two parties need to create a multi-signature wallet and they can access it with their private keys. At least one of them must deposit some amount of cryptocurrency into that wallet. After every payment, the amount will be deducted from the wallet if both do signing with their private keys. They can do any number of transactions on this channel. They can use this channel as long as they need. Anyone of them can close the channel. After closing, the latest balance sheet of wallet that was signed by both parties will be broadcast to the network. Miners will check balance sheet and if found everything right, will release the funds to the respective parties. This will be considered as a single transaction on blockchain. So in this way, the Lightning Network can reduce the load on blockchain (Poon, Dryja, 2016).

The above discussion concludes that Satoshi Nakamoto proposed 1 MB limited block size in 2008. James A. Donald, First-person who interact on a forum with Satoshi Nakamoto, commented: "the way I understand your proposal, it does not seem to scale to the required size." After a decade, scalability is still a serious issue for Bitcoin and other cryptocurrencies. The experts are trying to get an optimal and permanent solution but still not achieved. Block size and security are a trade-off. Many latest implementations are yet unproven.

Scalability Trilemma (figure 3) says that there is a trade-off between three important properties: decentralization, scalability, and security. Blockchain can have at most two of them (Tssandor, 2019).

Figure 3. The Scalability Trilemma: - Satisfying all three at the same time is difficult.

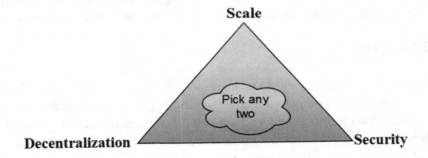

3.4 Fork

There are basically two types of fork, Soft fork and Hard fork. Any update in the chain that also supports previously blocks in the chain is termed as soft fork while an update that does not support previous blocks and make another chain is termed as Hard fork. Figure 4 illustrates both concepts. The user need not to upgrade the node on soft fork as it is compatible with the earlier version while Hard fork is must to update as it is not compatible with the earlier version. The hard fork is the result of the disagreement between the experts or users. Hard fork disturbs the harmony among users (Hamida, Brousmiche, Levard, & Thea, 2017).

Figure 4. Soft Fork and Hard Fork

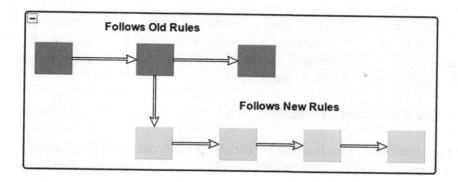

Many researchers are not happy with the restricted block size of the blockchain. They want to increase it. To achieve it, they did hard fork over blockchain and named it as Bitcoin Cash (BCH) in August 2017 with 8MB block size (Figure 5). Later, in May 2018, it fourfold and become 32 MB. As a result, it can process 61 tps. The worrying point is that it will generate 4.5 GB per day which need huge storage space and resources will be out of financial reach for common miners. Eventually, it will face the risk of centralisation.

Figure 5. BCH Fork (at block 478558)

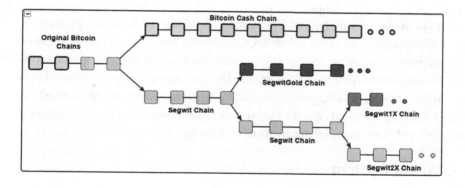

Segregated Witness (SegWit) is the result of soft fork. This protocol code was released in 2015 and updated on Bitcoin in August 2017. Initially, Bitcoin was suffering from a bug called transaction malleability. This bug mutates scriptSig in such a way that changes the transaction identifier (txid) but not the signature and content. Signature is known as witness. The SegWit fixes this bug. It keeps digital signature details outside and moved to the extended block while calculating the txid of the transaction data. So if an attacker tries to change the ScriptSig, it will not affect txid. The signature takes more than 50% of the transaction data. If we omit signature, we can process more number of transactions within a block. After implementing SegWit the max block size is about 4MB that results in a better throughput (Conti et al, 2018; Wuille, 2019).

3.5. Lack of Standardization

The numbers of users are increasing with the popularity of blockchain. Consequently, we have thousands of blockchain projects on different platforms with coding languages, consensus mechanism, protocols, and standards. So, it is a matter of concern on how these projects can interact with each other. Lack of interoperability creates problems for users and investors. The user must make n account for n platform. The ideal solution is to make a single account for n platforms. Standardization can unite the enterprises to collaborate on application development and consensus mechanism.

4. DISCUSSING BLOCKCHAIN ISSUES ON SPECIFIC APPLICATIONS

There exist various financial and non-financial applications of blockchain that hints how the blockchain taking over the world. BFSI, FX, FinTech, etc. from financial category to Healthcare, Land Registry, Identification from the non-financial category, it's all about the domination of blockchain applications. In the beginning, Banks and other sectors were skeptical about adapting blockchain but the scenario is now changed with time. Nowadays many financial and non-financial organizations and individuals are investing their resources in blockchain-based applications. However, such applications are facing various issues due to many reasons like infrastructure, lack of knowledge, fund, etc. In this section, some issues and challenges of basic financial and non-financial application will be discussed.

4.1. Voting System

The chemistry of blockchain with Voting sounds like a great solution. FollowMyVote, Votebook, VoteWatcher, Votem, Voatz, Agora are such projects based on blockchain platforms to solve the security and transparency of the Voting system. These projects may be norm someday but for now, many worries and vulnerabilities have to survive (Osgood, 2016).

The first one is the lack of knowledge and awareness among the citizens. Another issue is Coercion. M Green, cryptographer and security technologist, raises the query over it. Someone could be convinced by intimidating to vote in a certain manner and there is no solution to escape from that you did not do what they wanted.

Next issue, it is in the embryonic stage so the government and people are skeptical over it and don't want to be first. Although blockchain provides anonymously and maintaining the identity, public confidence and trust are necessary elements for blockchain-Enabled Voting's success. Due to its open-source voting platform nature, anybody can audit his recorded vote.

4.2. Healthcare

Healthcare is another non-financial application of blockchain. Gem Health Network, Guardtime, healthbank, healthureum are some major and nascent projects related to health based on blockchain. The primer issue is the financial crisis. The healthcare expenses grow uninterruptedly and Hospitals and clinics are not getting an adequate amount of fund to maintain the infrastructure and quality services. Many hospitals and clinics are not able to start or afford such advanced technology's features.

Such projects are worldwide and can be accessed from anywhere. The barrier is the law made by individual country. Some countries are favouring it and some are on the other side. The main concern is health providers and hospitals follow several regulations and laws. These regulations and laws should be supportive for the privacy of the patients (Mettler, 2016; Ahram, T., Sargolzaei, Sargolzaei, Daniels, & Amaba,2017).To access the health record, the patient uses a private key. If a person met an accident unfortunately and he is unconscious or in coma state then how the clinicians will come to know his health records.

The drug counterfeit issue is at its peak. According to a report, Pharmaceutical enterprises bear $200 million due to counterfeit drugs worldwide. A jillion of people died due to counterfeit drugs each year globally. Blockchain can reduce these fatalities with a great margin. Now a question pops up, why government and pharmaceutical enterprises are apathetic towards the adoption of blockchain?

4.3. Supply Chain

Despite the Supply chain is the natural application of blockchain still it is not in use too much. The supply chain has the potential to bring a new market and dominate the market. There exist thousands of e-services and they have their tied delivery services. Blockchain can be a boon for them.

Similarly, blockchain can track the food and diet and can analyse the effects of the diet. This analysis can bring reasons for illness. Which food she/he took before getting unwell, it can be known through the use of food tracking (Niranjanamurthy, Nithya, & Jagannatha, 2018). Additionally, it can also be noticed the nourishment and effect of diet on the patient.

The monger or salesman can track their products and they come to know who is using their products. Based on various such information, they can take the decision and can build their market. The consumer can verify the authenticity of the product directly. For example, recently, Nestlé has launched open blockchain to track the milk. Similarly, many other companies also launched their blockchain platform to track their products. Nevertheless, it is not in practice at the mass level.

4.4. Banking

The Financial industry has a well-established infrastructure already and it is a grand challenge for the cooperate world to switch on blockchain. No doubt, it will reduce the cost by a big margin (Nakamoto, 2008) and provide enough security but it needs skilled employees and new infrastructure. It needs an adequate amount of money to set up the initial blockchain infrastructure. While applying it on legacy systems, it still faces some challenges. Due to the new infrastructure, the maintenance value is high. It will take some time to adapt to the new environment. Many financial organisations have skeptical about its adoption. However, if they have long planned then obviously adoption of blockchain is more fruitful (Zheng, Xie, Dai, Chen, & Wang, 2017).

Although there are abundant benefits of blockchain in financial applications, there exist some barricade and challenges as well. These challenges need to be addressed before implementing globally. These challenges include security, scalability, interoperability, cost, efficiency etc.

4.5 Regulations and Governance

Many countries consider blockchain as important assets for their country and some countries don't. The economy of countries relies on a set of policies and regulations. The regulations vary with country. Japan was the first nation to use Bitcoin as cryptocurrency and presently about 2k cryptocurrencies are in the market. In contrary to it, the business of cryptocurrencies is considered illegal in many countries. Conclusively, rules and regulations of the individual country are denying the adoption of blockchain globally (Conti et al, 2018).

Because of the lack of standard rules and regulations, scams and market manipulation have been commonplace in the crypto world. As a result, we have myriad scams like Ponzi scheme, BitKRX, Mt. Gox etc., which stole millions from investors (Conti et al, 2018; Lansky, 2018). And, investors neither claim to website owner nor the government.

4.7. Blockchain Integrations With IoT

Blockchain and Internet of things both are significant fields and amalgamation of both are opening a huge number of possibilities for the future. In this direction IOTA, a new blockchain IoT based platform is introduced. IOTA has the capability to overcome the blockchain drawbacks. Scalability and low-cost communication between the different things/nodes of the internet is done by maintaining a common ledger. Low cost communication among the things enhances and gives an insight into the bright future of blockchain Internet of things platforms.

Interoperability among the node persists a major drawback in the field of blockchain and internet of things. Progressive work is carried by a lot of researchers to overcome these drawbacks. (Makhdoom, Abolhasan, Abbas, & Ni, 2018). The advancement of new technologies has made a huge leap in recent decades. It brings about a drastic change in every phase of human life that is capable of intelligent tasks. Blockchain and internet of things (IoT) both are disruptive technologies that have received a lot of attention from industrial, academic and financial technologies (Shrestha & Kim, 2019).

In the centralized IoT system, there is a risk of loss of privacy of sensitive information because centralized servers can access plain text data from various IoT devices. There is a huge interest in implementing blockchain to the IoT system to ensure the privacy of IoT data and the decentralized access model (Reyna, Martín, Chen, Soler & Díaz, 2018). Blockchain technology is used to retrieve information and store this information in blocks from different IoT devices to ensure transparency among global users (Rathee, Sharma, Kumar & Iqbal, 2019). In the last decade, numerous security techniques and approaches have been highlighted. Blockchain plays an important role in the securing of many IoT applications (Minoli & Occhiogrosso,2018).

The decentralized architecture of the Blockchain-based IoT system can offer security and many other benefits. The benefits of the integration of IoT with Blockchain are Data Integrity, Transparency, Security, Decentralization, Autonomy, Identity Management, Immutability, Resilience, Anonymity and Cost Reduction. The Internet of things (IoT) systems suffer mainly from security aspects. Blockchain plays an imperative role in mitigating the challenges associated with security. Using smart contacts Blockchain can easily handle and monitor the security aspects of IoT systems.

5. CONCLUSION

This chapter explains the basic knowledge of blockchain, 51% and scalability issues. Next, it describe the adaptation issues in specific application of blockchain. Blockchain encompasses a huge number of possibilities and possesses a very bright future. The use cases of this field are countless and the way it is been adapted by other technologies and industries is hyperphysical. This technology has the potential to do miracles in future. There are an ample amount of opportunities blockchain offers but at the same time, it suffers from various challenges and limitations such as scalability, security, and privacy, compliance and governance issues. These issues and challenges need to be thoroughly explored and addressed.

REFERENCES

Ahram, T., Sargolzaei, A., Sargolzaei, S., Daniels, J., & Amaba, B. (2017, June). Blockchain technology innovations. In 2017 IEEE Technology & Engineering Management Conference (TEMSCON) (pp. 137-141). IEEE. doi:10.1109/TEMSCON.2017.7998367

Alketbi, A., Nasir, Q., & Talib, M. A. (2018, February). Blockchain for government services—Use cases, security benefits and challenges. In 2018 15th Learning and Technology Conference (L&T) (pp. 112-119). IEEE.

Apostolaki, M., Zohar, A., & Vanbever, L. (2017, May). Hijacking bitcoin: Routing attacks on cryptocurrencies. In 2017 IEEE Symposium on Security and Privacy (SP) (pp. 375-392). IEEE. doi:10.1109/SP.2017.29

Chanti, S., Anwar, T., Chithralekha, T., & Uma, V. (2020). Global Naming and Storage System Using Blockchain. In Transforming Businesses With Bitcoin Mining and Blockchain Applications (pp. 146–165). IGI Global. doi:10.4018/978-1-7998-0186-3.ch008

Conti, M., Kumar, E. S., Lal, C., & Ruj, S. (2018). A survey on security and privacy issues of bitcoin. *IEEE Communications Surveys and Tutorials*, *20*(4), 3416–3452. doi:10.1109/COMST.2018.2842460

Crosby, M., Nachiappan, Pattanayak, P., Verma, S., & Kalyanaraman, V. (2016). Blockchain technology: Beyond bitcoin. *Applied Innovation Review*, *2*(6-10), 71.

Gaurav, A. B., Kumar, P., Kumar, V., & Thakur, R. S. (2020). Conceptual Insights in Blockchain Technology: Security and Applications. In Transforming Businesses With Bitcoin Mining and Blockchain Applications (pp. 221-233). IGI Global.

Gupta, S., & Sadoghi, M. (2018). Blockchain transaction processing. In Encyclopedia of big data technologies, (pp. 1–11). doi:10.1007/978-3-319-63962-8_333-1

Hamida, E. B., Brousmiche, K. L., Levard, H., & Thea, E. (2017, July). Blockchain for enterprise: overview, opportunities and challenges. Academic Press.

Lansky, J. (2018). Possible state approaches to cryptocurrencies. *Journal of Systems Integration*, *9*(1), 19–31. doi:10.20470/jsi.v9i1.335

Lu, Y. (2018). Blockchain: A survey on functions, applications and open issues. *Journal of Industrial Integration and Management*, *3*(04), 1850015. doi:10.1142/S242486221850015X

Makhdoom, I., Abolhasan, M., Abbas, H., & Ni, W. (2018). Blockchain's adoption in IoT: The challenges, and a way forward. *Journal of Network and Computer Applications*.

Mettler, M. (2016, September). Blockchain technology in healthcare: The revolution starts here. In 2016 IEEE 18th International Conference on e-Health Networking, Applications and Services (Healthcom) (pp. 1-3). IEEE.

Minoli, D., & Occhiogrosso, B. (2018). Blockchain mechanisms for IoT security. Internet of Things, 1-2, 1–13. doi:10.1016/j.iot.2018.05.002

Moubarak, J., Filiol, E., & Chamoun, M. (2018, April). On blockchain security and relevant attacks. In 2018 IEEE Middle East and North Africa Communications Conference (MENACOMM) (pp. 1-6). IEEE. doi:10.1109/MENACOMM.2018.8371010

Nadeem, S., Rizwan, M., Ahmad, F., & Manzoor, J. (2019). Securing Cognitive Radio Vehicular Ad Hoc Network with Fog Node based Distributed Blockchain Cloud Architecture. *International Journal of Advanced Computer Science and Applications*, *10*(1), 288–295. doi:10.14569/IJACSA.2019.0100138

Nakamoto, S. (2008). Bitcoin: A peer-to-peer electronic cash system. Retrieved from https://bitcoin.org/bitcoin.pdf

Niranjanamurthy, M., Nithya, B. N., & Jagannatha, S. (2018). Analysis of Blockchain technology: Pros, cons and SWOT. *Cluster Computing*, 1–15.

Osgood, R. (2016). The future of democracy: Blockchain voting. COMP116: Information Security, 1-21.

Poon, J., & Dryja, T. (2016). *The bitcoin lightning network: Scalable off-chain instant payments*. Academic Press.

Rathee, G., Sharma, A., Kumar, R., & Iqbal, R. (2019). A Secure Communicating Things Network Framework for Industrial IoT using Blockchain Technology. *Ad Hoc Networks*, *94*, 94. doi:10.1016/j.adhoc.2019.101933

Reyna, A., Martín, C., Chen, J., Soler, E., & Díaz, M. (2018). On blockchain and its integration with IoT. Challenges and opportunities. *Future Generation Computer Systems*, *88*, 173–190. doi:10.1016/j.future.2018.05.046

Shrestha, R., & Kim, S. (2019). Integration of IoT with blockchain and homomorphic encryption: Challenging issues and opportunities. Role of Blockchain Technology in IoT Applications, 115, 293–331. doi:10.1016/bs.adcom.2019.06.002

Tssandor (.2019). Retrieved 24 July 2019, from https://steemit.com/blockchain/@tssandor/a-gentle-introduction-to-blockchain-scalability-part-i

Vujičić, D., Jagodić, D., & Ranđić, S. (2018). *Blockchain technology, bitcoin, and Ethereum: A brief overview. In 2018 17th International Symposium Infoteh-Jahorina (INFOTEH)*. IEEE., doi:10.1109/INFOTEH.2018.8345547.

Wuille, P. (2019). Segregated-witness-and-its-impact-on-scalability. Retrieved 24 July 2019, from https://diyhpl.us/wiki/transcripts/scalingbitcoin/hong-kong/segregated-witness-and-its-impact-on-scalability/

Yli-Huumo, J., Ko, D., Choi, S., Park, S., & Smolander, K. (2016). Where is current research on blockchain technology?—A systematic review. *PLoS One*, *11*(10), e0163477. doi:10.1371/journal.pone.0163477 PubMed

Zheng, Z., Xie, S., Dai, H., Chen, X., & Wang, H. (2017, June). An overview of blockchain technology: Architecture, consensus, and future trends. In 2017 IEEE International Congress on Big Data (BigData Congress) (pp. 557-564). IEEE. doi:10.1109/BigDataCongress.2017.85

Chapter 3
Blockchain–Enabled Secure Internet of Things

Vinod Kumar
Madanapalle Institute of Technology and Science, India

Gotam Singh Lalotra
Government Degree College for Women, Kathua, India

ABSTRACT

This century is the time of ubiquitous, smart, and intelligent devices. These devices have a wide variety of applications in different fields like business, manufacturing, healthcare, retail, education, security, transportation, etc. Internet of things is now becoming the inexorable part of the all these fields. But security has always been a major concern in embracing these technologies. The blockchain technology is the next frontier for securing the internet of things. It will play a pivotal role to secure the communication in internet of things ecosystem. This chapter discusses the blockchain-enabled secure internet of things (IoT).

1. INTRODUCTION

IoT is an internet technology connecting devices, machines and tools to the internet by means of wireless technologies. IoT is the one of the greatest phenomena of this century.

"According to Gartner research, The Internet of Things (IoT) is the network of physical objects that contain embedded technology to communicate and sense or interact with their internal states or the external environment." (Gartner, 2019)

DOI: 10.4018/978-1-7998-2414-5.ch003

IoT is offering new opportunities and providing a competitive advantage for businesses markets. It touches everything—not just the data, but how, when, where and why you collect it. The things connected to internet are changing due to the technologies that have created internet of Things. The services are being offered by devices on the edge of network without the human intervention at different levels

As the data generation and analysis is indispensable to the IoT, Managing and handling information throughout its life cycle is a multifaceted exercise because data have to pass through many administrative boundaries. A serious thought is to be given for protection of data in its entire life cycle.

Considering IoT as system-of-system is a good practice as the different physical and technological components are involved in actually make up an IoT ecosystem. Providing business value to any organisation is not an easy task as the architect of these systems. The enterprise architects aim for designing integrated solutions which include Protocol, applications, transport, edge devices and analytical competencies for fully functional IoT system. With the increase of complexities, the challenges are posed to keep IoT secure without affecting the other system. (Internet of things beyond-bitcoin, 2019)

The security of data is vital as claimed by International Data Corporation (IDC) that 90% of organizations that implement the IoT have to suffer an IoT-based breach of back-end IT systems in the upcoming couple of years.

2. BACKGROUND

A blockchain is a distributed ledger that maintains a growing number of data records and transactions. As transactions are related to network participants, they are documented in blocks. They are arranged in the right sequence and assigned a record timestamp when they are added. It is a decentralised technology with the removal of intermediaries the tedious inconvenient banking process can be bypassed which is cost and time efficient. Cryptographic algorithms support the blockchain technology which ensure the prevention of data distortion and ensure high security. The intermediate block on the database cannot be replaces as every block has a hash to the previous block. A block can be extended but cannot be changed.

Generally, Blockchain Technology can be categorised in two core types- public blockchain and private blockchain. (Z Zheng, *et* al. 2017)

- In a **public** blockchain, everyone can read or write data. Some public blockchains limit the access to just reading or writing. Bitcoin, for example, uses an approach where anyone can write.

- In a **private** blockchain, all the participants are well known and trusted. This is useful when the blockchain is used between companies that belong to the same legal mother entity.

2.1. The Problem with the Current Centralized Model

The existing IoT ecosystems rely on centralized, brokered communication models also known as the server/client paradigm. All devices are identified, authenticated and connected through cloud servers that support huge processing and storage capacities. Connection between devices has to be established through the internet, whatsoever the distance in-between is.

While this model has connected generic computing devices for many years, and will support small-scale IoT networks for years to come, but will not cater the need of growing huge IoT ecosystems of future.

Current IoT solutions faces many challenges because the networking equipments, large server farms and centralised clouds involves very high expenditure for infrastructure development and their maintenance. As the IoT devices grow to billions consequently it will involve a large amount of investment.

Cloud servers will remain a bottleneck and point of failure for the entire network, even if the economic engineering and economic challenges are overcome. No single platform to support IoT. Diversity of ownership of devices and the assisting cloud infrastructure makes machine-to machine (M2M) communication difficult.

2.2. Decentralizing IoT Networks

To have more reliable network a decentralized network is solution to the above discussed challenges. A standardised peer-to-peer communication architecture for handling billions of transactions among the devices will reduce the cost significantly by distributing the load of computation and storage across the billions of devices.

Nevertheless, peer-to-peer communication will solves its own issues the principal issue is the security. IoT security is not just about the protection of sensitive data. The solutions offered have to maintain the security and privacy that propose some form of validation and consensus for transactions to prevent hoaxing and theft.

The decentralized approach have to support three fundamental functions:

- Peer-to-peer messaging
- Distributed file sharing
- Autonomous device coordination

The schematic diagram of decentralized approach for IOT system is shown in fig. 1.

Figure 1. Decentralized approach in IOT (Datafloq, 2019)

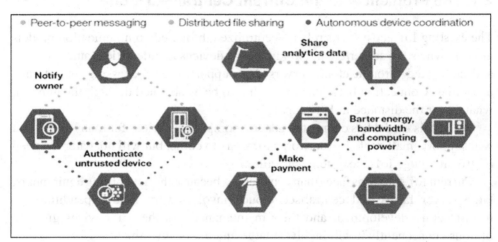

3. THE BLOCKCHAIN APPROACH

Blockchain the "distributed ledger" that support bitcoin has cropped up as an object of deep interest in the technical industry. This technology proposes a way of recording transaction that is secure, transparent, auditable and efficient; as such, it inherent the possibility of disrupting industries and enabling new business modes. The technology is young and changing very fast. To avoid troublemaking surprises decision makes across the industries and business should focus to investigate the application of technology. (A. B. Gaurav, et al., 2020)

The main components in Blockchain technology are listed here-

Network of Nodes

The transactions made on a blockchain network are collectively maintained by the nodes of the network and are checked by a protocol. 'Mining' adds the new transaction to the ledger and the other node on the network verify the proof of work.

Consensus

Consensus proposes the proof of work (PoW) and verifies the action in the networks.

Cryptography

It makes hard for unauthorized users to access or tamper Data bound by a crypto mechanism.

Shared ledger

The ledger is made publicly available and is incorruptible which is updated every time a transaction is made.

Distributed database system

The database is composed of blocks of information and is copied to every node of the system. Every block has a list of transactions, a timestamp and the information which links to the previous block.

Smart contract

It is used to verify and validate the participants of the network.

4. CHALLENGES TO SECURE IOT DEPLOYMENTS

Irrespective of the role your business has over the network, you need to know how to get advantage from this new technology that proposes such highly varied and rapidly changing opportunities.

Managing the large amount of existing and proposed data is a complex task. The aim of turning the huge data into valuable information is tedious and complicated because of many challenges. Mitigating IoT risks through existing security technology is not enough. The goal is to have data secure at the right place, right time and in right format. Figure 2 shows the transition of approach from centralized model to decentralized model in IOT infrastructure (Datafloq, 2019)

a.   Dealing with the Challenges and Threats

It is anticipated that more businesses will deploy security solutions for protection of IoT devices and services in future. As the number of online devices shall be increasing the organisation involved in the business have to broaden their scope of security.

Businesses have to adopt security as per the capabilities and risk associated with the devices involved. Business Intelligence presumes that spending on security solutions of IoT devices to increase five times in the next four years

b.   The Optimum Platform

Providing solutions to the IoT need unparallel collaboration, coordination and connectivity for each piece in the system. Though it is possible, but cost and time parameters make it difficult, until and unless new approach is applied.

Figure 2. Transition from centralized model to decentralized model

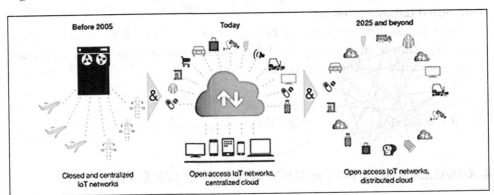

5. IS BLOCKCHAIN THE ANSWER TO IOT SECURITY?

Security is the ongoing issue for IoT. The huge market offers the ample amount of risk for device hacking in the unregulated market. We are talking of smart cars and smart homes, then the individual's privacy and security is a real concern. The data that is collected, processed and passed among IoT device over network the security becoming a huge concern (V. Kumar, et al., 2017).

Among many security recommendations for IoT devices, like biometric, two factor authorization one of the potential answer is blockchain IoT security. Blockchain is quite familiar for bitcoin and Ethereum, offering solution for the security of IoT. It provides protection against data tempering, locking access to Internet of Things devices and allowing compromised devices to be shut down in an IoT network. Hyundai has recently backed HDAC (Hyundai Digital Access Currency) a start-up specifically designed for IoT security. It has help creating a permissioned private network.

"Some of the distinguishing characteristics of the HDAC are as follows (a) PoW mining algorithm which lessens mining monopolization (b) Three minute blocks (c) Has a private/public/permissioned blockchain" @ ecurrencyholder.

Thomas Hardjono, Chief Technology Officer of MIT Connection Science advised there is need of infrastructure development for managing devices and data access. He proposed a blockchain based IoT framework known as ChainAnchor in one of his publication. The proposed framework handles device security by activation and security layers supported by manufacturers, data providers and third parties. The layer of access in this framework keeps away the unauthorised devices or bad actors from the network. It also contains cases for safely selling and removing devices from blockchain.

There are many issues apart from the blockchain IoT security like the issue of processing power. Many IoT devices lack the power required. The present blockchains are unable to control if a group of miners control more than 50% of the network's mining hash rate. The wide spread network of nodes in a blockchain make it very difficult, but the processing power of an IoT blockchain at home can easily hacked.

Yes the IoT security definitely continue to evolve as regulations to their development. But the possibility of security system of a blockchain IoT security hold the great potential in present scenario.

6. THE BLOCKCHAIN AND IOT

Blockchain technology provide the solution to settle the issues of Privacy, reliability and scalability in the Internet of Things. The blockchain technology could be the only technology in present era that is needed by the IoT industry. Because this technology can provide the processing of billions of transaction, trace the billions of devices over network and can make coordination among the large network of devices, thereby saving significantly for IoT industry. Moreover, the decentralized approach would remove the single point failure, making a more reliable ecosystem for devices over network. The data of the users would be more secure on the network as the blockchain technology uses cryptographic algorithm. (Choi, S. et. al., 2018 & Kumar, V., & Thakur, R. S. 2017)

The ledger cannot be tampered and altered easily by malicious users as the ledger is not lying at single location, as there is no single line of communication that can be intercepted. Moreover, blockchain has proven it worth in the financial services through cryptocurrencies such as bitcoin, where the trustless peer-to-peer messaging is made possible without the intervention of third party.

It not surprising that blockchain technology has been embraced quickly by the enterprise IoT technologies. This is all because of the capabilities like decentralized, trustless and autonomous that has made it a fundamental element of IoT solutions.

Fig.3 describes the universal digital ledger in distributed transaction ledger for various IOT Transactions (Datafloq, 2019)

Figure 3. Distributed transaction ledger for various IOT Transactions (Datafloq, 2019)

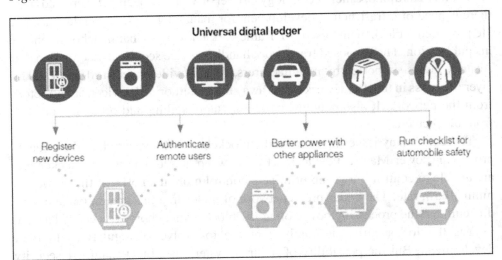

The blockchain can create an indisputable record of the past of smart devices over the IoT network. There is no centralized control or authority required for the functioning of autonomous devices. This results in the opening of the doors to a series of IoT set-ups that were really difficult, or even beyond imagination to implement.

Implementing the blockchain to the maximum capabilities, IoT solutions can empower trustless and secure messaging among devices in an IoT network. The message is treated as financial transaction in a bitcoin network in this framework. The smart contracts are used for the message exchange after the agreement between the two parties.

This condition can provide the control from distant location, in order to control the flow of water based on the conditions in the crop, the communication can directly be established with the irrigation system. On the similar lines data exchange can make adjustment based on the weather conditions in different fields.

Implementing the blockchain will make true autonomous smart devices capable of financial exchanges and data transfers without the intervention of centralized party. The blockchain provides this autonomy because nodes in the network verify and validate the transactions of their own without depending on centralized authority

In this context, the smart devices can be imagined to place orders for repairing its parts without the intervention of human or third party. Likewise, smart vehicles will be able to deliver a complete report about the replacement of most important part after arriving at a workshop.

One of the most exciting competencies of the blockchain is the capability to maintain an exact trusted and decentralized ledger of all transactions in a network.

This ability is necessary to assist many agreements and regulatory requirements of industrial IoT applications without relying on centralized authority.

7. RESOLVING IOT SECURITY ISSUES WITH BLOCKCHAIN TECHNOLOGY

7.1 The Problems of a Centralized IoT Network

The present IoT ecosystem is the centralized model. In this model the different devices are connected, recognized and verified through cloud services that provide high computation and storage capabilities. The internet is the fundamental requirement for information passage. A very high cost in term of infrastructure and maintenance of integrate IoT solutions is involved in the centralized model. (Zhao, S., et al., 2019).

The number of IoT devices is also one of the important issue to be undertaken. The cost involved when the number of internet connected devices reaches to millions, the communication channels will also be increased, resulting in the issue of scalability, economics and engineering.

Even if these issues are resolved one more issue is the cloud services which can disturb the entire network. Henceforth, IoT devices security will be even more difficult.

Applying centralized model to small sized IoT can be successful in saving cost because there would not be the problems of scalability and maintenance. Nevertheless, large IoT ecosystems will encounter these associated issues. Which calls for a decentralized framework.

Different areas of economy are investing largely in blockchain technology. The various countries of the world, corporations and universities have found reasons to invest in this technology.

7.2 Protecting IoT With a Decentralized Blockchain Approach

The most important emerging trend is the unification of blockchain and the Internet of Things. To solve the most of the security issues the decentralization of an IoT network is the solution. Though the decentralization, autonomy, trustworthiness and scalability potentially make it a component of the overall IoT ecosystem. (Bahga, A., & Madisetti, V. K., 2016).

When we are considering the Internet of Things, the Blockchain technology can be implemented for the successful connection, tracking, and coordination of millions of smart devices. The blockchain technology investment by the IoT industry can guarantee the appropriate management of data at various levels.

The integration of Blockchain technology into IoT networks can offer more security and privacy because this technology is based on cryptographic algorithms. The transactions are recorded orderly and carefully by which the connected devices history can be recorded.

Merging this with the fact that there is no need of central authority for the implementation of blockchain technology you will see the integration potentials and benefits are really limitless.

7.3 Two Basic Setups

There are two main schemes for using blockchain technology for providing IoT network security. In first scheme, a company integrates its connected devices to get and transmit data, then it connects them to a blockchain network. This technology smart devices exchange messages, make order and complete transactions. In the second scheme, the Ethereum smart contacts are employed by a company for automation of the process. This provides endless and safe exchanges of messages between connected devices like blockchain based financial transactions.

8. CONCLUSION

The implementation of a blockchain technology decentralized approach to an entire IoT network can help in different ways to secure the IOT infrastructure. It will guarantee proper security by ensuring the privacy and protection of data at all levels. In addition, blockchain technology can help resolve scalability issues and provide an effective functioning of the system and can solve the economic issues of the world.

REFERENCES

Bahga, A., & Madisetti, V. K. (2016). Blockchain platform for industrial internet of things. *Journal of Software Engineering and Applications*, *9*(10), 533–546. doi:10.4236/jsea.2016.910036

Choi, S. S., Burm, J. W., Sung, W., Jang, J. W., & Reo, Y. J. (2018). A blockchain-based secure Iot control scheme. In *2018 International Conference on Advances in Computing and Communication Engineering (ICACCE)* (pp. 74-78). IEEE. 10.1109/ICACCE.2018.8441717

Datafloq. (n.d.). https://datafloq.com/read/securing-internet-of-things-iot-with-blockchain/2228

Gartner Research. (n.d.). https://www.gartner.com/it-glossary/internet-of-things/

Gaurav, A. B., Kumar, P., Kumar, V., & Thakur, R. S. (2020). Conceptual Insights in Blockchain Technology: Security and Applications. In Transforming Businesses with Bitcoin Mining and Blockchain Applications (pp. 221-233). IGI Global.

Internet of things beyond-bitcoin. (n.d.). https://www.cio.com/article/3027522/ internet-of-things/beyond-bitcoin-can-the-blockchain-power-industrial-iot.html

Kumar & Thakur. (2017). A brief Investigation on Data Security Tools and Techniques for Big Data. *International Journal of Engineering Science Invention, 6*(9), 20–27.

Kumar, V., & Thakur, R. S. (2017). Jaccard Similarity based Mining for High Utility Webpage Sets from Weblog Database. *International Journal of Intelligent Engineering and Systems, 10*(6), 211–220. doi:10.22266/ijies2017.1231.23

Zhao, S., Li, S., & Yao, Y. (2019). Blockchain enabled industrial Internet of Things technology. *IEEE Transactions on Computational Social Systems, 6*(6), 1442–1453. doi:10.1109/TCSS.2019.2924054

Zheng, Z., Xie, S., Dai, H., Chen, X., & Wang, H. (2017). An Overview of Blockchain Technology: Architecture, Consensus, and Future Trends. *2017 IEEE International Congress on Big Data (BigData Congress),* 557–564.

KEY TERMS AND DEFINITIONS

Block: It is a container data structure which contain series of transactions. Each transaction within a block is digitally signed and encrypted and verified by the peer node of blockchain network.

Blockchain: It is a decentralized computation and information sharing platform that enables multiple authoritative domains, who don't trust each other, to cooperate, coordinate and collaborate in a rational decision-making process.

Internet of Things: Internet technology connecting devices, machines and tools to the internet by means of wireless technologies.

Private Blockchain: All the participants are known and trusted. This is useful when the blockchain is used between companies that belong to the same legal mother entity.

Public Blockchain: Everyone can read or write data. Some public blockchains limit the access to just reading or writing. Bitcoin, for example, uses an approach where anyone can write.

Chapter 4
Securing IoT Applications Using Blockchain

Sreelakshmi K. K.
Department of Computer Science and Information Systems, Birla Institute of Technology and Science, Pilani, India

Ashutosh Bhatia
Department of Computer Science and Information Systems, Birla Institute of Technology and Science, Pilani, India

Ankit Agrawal
Department of Computer Science and Information Systems, Birla Institute of Technology and Science, Pilani, India

ABSTRACT

The internet of things (IoT) has become a guiding technology behind automation and smart computing. One of the major concerns with the IoT systems is the lack of privacy and security preserving schemes for controlling access and ensuring the security of the data. A majority of security issues arise because of the centralized architecture of IoT systems. Another concern is the lack of proper authentication and access control schemes to moderate access to information generated by the IoT devices. So the question that arises is how to ensure the identity of the equipment or the communicating node. The answer to secure operations in a trustless environment brings us to the decentralized solution of Blockchain. A lot of research has been going on in the area of convergence of IoT and Blockchain, and it has resulted in some remarkable progress in addressing some of the significant issues in the IoT arena. This work reviews the challenges and threats in the IoT environment and how integration with Blockchain can resolve some of them.

DOI: 10.4018/978-1-7998-2414-5.ch004

I. INTRODUCTION

The rapid advancements in networking technologies have led to an increased number of devices or things being able to connect to the Internet, which forms the Internet of Things, commonly known as IoT. Some of the leading IoT applications are Smart-grid, smart-homes, Industrial IoT, smart healthcare, etc. At a high-level, a typical IoT ecosystem consists of devices like sensors that collect data, actuators, and other devices that perform control and monitoring specific to the application area, communication infrastructure guided by the network protocols and local or centralized storage (cloud) that collects data from different devices and processes it for further analysis. The data generated by the various IoT devices is characterized by its vast volume, heterogeneity, and dynamic nature. Each device in an IoT environment has a unique identifier associated with it. A review work Colakovic and Hadialic (2018) gives a detailed and technical description of IoT and its enabling technologies. To build a sustainable IoT ecosystem that can adapt and perform well in a particular application area is a challenging task. With various smart solutions using a large number of devices, the problem of maintaining security for private or user data in the centralized cloud storage is a very tedious task that needs significant attention. The stakes are high if the private data falls into the hands of malicious entities. Another issue that draws concern is the resource and energy constraints of devices, which make it challenging to run massive cryptographic algorithms that strengthen the security of the data generated. The other challenges that need to be dealt with in specific situations such as a disaster are the fault tolerance and recovery of devices located at remote locations. Also, the diverseness in the IoT application areas and the uncertainty about the technology and the solutions offered creates a lack of trust in these solutions. Thus the need for a decentralized solution to ensure the security in an IoT ecosystem is an essential requirement of any IoT application.

The concept of Blockchain has been very active in cryptographic and security since its revelation in 2008. The remarkable advancements made in the Blockchain research have made cryptocurrencies a reality using BitCoin. The BitCoin with a current value of 5431.43 USD and holding around 5.7 million blocks is continuously increasing at a rapid rate with the help of more hashing power and mining pools. Software giants like Linux Foundation are already hacking the potential of Blockchain by researching on applications like HyperLedger (Blummer et al., 2018). With the Software industry predicting a promising future for the blockchain technology, it is essential that we investigate in detail the applicability of Blockchain in IoT to address the main security issues and how far it can be successful in solving them.

When Blockchain meets IoT, some of the expected benefits with this convergence are the building of trust between entities, completeness, consistency, and integrity of stored data, immutability or tamper-proof preservation of private data, reduction in expenses and thereby cheaper solutions, enhanced security and faster processing of Big Data.

The major objectives of the review work presented in this paper are:

- To investigate the security issues and challenges currently present in IoT applications.
- To highlight the decision criteria for applying Blockchain in IoT.
- To survey the scope of solutions that can be achieved through the convergence of Blockchain with IoT.
- To demarcate what IoT applications need and what distributed ledger technology (DLT) can offer.
- To present the state of the art in the integration of Blockchain with IoT.
- To identify and categorize IoT applications based on the issues addressed by Blockchain in the particular application area.

The rest of the paper is organized as follows: Section 2 discusses the security challenges in IoT, Section 3 presents the functioning of Blockchain, and Section 4 describes the need for using Blockchain in IoT. Section 5 discusses state of the art and the existing surveys and research that has gone in integrating Blockchain and IoT Blockchain; it analyses by taking some application domains of IoT where the application of Blockchain has succeeded in bringing trust and security among the different parties involved.

II. CHALLENGES AND SECURITY THREATS IN THE IOT ECOSYSTEM

Fig. 1 shows the primary security issues at different levels of IoT layered architecture. Safeguarding the device-level security of IoT objects is a cumbersome job considering the whole IoT assets and the possible vulnerabilities they hold. IoT applications should be developed, keeping in mind the design considerations such as storage space, computational power, physical security, communication bandwidth, cost, and latency. The total absence or the lack of regular firmware updates for the installed devices makes it easy for the attackers to exploit the weaknesses in them. The data generated by the devices can be leaked during transmission. The recently instigated Mirai botnet attack, which was one among the biggest distributed denial-of-service (DDoS) attacks in which malicious aggressors intruded into the network by manipulating IoT devices, which were poorly secured, emphasizes the need for strengthening the device-level security in the IoT domain (Fruhlinger, 2018). The low level of security and the high connectivity among the devices made it easy for the attackers to manipulate a few of the devices to obtain the data and make it dysfunctional. A malware named Mirai was installed in the IoT devices using network data from a "zombie network" through Telnet and elementary dictionary attack procedures. Those devices whose security was compromised became part of the botnet, which was then exploited to continue the DDoS attack.

Figure 1. Security Challenges at different levels of IoT layered architecture

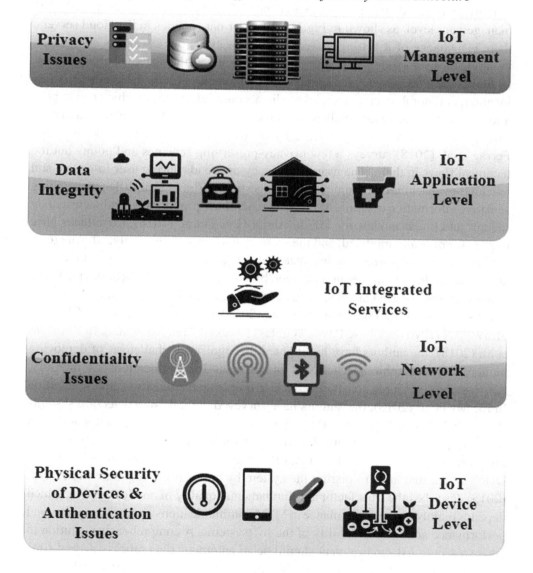

To provide end-to-end host security at the transport layer, Transport Layer Security (TLS) and Datagram Transport Layer Security (DTLS) can be used, thus ensuring host anonymity. Nevertheless, the problem with solutions like TLS and VPNs is that it proves to be unsuitable for many applications because they are not scalable (Miraz,2019). The existing solutions suggest the usage of the Secure Socket Layer (SSL) protocol encrypts the user's data while relaying to the cloud storage. This can be used for ensuring secure communication between the devices and the cloud. At the application level, ensuring integrity becomes a significant problem as more and more data gets aggregated from different devices. However, in the IoT management level, as shown in Fig.1, while user-data resides in the cloud servers, there is a chance of it getting shared between or even sold to various companies, violating the user's rights for privacy and security and further driving public distrust. In most cases, the devices may require the end user's private data such as name, location, cell number, etc. or social media account information, which can expose a lot about the user to any malicious attacker who gets it. Thus, there is a lack of trust in the level of privacy offered by centralized infrastructures like a cloud. Ferrag et al. (2018) surveys a few privacy-preserving schemes and points out the technical flaws in them. The usage of privacy-aware ids during user-to-device and machine-to-machine communication is suggested in (Elrawy et al. 2018) for avoiding sensitive information tracking. Many researchers have proposed several security risk models and threat models for IoT. In Abdul-Ghani et al. (2018), IoT attacks have been systematically modeled, and the security goals have been analyzed. An attack taxonomy and the corresponding measures to tackle them have been listed. The attacks in the IoT environment have been broadly aligned as Physical-device based attacks, Protocol-based attacks, Data at rest-based attacks, and Application-based attacks. The work by Pongle and Chavan (2015) surveys the attacks on RPL and 6LoWPAN (IPv6 over Low-Power Wireless Personal Area Networks). In Kouicem et al. (2018), the authors have highlighted the significant challenges of deploying modern cryptographic mechanisms in different IoT applications as mobility, heterogeneity, resource constraints, lack of proper standardization, and scalability. In Elrawy et al. (2018), the authors have surveyed the intrusion detection systems (IDS) for IoT based systems. They claim that IDS can be a potential solution to reducing the network-level attacks on RPL (Routing Protocol for low power and lossy network). It has been shown that IDS can also reduce the chance of a DoS or DDoS attack that aims to disrupt the system by bombarding requests. Bassi et al. (2013) describes the trust factor as a fundamental quality of any IoT system, which depends mainly on the performance in M2M communications and the computational performance and interoperability of the IoT systems. A comprehensive solution to create a secure IoT environment should be an automatic data processing real-time platform that encompasses services like data encryption and authentication, thus promising data integrity, access control, privacy, and it should be scalable and less expensive. The ability to promptly detect and isolate the devices whose security has been compromised is a much-needed requirement to ensure device-level security in any IoT application. The emergence of Blockchain has paved the way for exploring its potential in providing some or all of these security services in the IoT system.

III. BLOCKCHAIN CONCEPTS

Although numerous papers have elaborated on the techniques and concepts of Blockchain and smart contracts, we must highlight the basics. Fernandez-Caramez and Fraga-Lamas (2018) gives a good description of the blockchain functioning.

A blockchain is a distributed ledger of immutable records that are managed in a peer to peer network. All the nodes in the network ensure the integrity and correctness of the Blockchain through consensus algorithms. This method of placing trust in a network of nodes strengthens the security of the Blockchain. Blockchains can be classified into public, private, or consortium based on whether the membership is permissioned or permissionless. In public blockchains, any user can become a member. There are no membership restrictions, and they are only pseudo-anonymous. Bitcoin and Ethereum are good examples of public blockchains. However, private blockchains are owned and operated by a company or organization, and any user who wants to join the network has to request for membership through the concerned people.

Thus there is only partial immutability offered. Private and consortium blockchains are faster in transaction processing compared to the public counterparts, due to the restricted number of members. Examples of some permissioned blockchains are HyperLedger (Fabric Blummer et al., 2018, Hyperledger, 2017) and R3 Corda (Brown et al., 2016). Some private blockchains impose read restrictions on the data within the blocks. Consortium blockchains are owned and operated by a group of organizations or a private community. Blockchain users use asymmetric key cryptography to sign on transactions. The trust factor maintenance within a distributed ledger technology (DLT), can be attributed to the consensus algorithms and the key desirable properties achieved thenceforth. Wüst and Gervais (2018) gives a good description of these properties. Some of them are Public Verifiability, Transparency, Integrity. The main terminologies in Blockchain are discussed below:

A.   Terminologies in Blockchain:
   1.   ***Blocks:*** The transactions that occur in a peer-to-peer network associated with a blockchain are picked up from a pool of transactions and grouped in a block. Once a transaction has been validated, it cannot be reverted

back. Transactions are pseudonymous as they are linked only to the user's public key and not to the real identity of the user. A block may contain several hundreds of transactions. The block-size limits the number of transactions that can be included in a block. Fig.2 shows the general structure of a block in a blockchain. A block consists of the version no., hash of the previous block, the Merkle root tree to trace the transactions in the block, hash of the current block, timestamp and nonce value. A blockchain starts with a genesis block.

2. *Mining:* Mining is a process in which the designated nodes in the blockchain network called miners collect transactions from a pool of unprocessed transactions and combine them in a block. In mining, each miner competes to solve an equally difficult computational problem of finding a valid hash value with a particular no. of zeroes that is below a specific target. In Bitcoin mining, the number of zeroes indicates the difficulty of the computation. Many nonce values are tried to arrive at the golden nonce that hashes to a valid hash with the current difficulty level. When a miner arrives at this nonce value, we can say that he has successfully mined a block. This block then gets updated to the chain.

3. *Consensus:* The consensus mechanism serves two main purposes, as given in Jesus et al. (2018): block validation and the most extensive chain selection. Proof-of-Work is the consensus algorithm used in Bitcoin Blockchain. The proof-of-stake algorithm is much faster than Proof-of-Work and demands less computational resources. The Ethereum blockchains use a pure proof-of-stake algorithm to ensure consensus. Besides Proof-of-Work, there are other consensus algorithms such as Proof of Byzantine Fault Tolerance (PBFT), proof- of activity, etc. Anwar(2018) presents a consolidated view of the different consensus algorithms. Proof-of-Work is a kind of a signature which indicates that the block has been mined after performing computation with the required difficulty level. This signature can be easily verified by the peers in the network to ensure a block's validity. The longest chain is always selected as the consistent one for appending the new block.

4. *Smart Contracts:* They are predefined rules deployed in the Blockchain network that two parties involved in a settlement must agree to priorly. Smart contracts were designed to avoid disagreement, denial, or violation of rules by the parties involved. They are triggered automatically in the Blockchain, on the occurrence of specific events mentioned in the rules.

B. Overall functioning:

Users connect to the Blockchain and initiate a transaction signed with their private key. This transaction is sent to a pool of transactions where it resides

Figure 2. Structure of a Block in a Blockchain

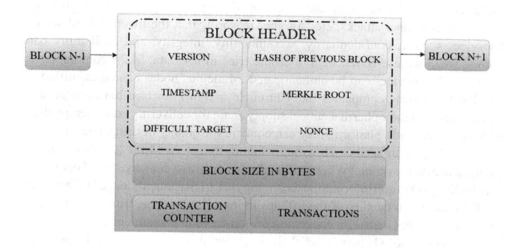

until it is fetched into a block by a miner. The miner then generates a new block after gathering transactions from the pool and computing the valid hash of the block. When a miner succeeds in generating a new block, the new block is broadcast to the nodes in the P2P network. All nodes in the network verify the block using a consensus algorithm, and upon successful validation, update it to their copy of the chain, and the transaction attains completion.

IV. WHY DO WE NEED BLOCKCHAIN IN IOT?

According to Agrawal et al. (2018), the major barricade in the decentralized environment of IoT is the lack of privacy and security of sensitive data that is transferred when connected devices communicate with each other or with the cloud. Data shared cannot be securely encrypted due to the lack of computational power and energy to run encryption algorithms. Thus ensuring data privacy and security is a requirement in any IoT application. The authors in Agrawal et al. (2018) have modeled a security solution using Smart Contracts and Blockchain to ensure continuously secured user-device communications in a smart city and smart home scenario. Using IoT hubs or edge nodes that enable the constrained device to connect to the Blockchain (Agrawal et al., 2018), thus mitigating the necessity to become full nodes, they have tackled the issue of resource and energy constraints. Also, in a distributed environment like blockchain possibility of detecting attacks and restraining further damage is easy since achieving consensus among peers is a necessary condition. Introducing Blockchain in IoT would eliminate the possibility of attacks like DDoS attack, device spoofing, impersonation, injecting malicious code, side-channel attacks, etc. Another reason is that the much-needed security services such as confidentiality, accountability, integrity, and availability come along when we use Blockchain to ensure trust in IoT data. M2M communication between IoT devices can be authenticated. Malicious nodes can be identified and isolated. Recently companies like Chronicle in San Francisco have started using blockchains in their pharmaceutical supply chain for delivering gene therapy drugs. Using a secure IoT platform, they can confirm the quality of drugs and ensure that they don't get damaged or go wrong while in transit. In Miraz (2019) the authors emphasize on the point, "Where IoT is often viewed as a convergence of operational technology (OT) and information technology (IT), Distributed Ledger Technology's (DLT) role as an enabler of the IoT lies in its ability to forge trust, not only at the product level but across an ecosystem of non-trusting constituents."

To determine whether Blockchain is essential in a particular IoT application domain, Ferrag et al. (2018) presents a flow diagram. The consolidated thoughts of it can be briefed as follows: If an IoT application requiring a decentralized security framework demands verification of records between multiple parties who do not trust each other nor a centralized third party and the documents need to be synchronized among these entities, then Blockchain can be applied to arrive at a presumed consensus. However, it should be noted that though the democratic blockchain platform can be used to limit the implications of attack by promoting easier detection, it cannot be taken as an ultimate solution to ensuring IoT security.

Blockchain should not be applied in IoT for merely performing transaction processing or as a substitute for a replicated database requirement. If a traditional database can solve the problem or if all participant trusts a centralized authority, then there's no need for Blockchain in such a scenario. Blockchain should not be used in applications where raw data needs to be gathered in real-time as these incur high latency overheads.

V. STATE OF THE ART AND EXISTING RESEARCH IN BLOCKCHAIN BASED IOT (BIOT)

Quite a lot of research papers have been written on the convergence of Blockchain with IoT. Blockchain technology, in its current form, cannot be directly absorbed into the IoT domain as most of the IoT applications operate in real-time, and the introduction of Blockchain increases latency, demands high computational power and bandwidth. However, some real implementations though at their nascent level Gundersen (2011) and Hanada et al. (2018) have shown results of a promising future that can be achieved through the convergence of the two technologies. Hence, research continues to delve deep into its use cases, such as the applicability of smart contracts to resolve the majority of the existing business matters like a violation or bypass of policies, forgery, frauds, etc. Many IoT applications may have the requirement of tracking and keeping the participating entities updated on the essential activities that occur in the system. A lot of discrepancies arise in business transactions while procuring products and services, e.g., selling counterfeit products or cheating a manufacturer by demanding payment before the completion of the required service, etc. These discrepancies can be taken care of using sensory data linked with smart contracts. With smart contracts, organizations can safely ascertain funds for current and future operations, the trust factor now being ensured. Bodkhe et al. (2020) survey various consensus algorithms and their applicability in a Cyber-physical system. They also address the challenges and security issues in various CPS application domains.

Dai et al. (2019) discuss the main opportunities that arise in the IoT ecosystem when it is converged with Blockchain, namely: Enhanced interoperability, improved security, traceability, and reliability of IoT data, Autonomic interactions of entities in IoT system. It also describes the architecture of Blockchain of things consisting of data sublayer, network sublayer, consensus sublayer, incentive sublayer, and service sublayer. Makhdoom et al. (2019) discuss methods, like Sharding to reduce transaction processing time, to overcome the challenges associated with the integration of Blockchain and IoT.

Hang and Kim (2019) introduce an IoT platform to assure data integrity of data sensed by IoT devices. It uses HyperLedger Fabric along with a proof of consensus method to achieve consensus. The solution is appropriate to be used in a resource-constrained environment. Rejeb et al. (2019) highlight the emerging research areas that arise with the integration of IoT with Blockchain as Scalability, Security, Immutability, and Auditing, Effectiveness and Efficiency of Information flows, Traceability and Interoperability and Quality

Maroufi et al. (2019) discuss the main challenges in blockchain and IoT integration. Its introduction helps to build a decentralized, scalable, secure, immutable ledger. The heterogeneity of IoT solutions is one of the main challenges involved with the convergence of the two technologies. Panarello et al. (2018) categorize the utility of Blockchain in smart environments into two: Device manipulation and data manipulation. Data manipulation uses Blockchain as a history keeping system, and device manipulation uses smart contracts to make autonomous decisions based on business logic.

Atlam et al. (2018) describe the comparison between Blockchain and IoT and elaborates on the benefits such as publicity, decentralization, resiliency, security, speed, cost minimization, immutability, and anonymity, of converging the two technologies. Yu et al. (2018) discuss various application domains for the integration of IoT and

Blockchain and the main security challenges it solves in an IoT ecosystem. It also gives a view of the Blockchain and IoT integrated framework addressing each layer in the IoT architecture in detail.

Minoli and Occhiogrosso (2018) categorize the different frameworks for IoT blockchain integration into categories such as end-to-end blockchains, Analytics/storage-level, Gateway-level, Site-level, and Device level. A fast payment system for Blockchain backed edge IoT systems is proposed, which ensures security and reliability (Hao et al., 2018). The different phases of the protocol, such as Prepare Phase, Deposit Phase, Fast Payment Phase, Transfer Phase, are described. To prevent double spending problem, a Broker is designated with a pool of deposits. The Broker is responsible for The system ensures security and punishes Brokers. In case they violate the rules of the system.

Figure 3. Relationship between offerings of blockchain and security requirements

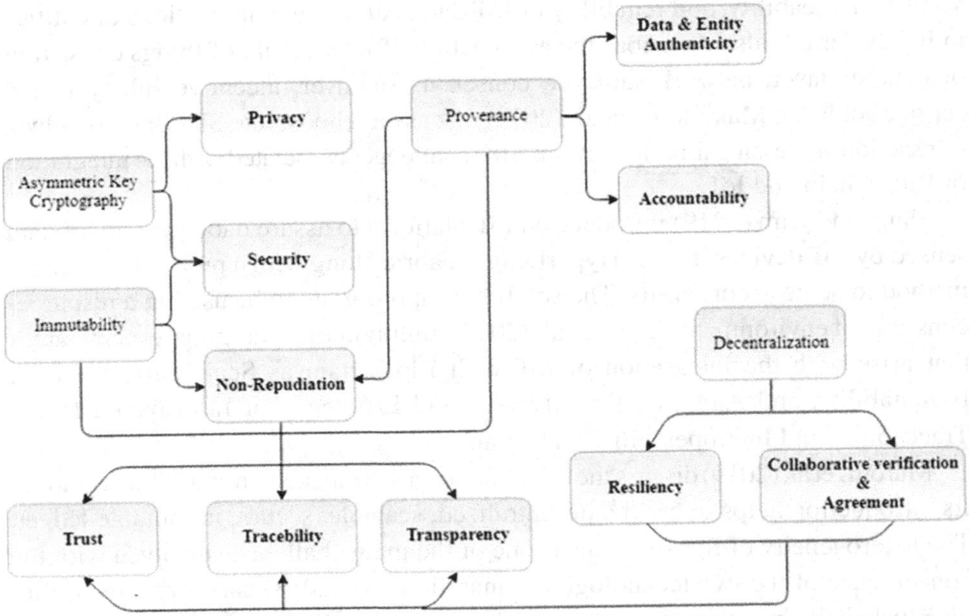

The potential of Blockchain to resolve problems in ensuring trust in the clinical trials in the healthcare industry has been discussed in many papers. Blockchain can not only provide automatized solutions but also establish trust among the different stakeholders such as patients, drug dealers, hospitals, and lab staff and also protect data privacy. According to Benchoufi and Ravaud (2017), Blockchain enables the patients to ensure trust in their private data through access control policies. A proof-of-concept methodology for collecting consent from the concerned people is explained in this context to enable differential privacy. Some of the companies that are currently working on converging the technologies of Blockchain and IoT are:

- Robonomics (Lonshakov et al., 2018): Robonomics platform implements DApp for smart cities and industries
- IoTeX (Dagher and Adhikari, 2018): It is an IoT-oriented blockchain platform that provides application-specific services such as scalability, isolating nodes, deploying applications.
- IoT Chain (Alphand et al.,2018): Uses a lite OS, the Practical Byzantine Fault Tolerance (PBFT), and CPS technology.
- Filament (2018) a startup that's working towards the goal of building a smart economy has their Blockchain solution kit that consists of hardware and software technologies which can be integrated into edge nodes and IoT devices to ensure a secure transaction execution environment (TEE) through Ethereum or HyperLedger blockchains. A hardware plug and play device has been built to enable tracking of events in autonomous vehicles such as vehicle tracking, charging, and making M2M payments. The main functional aspects associated with it are: assigning secret identities to IoT devices, hardware acceleration to reduce computational latency, manage M2M transactions, built-in quality assessment and compliance audit system and key management systems used to connect to Blockchain and obtain Carbon credits, encryption support for ECDSA (Elliptic curve Digital Signature Authentication), ECDH (Elliptic curve Diffie Hellman) and SHA-256 with HMAC option. With this technology, IoT devices can securely communicate valid attested data, which can be verified.
- Xage: A California based cyber-security startup founded in 2016, exploits Blockchain for connecting industrial machines from oil-wells to smart meters. The perk that comes with decentralization is that the security of every device connected will have to be compromised to obtain control of the data in Blockchain. The security of M2M communication at the network and transport layer is secured as they happen over the Blockchain. The Xage Security Fabric provides a comprehensive solution for modern industrial operations. The main features of the fabric include: safeguarding all equipment from the latest IoT devices to vulnerable legacy systems, identity management, single sign-on, and access control. The company provides two new innovative mechanisms to ensure security: hierarchical tree system and super-majority consensus (Xage, 2019).

- Grid+ (Daley, 2019): Using the Ethereum blockchain, it grants consumers permission to access low powered, energy-saving IoT devices.
- Hypr (Daley, 2019): Being a New York-based company, it stores unique biometric login information such as palm, face, eye, a voice in Blockchain, and implemented a DLT digital key to allow homeowners to have single-point access to smart doors and smart entertainment centers.
- ShipChain (Lawrence, 2020): The Company combines a ship and trace platform based on Blockchain with information from near field communication (NFC) tags that observes and shares the temperature of goods throughout the supply chain, thus providing visibility and trust between producers, transporters, and consumers.
- Chronicled (Daley, 2019): The San Francisco based Company focuses on tracing and managing the supply chain for pharmaceuticals and food supply using Blockchain. It uses IoT enabled shipping containers and sensors for this.
- Netobjex (Daley, 2019): The Company created a standard mechanism for M2M communication for IoT devices. It uses IoToken to enable customers in a restaurant to pay their bill, and in drone delivery, it marks the point of delivery and the transaction for payment.
- Some of the companies like BIMCHAIN, Briq, ULedger, Hunter Roberts OEG & Gartner Builders, Probuild, Tata Steel, Lifechain by Costain are working towards the integration of Blockchain & IoT in the construction sector to improve verification of identities and keep track of the progress of their work (Mazhanda, 2019).
- Eight companies namely, Cisco, Asterix, Radiflow, Xage Security, Sumo Logic, BlackRidge Technology, TDi Technologies, Spherical Analytics, have been selected by the National Cybersecurity Center of Excellence (NCCoE) for working towards securing Industrial Internet of Things (IIoT). The main reasons for introducing Blockchain in IIoT is to secure M2M communication, authenticating, and authorizing a transaction.

Ellervee et al. (2017) presents a good comparison of some blockchains and describes the scope of Blockchain, clearly defining what Blockchain can do and what it cannot. Users and block validators or miners represent the actors in the Blockchain. It also describes the processes that occur in the system like network discovery, creating transactions, signing, issuing assets, mining, and assigning permissions, platforms (permissioned or permissionless), and data models. Fig. 3 represents the outline of how we can manipulate Blockchain to ensure security. The figure helps in understanding the relationship between offerings such as immutability, provenance, etc. and which aspect is needed to satisfy the specific security requirements in user applications.

In the following, we present some use-cases, that provide an overview of how Blockchain can be integrated into IoT. We have classified them based on the functional aspects of Blockchain that they utilize and present a sample system model wherever necessary. Some general issues, such as usage of Blockchain for authorization, access control, device identification, data security, secure M2M communication, have been mentioned in various research papers. However, their practical implementation is still in question. Hence these use cases are not discussed in detail.

A. Blockchain to ensure Privacy, Security, Non-Repudiation and Identification and Isolation of malicious nodes

Generally speaking, privacy is a primary concern in any IoT application. Here, we present some major IoT applications where the loss of confidentiality can result in catastrophes and describe how Blockchain can help in avoiding it. We have highlighted the lack of privacy in IoT and described its reasons in detail in Section II.

1) *Intelligent Transport System:* In an intelligent transport system (ITS), we have vehicles communicating with one another to exchange safety messages and navigation information in real-time such as road conditions, navigation information, traffic jams, accident cases, etc. When vehicles communicate with one another, they share information such as location and user's personal information to identify each other. Hence privacy-preserving schemes are required to protect such sensitive data. Similarly, messages circulated in the network can also be forged. To avoid this and improve trusted communication in VANETs, we look into the applicability of Blockchain in ITS and to what extent it succeeds in solving the problem of Privacy, Security, and Trust.

    System Model: The system model has been explained pertaining to the framework mentioned in Singh and Kim (2017). Here the actors are the vehicles. In this work, Blockchain has been put to use in a vehicular network of autonomous vehicles as a secure data-sharing framework. Here the distrust is between vehicles spreading the information and vehicles receiving this information and using it to perform actions such as taking a lane diversion. Certain vehicles have been designated as Miner nodes based on their willingness to contribute to the network. Consensus achieved in Blockchain helps to ensure trust in the navigation message disseminated and to decide which autonomous vehicle can cross an intersection. The framework implemented has negligible latency associated with it.

Other use-cases of Blockchain in ITS is for vehicle leasing, parts provenance, vehicle tax payment, ride-sharing, performing automatic payments at parking areas and fuel station, or charging station in case of electric vehicles.

The works in Li et al. (2018), Singh and Kim (2017) and Huang et al. (2018) present different methodologies by which Blockchain has been used in VANETS and intelligent transport systems for secure communication and transaction processing. In Singh and Kim (2017), the issues identified in smart vehicle communication are lack of trust, reliability, and data privacy. The authors have introduced a unique identifier called Intelligent Trust Point (IV-TP) similar to a Bitcoin id to ensure privacy in inter-vehicular communication. They have also brought out a proof of driving consensus protocol to maintain consensus. In Yuan and Wang (2016), the authors have elaborated on the design of a blockchain-based framework for ITS. They have presented a seven-layer conceptual model and considered the integration of Blockchain with ITS for creating a parallel transportation management systems (PTMS). A ride-sharing Dapp called La'zooz has also been exemplified. The authors of Lu et al. (2018) investigate the privacy-preserving schemes that can be applied in VANETs to ensure trust and anonymity. They have validated the entity-centric model, which is based on a reputation mechanism to judge the trustworthiness of a vehicle and data-centric model in which trust in the message propagated is computed through various metrics. Finally, they have used a protocol that places faith in a message using a mixture of these two techniques. They have formulated a proof of presence to arrive at a consensus. However, the model proposed by them assumes that the road-side units have adequate computing power. Hanada et al. (2018) studies a decentralized application (DApp) using Blockchain and smart contracts for automatic gasoline purchases in a smart transport system.

They have used smart contracts to counter the problems that affect the aspects of trust and transparency in the services provided by IoT applications.

For making this clearer, let's take the example of a fuel station that delivers its services based on smart contracts and IoT. Consider an interface between the fuel pump and the customer's car. The entities involved in the IoT ecosystem are the sensors that sense the level of fuel in the car and the fuel pump that stops when the fuel is filled. A DApp developed for

performing transactions between the IoT nodes can be deployed on the car kit and the fuel pump. The fuel station can then verify payment deposited, and based on this, it can circulate the fuel consumption details to a smart contract. A list of fuel stations based on the user's current location can be checked in the DApp for filling gas.

In Li et al. (2018), CreditCoin, a privacy-preserving incentive announcement network based on Blockchain, has been proposed to report traffic issues and accidents using VANETS. It includes two components: the announcement protocol and

Table 1. Solutions Offered by Blockchain in Various Applications in IoT

Sl No.	IoT Application Domains	Identification & Isolation Of Malicious Nodes	Provenance	Security	Privacy	Traceability	Trust	Transparency	Non-Repudiation	Accountability
1	Smart city	✓	✓	✓			✓	✓		
2	Smart Grid		✓			✓	✓	✓	✓	✓
3	Smart Healthcare		✓	✓	✓	✓	✓	✓	✓	✓
4	Supply chain management		✓	✓		✓	✓	✓	✓	✓
5	Intelligent Transport Systems	✓	✓	✓	✓		✓	✓	✓	✓
6	Smart homes & Buildings	✓	✓		✓		✓		✓	
7	Industrial IoT & Smart Manufacturing		✓				✓		✓	

incentive mechanism. In this system, the users who complete successful missions are rewarded with credit coins, which actively allows consistent traffic incidents to be reported and verified.

Hîrțan et al. (2020) propose a reputation system that focuses on preserving the privacy of users in an Intelligent Transport System in the cities of San Francisco, Beijing, and Rome. It introduces a consensus mechanism for traffic data sharing, that uses the reputation of the node and the validated answer received from each node in the cluster to achieve consensus in a system of unreliable nodes.

The introduction of Blockchain in ITS helps tackle the privacy concern by introducing anonymity and dynamic heterogeneous key management schemes for ensuring the security of messages in transit.

2) Smart Homes and Smart Buildings:

System Model: A typical home network in smart homes of the future, consists of smart doors and gates, smart lights, smart walls, wearable devices, smart ventilation system, smart home appliances such as refrigerator, AC, Washing machine, etc., smart gardening system, smart surveillance and intrusion detection system (IDS), smart garage, smart washrooms and toilets, smart baby and old people tracker and smart whatnot. These devices communicate with each other and with the user to enhance comforts and living experience. Normally, a smart device in a home network may have shared users, and to personalize the experience, it may be configured with the user profile of its current user, and this data may be shared with other devices for understanding user's choices. However, this collaborative data collection and decision making in the home network comes at the cost of compromising privacy. Hence we use Blockchain to secure the communication between IoT devices. The data in the block consists of the data exchanged between devices, transaction information in case devices perform transactions with the outside world.

The private details of a user can be manipulated by attackers who hack into these devices to perform malicious activities. The stakes are high, including detecting the presence of people at home. Apart from this dangerous compromise in privacy, we also need to take care of the security of devices as they relay information about the location of the smart home for various application purposes. Ensuring device security is another major challenge in a smart home ecosystem. Most vendors do not provide regular security updates for the firmware in smart devices, which leaves vulnerabilities. Hence it is necessary to confirm the security of the connected network of devices installed in a smart home be firmly ascertained. Even more critical is ensuring the security and privacy of devices in smart buildings where numerous employees work.

For this, Dorri et al. (2017) have proposed a scheme using shared keys with a particular lifetime to allow only trusted devices to communicate in a smart home network. Each device in the home network is registered with a home miner. The smart homes are connected to an overlay that enables provide hierarchical and distributed processing. Leiding et al. (2016) presents an access control mechanism that can be applied to Blockchain-based home networks where Security access managers (SAM) are used to identify malicious nodes and prevent them from generating any further transactions in the network. This strategy can be very useful to enable device-level trusted interoperability in smart homes and smart buildings and also in other use-case scenarios such as ITS, in general. Zhou et al. (2018) and Bastos et al. (2018), the authors have used smart contracts and Blockchain to bring about a secure solution for securing communication in a home network.

3)   Smart Healthcare:
System Model: When we talk about smart healthcare, it is characterized by the vast volume of data from heterogeneous sources varying from wearable devices that track the personal health status of the user to the Doctor's diagnosis and evaluation data and prescriptions. Electronic Health Records are used to integrate and store all this data in digital form. However, since patients may visit different hospitals for different types of diseases and treatments, this data gets fragmented and inconsistent. If we use a central database to store and access

this data, it invites security and privacy problems as the data may be accessed or modified by unauthorized parties. Many such cases are stated in papers where the patient data is sold to people in return for money and personal benefits. Hence there's a need for controlling access to such important information to ensure that patients receive proper healthcare services.

Numerous techniques have been proposed on Blockchain to promote a trusted medical data-sharing platform. Most solutions define a publisher-subscriber or patient-requester relationship between the communicating entities involved (Rifi et al., 2018, Shen et al., 2019). In Rifi et al. (2018), the author have proposed and implemented a method using edge servers to overcome the computational power constraint in a smart healthcare data collection network. They have defined the main actors in their network as publishers who are the patients whose health is monitored using sensors and subscribers who require the publisher's data to perform health monitoring and diagnosis. The subscribers who can have access to the health data are added by the publisher to their corresponding address. Thus only subscribers authorized by the publisher gain access to the health data. The patients are monitored within the premises of their smart home. The smart home has a local gateway that connects to an edge server for performing computationally intensive tasks. Using three types of smart contracts, namely: Publisher contract, client contract, and subscriber contract, they have defined the terms and permissions of each actor in the system. For ensuring privacy, the subscriber id and publisher id are verified. In MedChain, a Blockchain-based health data sharing system that uses session keys to safeguard the privacy is introduced (Rifi et al., 2018). In this, a healthcare provider collects data from the sensor devices and performs the mining process. Sessions are used to grant access to the requester of the data.

Ray et al. (2020) discuss Blockchain use cases in healthcare like accessing medical records, EHR claim and bill assessment, Clinical Research, Drug Supply Chain Management, IoBHealth, a dataflow architecture bringing together Blockchain and IoT is proposed, for accessing, storing and managing e-healthcare (EHR) data. Uddin et al. (2020) propose a three-layer architecture for leveraging Blockchain in eHealth services consisting of Sensing Layer, Edge processing layer, Cloud layer. A patient agent (PA) software implements a lightweight blockchain consensus mechanism and uses a task offloading algorithm for preserving privacy.

4) Smart Manufacturing and Industrial IoT:
    System Model: The evolution of Industrial IoT (IIoT) and smart cognitive and autonomous robots, augmented reality technologies in the manufacturing sector has led to the emergence of the 4th Industrial revolution. This has created a huge impact on the manufacturing sector. Smart factories are becoming a

reality with companies like Ubirch bringing automatization through smart strategies like a machine as a service, predictive maintenance, and verification of the condition of manufactured products. Smart devices aid manufacturing in design, manufacture maintenance, and supply of products. With IoT, the factory can be transformed into an ecosystem where everything is connected, well-monitored, secured and monetized. The advantages of this connected environment are: the quality of products can be ensured, and machines and services can be shared. In this shared, connected ecosystem, when machines engage in M2M communication, trust, security, and privacy become at stake. Hackers can target the surveillance or the machines for disrupting the factory operations.

Blockchain can be used to perform trusted communication and ensure privacy and security in the transactions performed in distributed manufacturing. Xu et al. (2019) and Liu et al. (2019) describe the security frameworks developed using Blockchain for IIoT. In Xu et al. (2019), a Blockchain-based Service Scheme is presented. A non-repudiation scheme is proposed, which works based on a homomorphic hash function to ensure whether a particular service promised is delivered or not. In Wan et al. (2019), presented a Blockchain-based security framework for ensuring privacy and security in a smart factory. They have given a layered division to the framework as the Sensing layer, Firmware layer, Management hub layer, Storage layer, and application layer. They have used a blacklist- whitelist mechanism to track and isolate malicious nodes and ensure privacy. They have shown how a lightweight private blockchain can be used to trace the operations of machines and M2M communications. They have combined two models: Bell-La Padula (BLP) model and Biba model to build the data security model using a dynamic identity verification mechanism.

B. Blockchain for Provenance, Accountability, Traceability, and Transparency

1) ***Blockchain for Smart Grid:*** Blockchains are used in Smart-Grid networks for secure trading of sustainable energy. The evolution of micro-grids and smart-grids have enabled small-scale production and selling of power. Provenance and accountability are the guiding factors that need to be brought into the transactions in the energy-trade microgrid network for efficient interoperability. ***System Model:*** The working of a smart-grid network in a city can be explained like this. Excess renewable energy such as solar energy or wind energy produced at homes can be stored in batteries, which can later be sold to other homes in the neighborhood or companies. A smart-meter installed keeps track of the

energy units produced or consumed in real-time and relays this information to the energy distributor for monitoring and billing. With smart-grids becoming a reality, there is a need for a secure energy-trading platform to establish trust and track transactions that occur in the smart grid network.

The state of the art of applying Blockchain to micro-grids and smart-grids brings us to the Brooklyn Micro-grid solutions offered by LO3 Energy (Gundersen, 2011). The smart-contracts linked to the local grid are used to tokenize the extra energy and decide where to buy the electric power from. The energy sharing market consists of four main concepts: Tokenization, P2P Markets, Prosumers, and Community Micro-grids, and Energy-service Companies (CMESC). Tokenization involves converting surplus energy to energy credits. The P2P markets are a network of nodes established in the smart-grid between neighbors and prosumers to energy-producing companies. Prosumers are called so because of the dual role they play as producers and consumers in the energy trading system. In Pieroni et al. (2018), Blockchain is applied for securing communication, transactions, and tokenization of energy. A Smart energy blockchain application prototype has been implemented in the work that connects to the Blockchain in the P2P network. Li et al. (2017) has given a good demonstration of the smart-grid detailing the entities involved as Smart meters, energy nodes, and energy aggregators. Using a consortium blockchain, a unified blockchain for the energy credits transferred has been presented, which can be deployed in the Industrial IoT ecosystem. This enables the user to trace their transaction history and transact with trusted prosumers or companies efficiently. Daghmehchi Firoozjaei et al.(2020) propose a privacy-preserving hybrid blockchain framework called Hy-Bridge, which uses subnetworks that preserve the privacy of IoT users in a microgrid. It separates transactions of the power grid from those of the micro grid. It has three layers IoT user layer, platform layer, and enterprise layer.

2) ***Smart Cities:*** A waste management system for a future smart city is presented in Lamichhane et al. (2017), which is characterized by smart garbage bins(SGB) involving the sensors that detect and alerts the garbage collection service when the bin is full, actuators and smart locks to lock the SGBs. The different entities involved in the system are citizens, Municipality, Waste management operators who dispatch driverless vehicles that perform garbage collection, recyclers who recycle the waste to obtain rewards. Blockchain can be used to record operations and trace the transactions associated with garbage collection and recycling. In Nagothu et al. (2018), collaborative smart surveillance has been presented which uses access control rules specified in the smart contracts to restrict access of unauthorized nodes at fog level to connect to a cloud node containing Blockchain that stores surveillance data in various places in a smart

city. In Nikouei et al. (2018), the authors have proposed an authentication scheme integrated into the Blockchain is used to share and aggregate the surveillance data in two trustless domains at the edge and fog level.

3)   Smart Supply Chain Management:

System Model: A smart supply chain consists of smart objects which have a unique identity and are connected through wireless technologies. They can store information about their conditions like temperature, humidity, etc. and communicate to the Internet through wireless technologies. Then there are suppliers, distributors, transportation services, and consumers. In a conventional supply chain environment, the condition of the products is not traced at each checkpoint. Hence huge loss is encountered by the buyers. Sometimes products transported get tampered or replaced. Thus to ensure the security of manufactured products throughout the supply chain, we need an automated decentralized system that helps to track and assess the quality of product real-time.

Blockchain has been employed in a food supply chain system to overcome this problem. In Lin et al. (2018), Blockchain-based food traceability is proposed. This system enables to ensure food safety by tracking the food product and storing its condition at each stage. Through smart contracts which it establishes between buyer and seller, it provides a transparent system to the buyer, which allows them to verify and ensure the quality of the food they buy. Blockchain and IoT sensors together provide both parties provenance, traceability, trust, and transparency. Through this system, the seller can also identify at which stage in the supply chain the product suffered damage so that they can take remedial methods to avoid the same in the future. They can also determine whether the product has been tampered by scanning the RFID and tracing the sensor values collected, which are stored as metadata in the blocks. Table I summarizes the most relevant security services offered by Blockchain in each IoT application discussed so far.

VI. FUTURE WORK

The applications discussed in the previous section, depict a bright future for the convergence of Blockchain and IoT. However, the inclusion of Blockchain always introduces the probability of a 51% vulnerability. The papers surveyed predict this as far from the possible case. Lightweight algorithms being researched extensively might help in tackling energy and power constraints in IoT environments. However, there's a need for developing a unified blockchain framework for IoT applications. Also, though many initial research works claim that Blockchain is impregnable, there have been many incidents of breach of security of Blockchain like key tampering attacks, Sybil attack, etc. which have been elaborated in (Ferrag et al. 2018). Since the Blockchain in its current form cannot guarantee ultimate security, research needs to focus on identification and resolution of flaws so that developers can build more successful secure versions of Blockchain, which, when integrated with IoT, can provide a secure and safe environment for the application users.

VII. CONCLUSION

The IoT applications face a lot of challenges in terms of security, which can be solved using Blockchain. We have iscussed the major security issues in IoT and exemplified how the application of Blockchain can help in addressing these issues. Many research texts that were surveyed have applied Blockchain to IoT applications without actually ensuring whether it is necessary. Careful assessment needs to be done before applying Blockchain for a particular application. We have analyzed the need for using Blockchain in a particular application area. We have presented the decision criteria and mentioned where it can be used and what offerings it can provide and what it cannot. Also, we have explained a general system model and supportive use cases that can help in the integration and development of Blockchain-based secure IoT solutions.

REFERENCES

Abdul-Ghani, H. A., Konstantas, D., & Mahyoub, M. (2018). A comprehensive IoT attacks survey based on a building-blocked reference model. *International Journal of Advanced Computer Science and Applications*, 355-373.

Agrawal, R., Verma, P., Sonanis, R., Goel, U., De, A., Kondaveeti, S. A., & Shekhar, S. (2018, April). Continuous security in IoT using blockchain. In *2018 IEEE International Conference on Acoustics, Speech and Signal Processing (ICASSP)* (pp. 6423-6427). IEEE. 10.1109/ICASSP.2018.8462513

Alphand, O., Amoretti, M., Claeys, T., Dall'Asta, S., Duda, A., Ferrari, G., . . . Zanichelli, F. (2018, April). IoTChain: A blockchain security architecture for the Internet of Things. In 2018 IEEE Wireless Communications and Networking Conference (WCNC) (pp. 1-6). IEEE. doi:10.1109/WCNC.2018.8377385

Anchor, B. I. S. T. (2019). Taraxa White Paper.

Anwar, H. (2018). *Consensus Algorithms: The Root Of The Blockchain Technology*. Retrieved from https://101blockchains.com/consensus-algorithms-blockchain

Atlam, H. F., Alenezi, A., Alassafi, M. O., & Wills, G. (2018). Blockchain with Internet of Things: Benefits, challenges, and future directions. *International Journal of Intelligent Systems and Applications*, *10*(6), 40–48. doi:10.5815/ijisa.2018.06.05

Bassi, A., Bauer, M., Fiedler, M., & Kranenburg, R. V. (2013). *Enabling things to talk*. Springer-Verlag GmbH. doi:10.1007/978-3-642-40403-0

Bastos, D., Shackleton, M., & El-Moussa, F. (2018). *Internet of Things: A survey of technologies and security risks in smart home and city environments*. Academic Press.

Benchoufi, M., & Ravaud, P. (2017). Blockchain technology for improving clinical research quality. *Trials*, *18*(1), 335. doi:10.118613063-017-2035-z PMID:28724395

Bodkhe, U., Mehta, D., Tanwar, S., Bhattacharya, P., Singh, P. K., & Hong, W. C. (2020). A Survey on Decentralized Consensus Mechanisms for Cyber Physical Systems. *IEEE Access: Practical Innovations, Open Solutions*, *8*, 54371–54401. doi:10.1109/ACCESS.2020.2981415

Brown, R. G., Carlyle, J., Grigg, I., & Hearn, M. (2016). Corda: an introduction. *R3 CEV, 1*, 15.

Čolaković, A., & Hadžialić, M. (2018). Internet of Things (IoT): A review of enabling technologies, challenges, and open research issues. *Computer Networks*, *144*, 17–39. doi:10.1016/j.comnet.2018.07.017

Dagher, T. G. G., & Adhikari, C. L. (2018). *Iotex: A decentralized network for internet of things powered by a privacy-centric blockchain*. White Paper: https:// whitepaper. io/document/131/iotexwhitepaper

Daghmehchi Firoozjaei, M., Ghorbani, A., Kim, H., & Song, J. (2020). Hy-Bridge: A hybrid blockchain for privacy-preserving and trustful energy transactions in Internet-of-Things platforms. *Sensors (Basel)*, *20*(3), 928. doi:10.339020030928 PMID:32050570

Dai, H. N., Zheng, Z., & Zhang, Y. (2019). Blockchain for internet of things: A survey. *IEEE Internet of Things Journal*, *6*(5), 8076–8094. doi:10.1109/JIOT.2019.2920987

Daley, S. (2019). *Blockchain and IoT: 8 examples making our future smarter*. Retrieved from https://builtin.com/blockchain/blockchain-iot-examples

Dorri, A., Kanhere, S. S., Jurdak, R., & Gauravaram, P. (2017, March). *Blockchain for IoT security and privacy: The case study of a smart home. In 2017 IEEE international conference on pervasive computing and communications workshops (PerCom workshops)*. IEEE.

Ellervee, A., Matulevicius, R., & Mayer, N. (2017). A Comprehensive Reference Model for Blockchain-based Distributed Ledger Technology. In *ER Forum/Demos* (pp. 306-319). Academic Press.

Elrawy, M. F., Awad, A. I., & Hamed, H. F. (2018). Intrusion detection systems for IoT-based smart environments: A survey. *Journal of Cloud Computing, 7*(1), 21. doi:10.118613677-018-0123-6

Fernández-Caramés, T. M., & Fraga-Lamas, P. (2018). A Review on the Use of Blockchain for the Internet of Things. *IEEE Access: Practical Innovations, Open Solutions, 6*, 32979–33001. doi:10.1109/ACCESS.2018.2842685

Ferrag, M. A., Derdour, M., Mukherjee, M., Derhab, A., Maglaras, L., & Janicke, H. (2018). Blockchain technologies for the internet of things: Research issues and challenges. *IEEE Internet of Things Journal, 6*(2), 2188–2204. doi:10.1109/JIOT.2018.2882794

Filament. (2018). *Blocklet USB Enclave Data Sheet*. Academic Press.

Fruhlinger, J. (2018). *The Mirai botnet explained: How teen scammers and CCTV cameras almost brought down the internet*. Retrieved from https://www.csoonline.com /article/3258748/the-mirai-botnet-explained-how-teen-scammers-and-cctv-cameras-almost-brought-down-the-internet.html

GSMAs Internet of Things Programme. (2018). *Opportunities and Use Cases for Distributed Ledger Technologies in IoT*. Academic Press.

Gundersen, T. (2011). *An introduction to the concept of exergy and energy quality*. Department of Energy and Process Engineering Norwegian University of Science and Technology, Version, 4.

Hanada, Y., Hsiao, L., & Levis, P. (2018, November). Smart contracts for machine-to-machine communication: Possibilities and limitations. In *2018 IEEE International Conference on Internet of Things and Intelligence System (IOTAIS)* (pp. 130-136). IEEE. 10.1109/IOTAIS.2018.8600854

Hang, L., & Kim, D. H. (2019). Design and implementation of an integrated IoT blockchain platform for sensing data integrity. *Sensors (Basel), 19*(10), 2228. doi:10.339019102228 PMID:31091799

Hao, Z., Ji, R., & Li, Q. (2018, October). FastPay: A Secure Fast Payment Method for Edge-IoT Platforms using Blockchain. In *2018 IEEE/ACM Symposium on Edge Computing (SEC)* (pp. 410-415). IEEE. 10.1109/SEC.2018.00055

Hîrţan, L. A., Dobre, C., & González-Vélez, H. (2020). Blockchain-based reputation for intelligent transportation systems. *Sensors (Basel)*, *20*(3), 791. doi:10.339020030791 PMID:32023997

Huang, X., Xu, C., Wang, P., & Liu, H. (2018). LNSC: A security model for electric vehicle and charging pile management based on blockchain ecosystem. *IEEE Access: Practical Innovations, Open Solutions*, *6*, 13565–13574. doi:10.1109/ACCESS.2018.2812176

Hyperledger Architecture Working Group. (2017). *Hyperledger Architecture* (Vol. 1). Introduction to Hyperledger Business Blockchain Design Philosophy and Consensus.

Jesus, E. F., Chicarino, V. R., de Albuquerque, C. V., & Rocha, A. A. D. A. (2018). A survey of how to use blockchain to secure internet of things and the stalker attack. *Security and Communication Networks*, *2018*, 2018. doi:10.1155/2018/9675050

Kouicem, D. E., Bouabdallah, A., & Lakhlef, H. (2018). Internet of things security: A top-down survey. *Computer Networks*, *141*, 199–221. doi:10.1016/j.comnet.2018.03.012

Lamichhane, Sadov, & Zaslavsky. (2017). *Smart Waste Management: An IoT and Blockchain based approach*. Academic Press.

Lawrence, C. (2020). *The Convergence of IoT and Blockchain is Transforming Industries*. Retrieved from https://www.codemotion.com/magazine/dev-hub/blockchain-dev/blockchain-and-iot-in-industry-use-cases/

Leiding, B., Memarmoshrefi, P., & Hogrefe, D. (2016, September). Self-managed and blockchain-based vehicular ad-hoc networks. In *Proceedings of the 2016 ACM International Joint Conference on Pervasive and Ubiquitous Computing: Adjunct* (pp. 137-140). ACM.

Li, L., Liu, J., Cheng, L., Qiu, S., Wang, W., Zhang, X., & Zhang, Z. (2018). Creditcoin: A privacy-preserving blockchain-based incentive announcement network for communications of smart vehicles. *IEEE Transactions on Intelligent Transportation Systems*, *19*(7), 2204–2220. doi:10.1109/TITS.2017.2777990

Li, Z., Kang, J., Yu, R., Ye, D., Deng, Q., & Zhang, Y. (2017). Consortium blockchain for secure energy trading in industrial internet of things. *IEEE Transactions on Industrial Informatics*, *14*(8), 3690–3700. doi:10.1109/TII.2017.2786307

Lin, J., Shen, Z., Zhang, A., & Chai, Y. (2018). Blockchain and IoT based Food Traceability System. *International Journal of Information Technology*, *24*(1), 1–16.

Liu, D., Alahmadi, A., Ni, J., Lin, X., & Shen, X. (2019). Anonymous reputation system for iiot-enabled retail marketing atop pos blockchain. *IEEE Transactions on Industrial Informatics, 15*(6), 3527–3537. doi:10.1109/TII.2019.2898900

Lonshakov, S., Krupenkin, A., Kapitonov, A., Radchenko, E., Khassanov, A., & Starostin, A. (2018). *Robonomics: platform for integration of cyber physical systems into human economy.* White Paper.

Lu, Z., Liu, W., Wang, Q., Qu, G., & Liu, Z. (2018). A privacy-preserving trust model based on blockchain for VANETs. *IEEE Access: Practical Innovations, Open Solutions, 6*, 45655–45664. doi:10.1109/ACCESS.2018.2864189

Makhdoom, I., Abolhasan, M., Abbas, H., & Ni, W. (2019). Blockchain's adoption in IoT: The challenges, and a way forward. *Journal of Network and Computer Applications, 125*, 251–279. doi:10.1016/j.jnca.2018.10.019

Maroufi, M., Abdolee, R., & Tazekand, B. M. (2019). *On the convergence of blockchain and internet of things (iot) technologies.* arXiv preprint arXiv:1904.01936

Mazhanda, F. (2019). *How Blockchain and IoT Are Opening New Capabilities in the Construction Industry.* Retrieved from https://www.iotforall.com/iot-in-construction/

Minoli, D., & Occhiogrosso, B. (2018). Blockchain mechanisms for IoT security. *Internet of Things, 1*, 1–13. doi:10.1016/j.iot.2018.05.002

Miraz, M. H. (2019). *Blockchain of Things (BCoT): The Fusion of Blockchain and IoT Technologies.* Cuhk Law.

Nagothu, D., Xu, R., Nikouei, S. Y., & Chen, Y. (2018, September). A microservice-enabled architecture for smart surveillance using blockchain technology. In *2018 IEEE International Smart Cities Conference (ISC2)* (pp. 1-4). IEEE. 10.1109/ISC2.2018.8656968

Nikouei, S. Y., Xu, R., Nagothu, D., Chen, Y., Aved, A., & Blasch, E. (2018, September). Real-time index authentication for event-oriented surveillance video query using blockchain. In *2018 IEEE International Smart Cities Conference (ISC2)* (pp. 1-8). IEEE. 10.1109/ISC2.2018.8656668

Panarello, A., Tapas, N., Merlino, G., Longo, F., & Puliafito, A. (2018). Blockchain and iot integration: A systematic survey. *Sensors (Basel), 18*(8), 2575.

Pieroni, A., Scarpato, N., Di Nunzio, L., Fallucchi, F., & Raso, M. (2018). Smarter city: Smart energy grid based on blockchain technology. *Int. J. Adv. Sci. Eng. Inf. Technol, 8*(1), 298–306. doi:10.18517/ijaseit.8.1.4954

Pongle, P., & Chavan, G. (2015, January). A survey: Attacks on RPL and 6LoWPAN in IoT. In *2015 International conference on pervasive computing (ICPC)* (pp. 1-6). IEEE. 10.1109/PERVASIVE.2015.7087034

Ray, P. P., Dash, D., Salah, K., & Kumar, N. (2020). Blockchain for IoT-Based Healthcare: Background, Consensus, Platforms, and Use Cases. *IEEE Systems Journal*, 1–10. doi:10.1109/JSYST.2020.2963840

Rejeb, A., Keogh, J. G., & Treiblmaier, H. (2019). Leveraging the Internet of Things and Blockchain Technology in Supply Chain Management. *Future Internet, 11*(7), 161. doi:10.3390/fi11070161

Rifi, N., Agoulmine, N., Chendeb Taher, N., & Rachkidi, E. (2018). Blockchain technology: Is it a good candidate for securing iot sensitive medical data? *Wireless Communications and Mobile Computing, 2018*, 2018. doi:10.1155/2018/9763937

Security, X. (2019). *Next-Generation Industrial Cybersecurity Introduces Hierarchical-Tree and Conditional Consensus in Blockchain for the First Time.* https://www. globenewswire.com/news-release/2019/10/10/1928089/0/ en/Xage-Security-Reveals-New-Blockchain-Innovation-to-Protect-Trillions-of-Industrial-Devices-and-Interactions.html

Shen, B., Guo, J., & Yang, Y. (2019). MedChain: Efficient healthcare data sharing via blockchain. *Applied Sciences (Basel, Switzerland), 9*(6), 1207. doi:10.3390/app9061207

Singh, M., & Kim, S. (2017). *Intelligent vehicle-trust point: Reward based intelligent vehicle communication using blockchain.* arXiv preprint arXiv:1707.07442

Uddin, M. A., Stranieri, A., Gondal, I., & Balasubramanian, V. (2020). Blockchain Leveraged Decentralized IoT eHealth Framework. *Internet of Things.*

Wan, J., Li, J., Imran, M., Li, D., & Fazal-e-Amin. (2019). A blockchain-based solution for enhancing security and privacy in smart factory. *IEEE Transactions on Industrial Informatics, 15*(6), 3652–3660. doi:10.1109/TII.2019.2894573

Wüst, K., & Gervais, A. (2018, June). Do you need a blockchain? In *2018 Crypto Valley Conference on Blockchain Technology (CVCBT)* (pp. 45-54). IEEE. 10.1109/CVCBT.2018.00011

Xu, R., Nikouei, S. Y., Chen, Y., Blasch, E., & Aved, A. (2019, July). Blendmas: A blockchain-enabled decentralized microservices architecture for smart public safety. In *2019 IEEE International Conference on Blockchain (Blockchain)* (pp. 564-571). IEEE. 10.1109/Blockchain.2019.00082

Xu, Y., Ren, J., Wang, G., Zhang, C., Yang, J., & Zhang, Y. (2019). A blockchain-based nonrepudiation network computing service scheme for industrial IoT. *IEEE Transactions on Industrial Informatics, 15*(6), 3632–3641. doi:10.1109/TII.2019.2897133

Yu, Y., Li, Y., Tian, J., & Liu, J. (2018). Blockchain-based solutions to security and privacy issues in the Internet of Things. *IEEE Wireless Communications, 25*(6), 12–18. doi:10.1109/MWC.2017.1800116

Yuan, Y., & Wang, F. Y. (2016, November). Towards blockchain-based intelligent transportation systems. In *2016 IEEE 19th International Conference on Intelligent Transportation Systems (ITSC)* (pp. 2663-2668). IEEE. 10.1109/ITSC.2016.7795984

Zhou, Y., Han, M., Liu, L., Wang, Y., Liang, Y., & Tian, L. (2018). Improving IoT Services in Smart-Home Using Blockchain Smart Contract. *IEEE International Conference on Internet of Things (iThings) and IEEE Green Computing and Communications (GreenCom) and IEEE Cyber, Physical and Social Computing (CPSCom) and IEEE Smart Data (SmartData)*, 81-87. 10.1109/Cybermatics_2018.2018.00047

Chapter 5
A Review on Bitcoin and Currency Encryption:
Bitcoin and Blockchain

Dharmendra Singh Rajput
Vellore Institute of Technology, India

Pankaj Shukla
Vellore Institute of Technology, India

Thippa Reddy G.
Vellore Institute of Technology, India

Rajesh Kaluri
Vellore Institute of Technology, India

Kuruva Lakshmanna
Vellore Institute of Technology, India

Praveen Kumar Reddy Kumar Maddikunta
 https://orcid.org/0000-0003-4209-2495
Vellore Institute of Technology, India

Harshita Patel
Vellore Institute of Technology, India

ABSTRACT

In today's world, security has become a major issue in our lives, and in this era, one cannot trust the government for handling their lifetime savings. That's where the bitcoin comes to our lives. In this chapter, the authors try to understand one of the famous innovative payment methods (Bitcoin), how it is used and the data structure (Merkle tree) that is used in it. Also, they discuss one of the most recent attacks that involved the use of bitcoin (Wanacry). Further, they try to understand how this hack succeeded in stealing 10,800 euros that is 8,74,290 rs from the hospital with the help of bitcoin. They also discuss the various bitcoin companies now emerging with their own security measures against such hacks.

DOI: 10.4018/978-1-7998-2414-5.ch005

1. INTRODUCTION

In today's world security had become a major issue in our lives and this era, one cannot trust the government for handling their lifetime savings. That's where the bitcoin comes to our life. A currency that is not controlled by any government or bank and thus the most secure way of doing the transaction. Through this chapter we will explain the overall aspect of bitcoin how it's being implemented, how much secure it is and how it will be in the future.

1.1 Cryptocurrency:

Let's break the above word into two simple words "Crypto" &" Currency". Crypto is a Greek originated word which means secret and currency (we all know!). Now if we combine this it becomes a secret currency. So what does a secret currency means? The secret currency here is regarded as a digital way of completing transactions that are nearly untraceable and are secure. Bitcoin is generally considered as the first cryptocurrency (Nakamoto, 2008 and Gord, 2016).

Figure 1. Bitcoin Logo [1]
https://en.bitcoin.it/w/images/en/2/29/BC_Logo.png

1.2 Why use Cryptocurrency-

Cryptocurrency like every other currency can be used for doing transactions but what makes cryptocurrency different is that it is decentralized. Now you would be thinking what does that mean? Simply, we can say that it can be said as the currency that is not issued by any government and is encrypted. But then how it is better than other currency? The answer to this is since cryptocurrency are not issued by any government, the governments do not have the right to take it away from you. This is the major advantage of cryptocurrency. Also in terms of security these currencies are way better than other currencies because they are very difficult to trace.

1.3 Blockchain

Before moving on to bitcoin we first need to understand what is blockchain (Zheng et al, 2017). Simply, a blockchain can be compared to the record or ledger of transactions being carried out. But in a way more complex method. Blockchain is a combination of a consensus algorithm, the protocol that the network implements and a group of nodes running that protocol. Hence this has to be differentiated from a database as 'database' is just a piece of software but the blockchain is an online encrypted transfer method consisting of an algorithm (Pilkington, 2016).

What makes blockchain more authentic is that each entry in the blockchain is immutable. This means one any entry of record is placed in ledger it cannot be removed replaced or re-entered. Blockchains follow very strict protocols so that none of its users can break the rule or use it against their advantage.

Let's see how it works:-

1. Every system that carries out the transaction is being considered as a node.
2. Nodes can be compared to account holders of the bank.
3. Each time a new node is added a majority of nodes first validate the new node.
4. Once the new node is validated it needs to download the entire digital ledger and sync with it.
5. Now each transaction that gets appended to a block (and the block subsequently to the blockchain) then the newly added node will have a copy of it and is in sync with the entire network.

The blockchain can be simply explained as a data structure where each block is linked with each other like a doubly linked list. Now for those of u who don't know what is doubly linked list, it is just a simple array of letter post which contains the address from where they were sent and the address to where they are going to be sent. Each blockchain solution has its level of encrypted algorithm. It depends on the network and the domain for which it's being used (Dhillon V. 2016 & Dhillon V. et al 2017).

1.4 Bitcoin

Blockchain systems use incentives like digital currency or redeem codes for transactions. It ensures that none of the participants can do betray or cheat other participants. Bitcoin was one of the first digital currency which implemented the method of the blockchain. Now if you have little knowledge about linked list then you would know that the structure of node remains the same for an element of a linked list. Bitcoin also consists of nodes usually know as blocks. These blocks usually contain the address of the previous cell and the next cell and other data like a digital fingerprint.

Bitcoin Block Structure:-

Figure 2. Bitcoin Block Structure
https://cdn-images-1.medium.com/max/1600/1*7hIidBDLF8bKpIll0Pp2Rg.jpeg

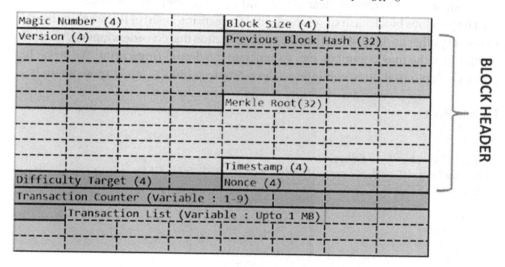

The above picture gives us an idea about the bitcoin block structure.

Let's see each of the parts briefly:

Magic Number: - the memory allocation for these magic number is 4 bytes. Now u would be thinking what does it contain? The magic number contains the identifier for the blockchain network or in simple language u can say it as an index of a record.

Block Size:- As the name says it indicates the size of the block generally its maximum size is fixed to 1 MB. But there proposals being made to increase the size by 2 MB. Since bitcoin was developed with consideration of scalability factor there won't be any problem while increasing the block size.

Version:-

Again as the name suggests each node of bitcoin follows a typical version of the bitcoin protocol and the information about the version is mentioned in this protocol. Also, the memory allocated for storing the version is 4 bytes.

Previous block hash:

Lets again break the terms "PREVIOUS BLOCK" & "HASH". Now we all know what does previous block mean. But what does hash means?

Hashing simply can be said as creating and assigning an index for particular data. How hashing assigns an index to data makes it much faster to search through the database for those of you who know about the time complexity it can reach to big O (1).

To know the meaning is clear you would ask what data does it stores?

The previous block hash stores the digital fingerprint(hash) of the previous block. Like every other hashing, it involves a hashing function that considers input as version, blocks size, the magic number, etc. to generate the digital fingerprint. We won't be going on depth in it but u can refer to the references links to study more about it.

Merkle Root:

Figure 3. Merkle Tree Diagram
https://cdn-images-1.medium.com/max/800/1*is44KCZhz3HXcPGgp8JERw.jpeg

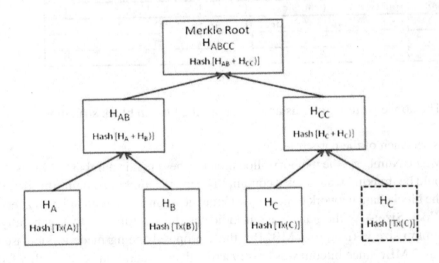

Now coming to the most important part of bitcoin that is data structure. We should never forget that in every complex program there is always a data structure that plays a key role. Now for those of you who studied data structure, it is the hash form of the binary tree. If we want to explain the Merkle tree in one line it can be defined as a hash of all the hashes.

Every summary of the transaction is stored in blocks (nodes). These blocks then become part of what we earlier studied blockchain. This also makes sure that once a block is connected to the blockchain it becomes immutable like strings which means it can't be changed by anyone. That is why blockchain is considered reliable. The decentralization of blockchain always makes sure that whatever transaction takes place is surely transparent.

The point that we should remember is that a Merkle tree doesn't store the data (list of all transactions) rather it stores a hash (digital fingerprint) of all transactions as a tree structure. This makes the search of transaction easier as we are using hashing. Also, the generated hash values by the algorithm are encrypted which makes sure that no one can hack or penetrate transactions.

Now since we know now a little bit about the implementation of bitcoin lets discuss some of the terms related to it. As we all know bitcoin is a digital currency thus at a time many people can do transactions. Now the problem is what if two-person does the transaction at the same time how does the system decide what to do next? To answer these questions we move to our next term FORKING.

FORKING

In cryptocurrency, there is one rule that always and always there would be only one path from the last added block to the first block (Genesis). When two blocks are created around the same time only one of the block is accepted and the other block is treated as an orphan block. Later when one of the blocks is linked to blockchain the remained block (orphan block) gets picked up by another block and thus each transaction gets successfully included in the network.

2. Literature Review

A purely peer-to-peer version of electronic cash would allow online payments to be sent directly from one party to another without going through a financial institution. Digital signatures provide part of the solution, but the main benefits are lost if a trusted third party is still required to prevent double-spending. Authors proposed a solution to the double-spending problem using a peer-to-peer network. The network timestamps transactions by hashing them into an ongoing chain of hash-based proof-of-work, forming a record that cannot be changed without redoing the proof-of-work. The longest chain not only serves as proof of the sequence of events witnessed but proof that it came from the largest pool of CPU power. As long as a majority of CPU power is controlled by nodes that are not cooperating to attack the network, they'll generate the longest chain and outpace attackers. The network itself requires minimal structure. Messages are broadcast on a best effort basis, and nodes can leave and rejoin the network will accepting the longest proof-of-work chain as proof of what happened while they were gone (Nakamoto, 2008).

Before moving to our next topic lets discuss some history of bitcoin. You may ask why history matters here. The most probable answer is that history tells what the necessity for the evolution of the technology was.

Bitcoin and cryptocurrencies aren't much old. Bitcoin wasn't the first originated cryptocurrency, there were many attempts trying to develop cryptocurrency but all of them were failed because of the improper system. The cryptocurrency before the bitcoin was somewhat centralized and that's why most people either fear to buy or don't have the trust in them Antonopoulos (2014).

Figure 4. Notable electronic payment systems
https://www.valuewalk.com/wp-content/uploads/2016/02/Bitcoin-And-Cryptocurrency-Technologies-1.
jpg

ACC	CyberCents	iKP	MPTP	Proton
Agora	CyberCoin	IMB-MP	Net900	Redi-Charge
AIMP	CyberGold	InterCoin	NetBill	S/PAY
Allopass	DigiGold	Ipin	NetCard	Sandia Lab E-Cash
b-money	Digital Silk Road	Javien	NetCash	Secure Courier
BankNet	e-Comm	Karma	NetCheque	Semopo
Bitbit	E-Gold	LotteryTickets	NetFare	SET
Bitgold	Ecash	Lucre	No3rd	SET2Go
Bitpass	eCharge	MagicMoney	One Click Charge	SubScrip
C-SET	eCoin	Mandate	PayMe	Trivnet
CAFE	Edd	MicroMint	PayNet	TUB
CheckFree	eVend	Micromoney	PayPal	Twitpay
ClickandBuy	First Virtual	MilliCent	PaySafeCard	VeriFone
ClickShare	FSTC Electronic Check	Mini-Pay	PayTrust	VisaCash
CommerceNet	Geldkarte	Minitix	PayWord	Wallie
CommercePOINT	Globe Left	MobileMoney	Peppercoin	Way2Pay
CommerceSTAGE	Hashcash	Mojo	PhoneTicks	WorldPay
Cybank	HINDE	Mollie	Playspan	X-Pay
CyberCash	iBill	Mondex	Polling	

Bitcoin was able to resolve this problem by making itself decentralized. Thus, got famous.

Now you may also want to ask what was the need of the crypto-currency itself ? The answer to this is very simple people wanted a currency that cannot be controlled by the government. Victims of strong banking rules and government regulations wanted a currency in which neither bank can interfere nor the government. Also, cryptocurrency was highly demanding in the dark world (dark web) which somewhat decreased its popularity initially.

Satoshi Nakamoto – the founder(s) of bitcoin

It would be bad if we discussed the history of the bitcoin without talking about its founder(s). A very little information is known about the bitcoin founder(s) Satoshi Nakamoto (Nakamoto, 2008) it is even not sure that there was only one person or group of people behind it. All we know is about a pseudo name which according to media leads to different people. There is no straight forward answer even after these many of the evolution of cryptocurrency. The problem that it was difficult to trace the founder(s) is that all of the people involved in discussions of bitcoin used anonymous mail ids were made it nearly impossible to figure who are the people behind this. One of the reasons that can be given for them being still anonymous is that it may be possible that they would keep a lot of bitcoin for themselves and don't want any government or private organization to gain access to their money. Whatever may be the reason the bitcoin founder(s) is as hard to track as the currency itself!

MOTIVATION

The reason we were motivated to write this chapter was that even today many people are unaware of cryptocurrency. We wanted to make readers aware of the power of cryptocurrencies in their financial lives. Also what excited us was the ideology of the founder of bitcoin and how they implemented it in their cryptocurrency. One of the major reasons was also to make readers aware of how cryptocurrencies can be used in illegal ways so that they can always take precautions while putting their life savings on buying cryptocurrencies. In the technical part what motivated us was the implementation of cryptocurrencies data structure and the concept of the blockchain.

Figure 5. anonmity across world
https://cdn-images-1.medium.com/max/800/1*k9EH4bSrWvJ0s-w0igB0yg.jpeg

BITCOIN AND DARK WEB

As soon as bitcoin came in the market it became a highly demanding currency in the dark web. But before moving forward for those who are new let me explain the term dark web. The dark web comprises the rest 96% percent of the web which we cannot access directly through our normal web browser (Why ?). Because of its dark!, meaning that there are websites that involve illegal activities such as selling drugs, cocaine, fake passports, and even human trafficking. Yes! people even do human trafficking through the web. The dark web always liked the bitcoin because bitcoin is near untraceable. That's the reason why bitcoin's popularity was declined initially.

One of the famous examples of this is the Silk Road which is famous for illegal activities like selling drugs and fake passports. There is even a recent link was paying some bitcoin will get GRE, TOFEL and sat scores at the top!. But these cannot be accessed directly you need to have a specific browser (TOR browser) to gain some access. We won't be going much on this topic but we can conclude that one of the biggest markets of the cryptocurrencies is dark web. Remember there are many things hidden from you if you start exploring dark web you'll find it out but I won't recommend that not until you have enough experience. Below I am pasting the actual screenshot of the silk road.

Now since we know a little bit about dark web lets move on to our next segment

Figure 6. Silk road website
https://theearloflemongrab.files.wordpress.com/2013/01/silk-road3.png?w=549

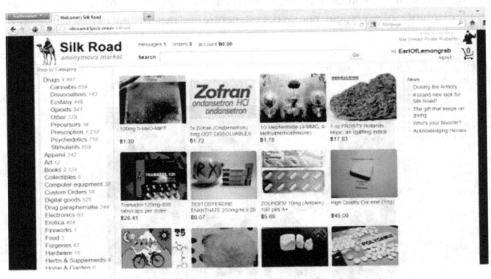

Figure 7. NSA logo
https://upload.wikimedia.org/wikipedia/commons/8/8d/Seal_of_the_U.S._National_Security_Agency.svg

WannaCry and bitcoin

Let's start by talking about what is WannaCry? It was a massive large scale ransomware attack that made the loss of up to 4 billion dollars to companies, hospitals, and other individuals. Let's try to understand how this attack got successful at such a large scale.

The ransomware attack exploited the vulnerability of Window's Server Message Block (SMB) whose exploit by was created by the NSA(National Security Agency)

The NSA named the exploit is Eternal Blue. Rather reporting the vulnerability to the Microsoft NSA wanted to use it for their profit. Later on, a group of hackers named "THE SHADOW BROKERS" released the exploit publicly. This exploit came under the radar of WannaCry developers. The WannaCry was written on Microsoft visual C++ so that there won't be any compatibility issues while attacking.

The WannaCry virus first tries to find a kill switch (a simple way of force shut down) if it is not found the ransomware encrypts your data and then tries to exploit the SMB (SERVER MESSAGE BLOCK) vulnerability to spread itself in other networks. The WannaCry virus comes itself with a self-transporting mechanism to spread itself. When it found its host it uses the eternal blue exploit and double pulsar tool to gain access to install and execute itself. Wannacry virus came with a display window like below where it asks it, users, to pay through the bitcoin and that's where our main part comes. Below is the picture of the display window you will get if you are attacked by a ransomware.

Figure 8. Example of WanaCry decrypt affected computer screen
https://upload.wikimedia.org/wikipedia/en/1/18/Wana_Decrypt0r_screenshot.png

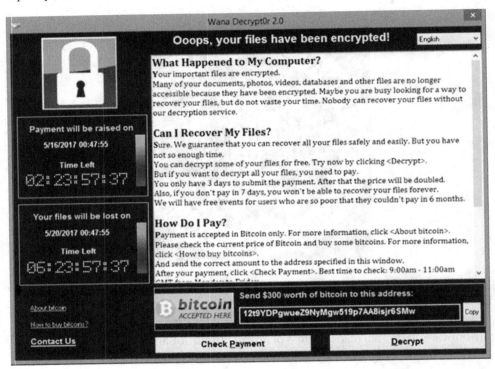

Before the Microsoft could eventually stop WannaCry was able to spread rapidly and we all know how much it cost. Now the major problem was that WannaCry attacked not only private organizations but hospitals. If the hospital loses it's patient's dose record it would the situation of life and death for patients that was the reason most of the hospitals paid the ransom.

WannaCry ransomware asks the user to pay through bitcoin. Now the problem was that bitcoin ledgers were public but from whom to whom the transaction goes was untraceable. That means suppose if the victim paid the attacker the ransomware we can see how many bitcoins are getting exchanged but we neither can track the attacker nor the victim.

The attackers exploit the advantage of bitcoin and that's why the ransomware was completely successful. It was the bitcoin at the end which made sure the attacker's identity remained secured. It is just like the money is floating in front of you but cannot see from where it is originating and where it is ending.

Although the ransomware was stopped by Microsoft emergency patches it still cost a lot of damage. After discussing this you may want to ask whether it's a good idea to continue cryptocurrency. Well, the answer to that can still be given as big YES! Because at the initial stage it was the NSA and the companies and who didn't respond to the situation properly. The NSA could have stopped it if they reported it to Microsoft, the hospitals and companies could have prevented It by continuously updating their software. At least I still believe cryptocurrency is still good. You have the right to disagree:).

The below map shows the countries that got initially affected by ransomware.

Figure 9. Countries that got affected with ransomware
https://upload.wikimedia.org/wikipedia/commons/thumb/2/20/Countries_initially_affected_in_WannaCry_ransomware_attack.svg/300px-Countries_initially_affected_in_WannaCry_ransomware_attack.svg.png

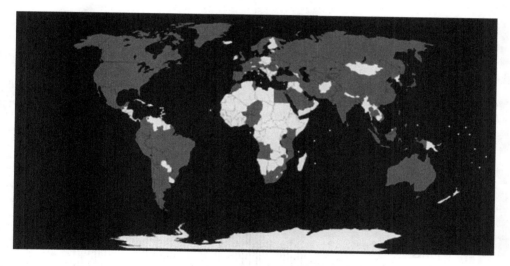

Whatever the attack cost it wasn't the last attack to be implemented. After many attacks were being carried out to big organizations some demanding only a single bitcoin to some demanding a huge amount that made companies stop their protection. Whatever happened the interesting part was that during 2017 when these ransomware attacks were continuing bitcoin price increased at a much higher rate whether it was for good or for bad.

Figure 10. Stock price of bitcoin
https://static.coindesk.com/wp-content/uploads/2017/12/coindesk-bpi-chart-22.png

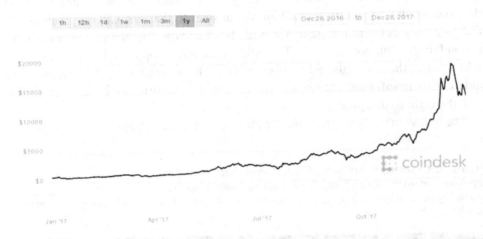

The above picture shows the stock price of bitcoin in 2017.

Figure 11. Bitcoin stock price during 2009-2017
https://en.bitcoinwiki.org/upload/en/images/thumb/e/e0/Transactions_per_month.png/450px-
Transactions_per_month.png

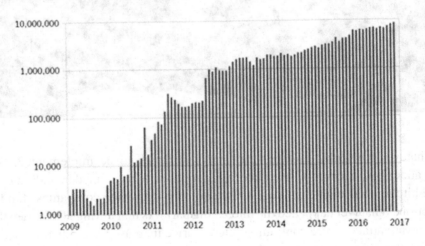

The above picture shows the comparison of bitcoin stock price with other respective years.

CONCLUSION

We will finally conclude this chapter by discussing the future of bitcoin. Bitcoin no doubt is one of the safest cryptocurrency but can it be implemented for mass usage well, for now, it may. Why? The answer is simple because of the cost of systems required to download every single transaction of bitcoin is usually high and as the bitcoin mining becomes expensive it may lead to freezing of the mining system.

The second important reason is that there is no proper authority to prevent the misuse of the bitcoin. That is the reason why bitcoin is usually preferred by the dark web. Also, the dark web requires anonymity which bitcoin provides in somewhat way you can say that bitcoin is helping criminals to perform the crime. One of the biggest examples for this can be what be discussed in the earlier silk route. This the reason why bitcoin has a low image in common public.

The third important reason can be given is the anonymous creators themselves. No one knows much about the founders of bitcoin does no one can estimate how much bitcoin would they owning. Any of the founders may suddenly come out reveal their bitcoins and may cause huge inflation in price.

The fourth reason is that bitcoin isn't cheap. In the time of writing this chapter one bitcoin worth's up to 3,963.78 United States Dollar or 2, 74,176.64 Indian Rupee thus not everyone can purchase bitcoin.

Thus we can say that maybe in future bitcoin can be a major currency but for now, it is not. I hope that you would have got some knowledge about bitcoin and security through this chapter.

REFERENCES

Antonopoulos, A. M. (2014). *Mastering Bitcoin* (1st ed.). O'Reilly Media.

Dhillon, V. (2016). *Blockchain-Enabled Open Science Framework*. O'Reilly Media. https://www.oreilly.com/ideas/blockchain-enabled-open-science-framework

Dhillon, V., Metcalf, D., & Hooper, M. (2017). *Blockchain in science. Blockchain Enabled Applications* (1st ed.). Apress. doi:10.1007/978-1-4842-3081-7

Gord, M. (2016). *Smart Contracts Described by Nick Szabo 20 Years ago now becoming Reality*. Bitcoin Magazine.

Nakamoto, S. (2008). *Bitcoin: A Peer to Peer electronic cash system*. https://bitcoin.org/bitcoin.pdf

Pilkington, M. (2016). *Blockchain technology: Principle and applications.* Research Handbook on Digital Transformations.

Zheng, Z., Xie, S., Dai, H., Chen, X., & Wang, H. (2017). An overview of blockchain technology: Architecture, consensus and future trends. *IEEE International Congress on Big Data (Big Data Congress).*

Chapter 6
Security Issues of IoT

Neha Gupta
Symbiosis University of Applied Sciences, Indore, India

ABSTRACT

Wireless communication networks are highly prone to security threats. The major applications of wireless communication networks are in military, business, healthcare, retail, and transportations. These systems use wired, cellular, or adhoc networks. Wireless sensor networks, actuator networks, and vehicular networks have received a great attention in society and industry. In recent years, the internet of things (IoT) has received considerable research attention. The IoT is considered as future of the internet. In the future, IoT will play a vital role and will change our living styles, standards, as well as business models. The usage of IoT in different applications is expected to rise rapidly in the coming years. The IoT allows billions of devices, peoples, and services to connect with others and exchange information. Due to the increased usage of IoT devices, the IoT networks are prone to various security attacks.

IOT – SECURITY

Every connected device creates opportunities for attackers. These vulnerabilities are broad, even for a single small device. The risks posed include data transfer, device access, malfunctioning devices, and always-on/always-connected devices. The main challenges in security remain the security limitations associated with producing low-cost devices, and the growing number of devices which creates more opportunities for attacks.

Security Spectrum: The definition of a secured device spans from the simplest measures to sophisticated designs. Security should be thought of as a spectrum of vulnerability which changes over time as threats evolve. Security must be assessed

DOI: 10.4018/978-1-7998-2414-5.ch006

based on user needs and implementation. Users must recognize the impact of security measures because poorly designed security creates more problems than it solves. Example: A German report revealed hackers compromised the security system of a steel mill. They disrupted the control systems, which prevented a blast furnace from being shut down properly, resulting in massive damage. Therefore, users must understand the impact of an attack before deciding on appropriate protection.

1.1 Challenges

Beyond costs and the ubiquity of devices, other security issues plague IoT:

i. **Unpredictable Behaviour** – The sheer volume of deployed devices and their long list of enabling technologies means their behaviour in the field can be unpredictable. A specific system may be well designed and within administration control, but there are no guarantees about how it will interact with others.

ii. **Device Similarity** – IoT devices are fairly uniform. They utilize the same connection technology and components. If one system or device suffers from a vulnerability, many more have the same issue.

iii. **Problematic Deployment** – One of the main goals of IoT remains to place advanced networks and analytics where they previously could not go. Unfortunately, this creates the problem of physically securing the devices in these strange or easily accessed places.

iv. **Long Device Life and Expired Support** – One of the benefits of IoT devices is longevity, however, that long life also means they may outlive their device support. Compare this to traditional systems which typically have support and upgrades long after many have stopped using them. Orphaned devices and abandon ware lack the same security hardening of other systems due to the evolution of technology over time (Weyrich & Ebert, 2015).

v. **No Upgrade Support** – Many IoT devices, like many mobile and small devices, are not designed to allow upgrades or any modifications. Others offer inconvenient upgrades, which many owners ignore, or fail to notice.

vi. **Poor or No Transparency** – Many IoT devices fail to provide transparency with regard to their functionality. Users cannot observe or access their processes, and are left to assume how devices behave. They have no control over unwanted functions or data collection; furthermore, when a manufacturer updates the device, it may bring more unwanted functions (Weyrich & Ebert, 2015).

vii. **No Alerts –** Another goal of IoT remains to provide its incredible functionality without being obtrusive. This introduces the problem of user awareness. Users do not monitor the devices or know when something goes wrong. Security breaches can persist over long periods without detection.

2. SECURITY REQUIREMENTS IN IoT

All the devices and people are connected with each other to provide services at any time and at any place. Most of the devices connected to the internet are not equipped with efficient security mechanisms and are vulnerable to various privacy and security issues e.g., confidentiality, integrity, and authenticity, etc. For the IoT, some security requirements must be fulfilled to prevent the network from malicious attacks. Here, some of the most required capabilities of a secure network are briefly discussed.

Resilience to attacks: The system should be capable enough to recover itself in case if it crashes during data transmission. For an example, a server working in a multiuser environment, it must be intelligent and strong enough to protect itself from intruders or an eavesdropper (Evans, 2011). In the case, if it is down it would recover itself without intimation the users of its down status.

- **Data Authentication:** The data and the associated information must be authenticated. An authentication mechanism is used to allow data transmission from only authentic devices.
- **Access control:** Only authorized persons are provided access control. The system administrator must control access to the users by managing their usernames and passwords and by defining their access rights so that different users can access only relevant portion of the database or programs.
- **Client privacy:** The data and information should be in safe hands. Personal data should only be accessed by authorized person to maintain the client privacy (Evans, 2011). It means that no irrelevant authenticated user from the system or any other type of client cannot have access to the private information of the client.

2.1 Iot Security, Privacy, Threats and Challenges

The era of IoT has changed our living styles. Although the IoT provides huge benefits, it is prone to various security threats in our daily life. The majority of the security threats are related to leakage of information and loss of services. In IoT, the security threats straightforwardly are affecting the physical security risk. The IoT consists of different devices and platform with different credentials, where every system needs the security requirement depending upon its characteristics. The privacy of a user is also most important part because a lot of personal information is being shared among various types of devices. Hence a secure mechanism is needed to protect the personal information. Moreover, for IoT services, there are multiple types of devices that perform communication using different networks. It means there are a lot of security issues on user privacy and network layer. User privacy can also be uncovered from different routes. Some security threats in the IoT are as follows:

1) E2E Data life cycle protection: To ensure the security of data in IoT environment, end-to-end data protection is provided in a complete network. Data is collected from different devices connected to each other and instantly shared with other devices. Thus, it requires a framework to protect the data, confidentiality of data and to manage information privacy in full data life cycle.

2) Secure thing planning: The interconnection and communication among the devices in the IoT vary according to the situation. Therefore, the devices must be capable of maintaining security level. For example, when local devices and sensors used in the homebased network to communicate with each other safely, their communication with external devices should also work on same security policy.

3) Visible/usable security and privacy: Most of the security and privacy concerns are invoke by misconfiguration of users (Atzori, Iera & Morabito, 2010). It is very difficult and unrealistic for users to execute such privacy policies and complex security mechanism. It is needed to select security and privacy policies that may apply automatically.

2.2 Security Threats in Smart Home

Smart home services can be exposed to cyber-attacks because majority of the service provider do not consider security parameters at early stages. The possible security threats in a smart home are eavesdropping, Distributed Denial of Service (DDoS) attacks and leakage of information, etc. Smart home networks are threatened by unauthorized access. The possible security threats to smart home are discussed as follows (see Fig. 3).

1) **Trespass**: If the smart door lock is effected by malicious codes or it is accessed by an unauthorized party, the attacker can trespass on smart home without smashing the doorway as shown in Fig. 4. The result of this effect could be in the form of loss of life or property. To get rid of such attacks, passwords should be changed frequently that must contain at least ten characters because it is

very difficult for attackers to break the long password. Similarly, authentication mechanism and access control may also be applied (Atzori, Iera & Morabito, 2010).

2) **Monitoring and personal information leakage**: Safety is one of the important purposes of a smart home. Hence there are a lot of sensors that are used for fire monitoring, baby monitoring, and housebreaking, etc. If these sensors are hacked by an intruder then he can monitor the home and access personal information as shown in Fig. 5. To avoid from this attack, data encryption must be applied between gateway and sensors or user authentication for the detection of unauthorized parties may be applied.

3) **DoS/DDoS**: Attackers may access the smart home network and send bulk messages to smart devices such as Clear To Send (CTS) / Request To Send (RTS). They can also attack targeted device by using malicious codes in order to perform DoS attacks on other devices that are connected in a smart home as shown in Fig. 6. As a result, smart devices are unable to perform proper functionalities because of draining resources due to such attacks (Adolphs et al., 2015). For avoidance from this attack, it is very important to apply authentication to block and detect unauthorized access.

4) **Falsification:** When the devices in smart home perform communication with the application server, the attacker may collect the packets by changing routing table in the gateway as shown in Fig. 7. Although the SSL (secure socket layer) technique is applied, an attacker can bypass the forged certificate. In this way, the attacker can misinterpret the contents of data or may leak the confidentiality of data. To secure the smart home network from this attack, SSL technique with proper authentication mechanism should be applied. It is also important to block unauthorized devices that may try to access smart home network. The IoT is a concept that depicts future where the physical objects connected to internet communicate with each other and identify themselves for other devices. The IoT system consists of smart objects, smartphones, tablets and intelligent devices etc. as shown in Fig. 3. Such systems use RFID, Quick Response (QR) codes or wireless technology to perform communication between different devices (Adolphs et al., 2015). The IoT helped to build connections from human to human, human to physical objects, and physical object to other physical objects. As per appraisal from IDC, there will be 30 billion internet connected devices by 2020. This rapid growth of internet data needs more valuable and secure network.

Figure 1.

Figure 2.

	IETF IoT Protocol Stack	TCP/IP Protocol Stack
Application Layer	IETF COAP	HTTP, FTP, DNS, SSH, SMTP, NTP, ...
Transport Layer	UDP	TCP, UDP
Network Layer	IPv6, IETF RPL	IPv4, IPv6
Adaption Layer	IETF 6LoWPAN	N/A
MAC Layer	IEEE 802.15.4 MAC	Network Access
Physical Layer	IEEE 802.15.4 PHY	

Figure 3. Examples of IOT

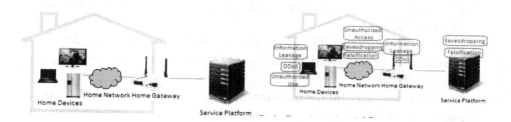

Figure 4.

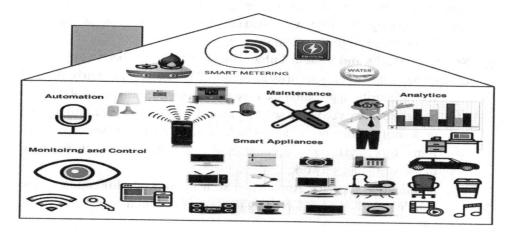

2.3. IoT Challenges

The security concern is the biggest challenge in IoT. The application data of IoT could be industrial, enterprise, consumer or personal. This application data should be secured and must remain confidential against theft and tampering. For example, the IoT applications may store the results of a patient's health or shopping store. The IoT improve the communication between devices but still, there are issues related to the scalability, availability and response time. Security is a concern where the data is securely transmitted over the internet. While transporting the data across international border, safety measure act may be applied by government regulation such as Health Insurance Portability and Accountability (HIPA) act. Among different security challenges, the most important challenges relevant to IoT are discussed.

1) **Data Privacy:** Some manufacturers of smart TVs collect data about their customers to analyze their viewing habits so the data collected by the smart TVs may have a challenge for data privacy during transmission.

2) **Data Security:** Data security is also a great challenge. While transmitting data seamlessly, it is important to hide from observing devices on the internet (Ackoff, 1971).

3) **Insurance Concerns:** The insurance companies installing IoT devices on vehicles collect data about health and driving status in order to take decisions about insurance.

4) **Lack of Common Standard:** Since there are many standards for IoT devices and IoT manufacturing industries. Therefore, it is a big challenge to distinguish between permitted and non-permitted devices connected to the internet.

5) **Technical Concerns:** Due to the increased usage of IoT devices, the traffic generated by these devices is also increasing. Hence there is a need to increase network capacity, therefore, it is also a challenge to store the huge amount of data for analysis and further final storage.

6) **Security Attacks and System Vulnerabilities:** There has been a lot of work done in the scenario of IoT security up till now. The related work can be divided into system security, application security, and network security (Ackoff, 1971).

   a) **System Security:** System security mainly focuses on overall IoT system to identify different security challenges, to design different security frameworks and to provide proper security guidelines in order to maintain the security of a network.

   b) **Application security:** Application Security works for IoT application to handle security issues according to scenario requirements.

c) **Network security:** Network security deals with securing the IoT communication network for communication of different IoT devices. In the next section, the security concerns regarding IoT are discussed. The security attacks are categorized into four broad classes.

2.4 ANALYSIS OF DIFFERENT TYPES OF ATTACKS AND POSSIBLE SOLUTIONS

The IoT is facing various types of attacks including active attacks and passive attacks that may easily disturb the functionality and abolish the benefits of its services. In a passive attack, an intruder just senses the node or may steal the information but it never attacks physically. However, the active attacks disturb the performance physically. These active attacks are classified into two further categories that are internal attacks and external attacks. Such vulnerable attacks can prevent the devices to communicate smartly (Fan, Wang, Zhang & Lin, 2014). Hence the security constraints must be applied to prevent devices from malicious attacks. Different types of attack, nature/behaviour of attack and threat level of attacks are discussed in this section. Different levels of attacks are categorized into four types according to their behaviour and propose possible solutions to threats/attacks.

1) Low-level attack: If an attacker tries to attack a network and his attack is not successful.
2) Medium-level attack: If an attacker/intruder or an eavesdropper is just listening to the medium but don't alter the integrity of data.
3) High-level attack: If an attack is carried on a network and it alters the integrity of data or modifies the data.
4) Extremely High-level attack: If an intruder/attacker attacks on a network by gaining unauthorized access and performing an illegal operation, making the network unavailable, sending bulk messages, or jamming network (Fan, Wang, Zhang & Lin, 2014). The Table I presents different types of attacks, their threat levels, their nature/behaviour, and possible solution to handle these attacks.

3. KEY ISSUES IN CYBER SECURITY AND PRIVACY

The Internet has grown from a useful research tool for universities into a fundamental utility, as important as electricity, water and gas. Wherever there is a valuable resource, there is also crime which seeks to gain value from the illicit use of that technology, or to deny the use of that resource to others. The interconnected nature

Table 1. Different Types of Attacks and Threat

	Threat	Property Violated	Threat Definition
S	Spoofing identify	Authentication	Pretending to be something or someone other than yourself
T	Tampering with data	Integrity	Modifying something on disk, network, memory, or elsewhere
R	Repudiation	Non-repudiation	Claiming that you didn't do something or were not responsible; can be honest or false
I	Information disclosure	Confidentiality	Providing information to someone not authorized to access it
D	Denial of service	Availability	Exhausting resources needed to provide service
E	Elevation of privilege	Authorization	Allowing someone to do something they are not authorized to do

of the Internet means that Internet resources can be attacked from any location in the world, and this makes cybersecurity a key issue. Cybersecurity revolves around three main themes.

Confidentiality is about keeping data private, so that only authorized users (both humans and machines) can access that data. Cryptography is a key technology for achieving confidentiality.

Authentication is about verifying that data has not been tampered with, and that the data can be verified to have been sent by the claimed author. Non-repudiation (i.e., avoiding denial by a sender that they actually sent a message) is sometimes considered separately, but we include it here as a subset of authentication (Fleisch, 2010).

Access refers to only allowing suitably authorized users to access data, communications infrastructure and computing resources, and ensuring that those authorized users are not prevented from such access.

The Information Security Breaches Survey is an annual cyber threat report commissioned by the UK Department for Business, Innovation and Skills and conducted by Price Waterhouse Coopers. The latest survey in 2015 shows that security breaches are on the rise; 90% of large organizations experienced cyber breaches in 2015 compared to 81% in 2014, and 74% of small businesses also suffered security breaches, indicating a double-digit year-on-year growth rate of 14%.

Now that the Internet has become a mission-critical component of modern business, cybersecurity has become an indispensable component of information systems (Gubbi, Buyya, Marusic & Palaniswami, 2013). However, as cybersecurity is enhanced, cybercrime is evolving to be more extensive, more destructive and more sophisticated. In Smart Homes, the ability of householders to manage their systems securely requires trusted and intuitive automated systems to assist in network management (Fleisch, 2010). Without such systems, the security and privacy threats of the Smart Home are likely to outweigh the advantages.

IoT Application Domains A number of application domains are particularly amenable to improved productivity through the deployment of IoT technology. Factory and plant automation applications are often grouped under the heading of Industrial Internet of Things. Xu et al. review this application area. Reliability, including through redundancy, security, and suitability for harsh environments are some of the key issues.

The networking of biomedical instruments and databases in hospitals has the potential to dramatically improve the quantity and availability of diagnostic and treatment decisions. It also has substantial implications for rural and remote clinics, providing ready access to specialist opinions. Extending medical instrumentation to the home has improved quality of life and reduced hospital readmissions.

The last two decades have seen a surge in the use of electronics in automobiles, based on dozens of networked microprocessors. The next stage of development will be communication between vehicles, and between vehicles and infrastructure. Standardization, security and cost are major drivers.

Transport and Logistics are already heavy users of RFID tags for the tracking of shipments, pallets and even individual items. The research direction here is into smart tags which can log and report transport conditions such as shock, tilt, temperature, humidity and pressure. Here the key driver is low cost, as well as orderly communication to hundreds or thousands of tags simultaneously.

IoT technology is having disruptive impacts on a very broad range of industries including entertainment, dining, public transport, sport and fitness, telecommunications, manufacturing, hotels, education, environmental science, robotics, and retail. In many of these industries, IoT is becoming a key enabler of innovation and success, (Fleisch, 2010) and industries are willing to invest in new technologies. Specialist IT support can be provided on staff or from external providers to ensure that the security and availability of their systems is sufficient for their business needs.

3.1 IoT and the Smart Home

This chapter deals with a very different environment—the Smart Home. Professional system design, installation and setup may be available when the smart electronics are included as part of a new home build. However, in most cases, Smart Home IoT technology is likely to be retrofitted to an existing home piece by piece as needs arise. Often, there is no ongoing professional support in either the design or operation phases of the IoT deployment in the Smart Home. While there are some reasonably widespread specialized Smart Home standards, such as X.10 powerline-carrier communications, these lack any type of security, and were designed before these home control networks were connected to the Internet . There are now a plethora of networking standards that can be used in a home (Zwave, Insteon, Bluetooth, Zigbee, Ethernet, Wifi, RS232, RS485, C-bus, UPB, KNX, EnOcean, Thread) . Each has its strengths and weaknesses, and expecting a heterogeneous network with many different protocols to be efficiently and securely managed by a non-expert presents significant challenges.

The Smart Home potentially provides additional comfort and security, as well as enhanced ecological sustainability. For example, a smart air conditioning system can use a wide variety of household sensors and web-based data sources to make intelligent operating decisions (Fleisch, 2010) rather than simple manual or fixed-schedule control schemes. The smart air conditioning system can predict the expected house occupancy by tracking location data to ensure the air conditioner achieves the desired comfort level when the house is occupied and saves energy when it is not.

In addition to enhanced comfort, the Smart Home can assist with independent living for the ageing. The Smart Home can assist with daily tasks such as cleaning, cooking, shopping and laundry. Low level cognitive decline can be supported with intelligent home systems to provide timely reminders for medication. Home health monitoring can signal caregivers to respond before expensive and disruptive hospitalization is needed. However, none of these benefits is likely to be taken up if the Smart Home system is not secure and trusted.

3.2 Security Threats in the Smart Home

Although the Smart Home is a very different environment, the overall nature of security threats is similar to other domains.

Confidentiality threats are those that result in the unwanted release of sensitive information. For example, confidentiality breaches in home monitoring systems can lead to the inadvertent release of sensitive medical data. Even seemingly innocuous data, such as the internal home temperature, along with knowledge of the air conditioning system operation parameters, could be used to determine whether a house is occupied or not, as a precursor to burglary. Loss of confidentiality in things such as keys and passwords will lead to unauthorized system access threats.

Authentication threats can lead to either sensing or control information being tampered with. For example, unauthenticated system status alerts might confuse a house controller into thinking that there is an emergency situation and opening doors and windows to allow an emergency exit, when in fact allowing illicit entry (Bauk, Dlabač, & Škurić, 2018). One issue that will be raised later is automated software updates—if these are not appropriately authenticated problems can arise.

Access threats are probably the greatest threats. Unauthorized access to a system controller, particularly at the administrator level, makes the entire system insecure. This can be through inappropriate password and key management, or it could be by unauthorized devices connecting to the network. Even if control cannot be gained, an unauthorized connection to a network can steal network bandwidth, or result in a denial of service to legitimate users. Since many Smart Home devices may be battery operated and wirelessly networked with a low operational duty cycle, flooding a network with requests can lead to energy depletion attack—a form of denial of service.

3.3 Vulnerabilities

A significant vulnerability is networked system accessibility. Because modern Smart Home systems are connected to the Internet, attacks can be conducted remotely, either by direct access to networked control interfaces, or by downloading malware to devices (Bauk, Dlabač, & Škurić, 2018).

System physical accessibility is also an issue. For both wireless and power-line carrier technologies, the networks can be physically accessed from outside the house, even if the house itself is securely locked.

The next vulnerability is constrained system resources. Device controllers have traditionally been small 8-bit microcontrollers with very limited computational and storage resources, limiting their ability to implement complex security algorithms.

System heterogeneity is a vulnerability. Devices come from many manufacturers, with different networking standards and different software update capabilities. Often the devices have little or no documentation about their internal software, operating systems, and installed security mechanisms.

Fixed firmware is another issue. There are very few smart home appliances which provide any regular software update service to patch security vulnerabilities. One suspects that there is currently little Incentive to continually patch software to stay ahead of security vulnerabilities for devices costing a few dollars.

Slow uptake of standards is a vulnerability. While some proprietary systems, such as a health monitoring sub-system, may have well-designed standards-compliant security, most current Smart Home devices implement few, if any, security approaches (Bauk, Dlabač, & Škurić, 2018).

We consider the largest vulnerability to be the lack of dedicated security professionals who can manage the complexities of a Smart Home network. Few householders can afford professional ongoing home network management assistance. Instead, amateur householders need to be able to self-manage their systems simply, safely and securely.

3.4 Vulnerability Example

As an example, a householder might assume that their web cam is only accessible by users who have been given its host name and port number. However, with the help of Internet device–scanning search engines such as Shodan (https://www.shodan.io) and Censys (https://censys.io) which legitimately search for accessible sensors, many devices are suddenly known and visible.

The conventional search engines such as Google and Bing crawl the Internet by retrieving webpages and follow the hyperlinks in those pages to index webpages, pictures or some popular file types. Internet device–scanning search engines, on the other hand, work like a network scanner, scanning the open ports of Internet nodes and indexing the header or banner information returned by connected devices; the headers or banners of the reply often include the device type, model, vendor, firmware version and other information. Apart from HTTP and HTTPS protocols, Internet device–scanning search engines use a variety of protocols (FTP, SSH, DNS, SIP and RTSP, etc.) to connect to the open ports of nodes. To facilitate access, these search engines also provide an application programming interface (API) to access their search results programmatically. Attackers can take advantage of these search engines to find vulnerable devices on the Internet. For example, using the search keywords "has_screenshot:true port:554" in Shodan will return a list of home surveillance cameras with their IP addresses, geographic locations and screenshots, as shown in Figure 1.

3.5 Some Existing Security Support for IoT

Due to their low cost, IoT computing devices generally are not as powerful as traditional desktop and laptop computers. Most IoT devices are low energy, use a low-end microcontroller and have limited memory. Such controllers are well-matched to the requirements of standalone controllers in a washing machine or air conditioner

However, these characteristics have made the move to networked IoT controllers more challenging as the existing Internet protocols are not typically designed for these embedded devices. Several Internet Engineering Task Force (IETF) working groups have been created to tackle these problems. IETF standardization work on IoT has played a vital role in the establishment of the necessary light-weight communication protocols for constrained environments over the existing IP network. These include IPv6 over Low-Power Wireless Personal Area Networks (6LoWPAN: RFC 6282) , IPv6 Routing Protocol for Low power and Lossy Networks (RPL: RFC 6550) and Constrained Application Protocol (CoAP: RFC 7252) (Ackoff, 1971). Figure 2 shows the comparison between IETF IoT and TCP/IP protocol stacks. Once devices are connected to the Internet, any of the security threats on the Internet could also compromise the security and privacy of IoT. In the following sections we review the current security implementations for these standard IoT protocols.

3.6 LoWPAN and Security

The Institute of Electrical and Electronics Engineers (IEEE) has defined the 802.15.4 standard for wireless personal area networks (WPANs). IEEE 802.15.4 defines how the physical and media access control layers should operate under the low-bandwidth, low-cost, low-speed and low-energy conditions typical of these networks. As such, 6LoWPAN is a light-weight protocol designed by the IETF to allow IPv6 packets to be transferred over IEEE 802.15.4 wireless networks

The Internet Protocol Security (IPsec) suite has defined Authentication Headers (AH) and Encapsulating Security Payloads (ESP) to enable data integrity, confidentiality, origin authentication and anti-replay protection for IPv6 packets (Fan, Wang, Zhang & Lin, 2014). The authors in proposed compressed AH and ESP features for 6LoWPAN to implement IPsec and thus provide end-to-end secure communications between wireless devices.

An enhanced authentication and key establishment scheme for 6LoWPAN networks (EAKES6Lo) has been proposed by the authors in . EAKES6Lo is divided into two phases to improve the security of 6LoWPAN networks. The two phases are: (1) system setup; and (2) authentication and key establishment. In Phase 1, the symmetric cryptography mechanism Advanced Encryption Standard (AES) is used to encrypt the data transfer in the network. To verify the integrity of the data, hash function Message Digest Algorithm 5 (MD5) or Secure Hash Algorithm (SHA) is employed. In Phase 2, six messages will be exchanged to finalize the authentication and key establishment process and establish a mutual authentication. Thus, 6lowPAN provides a template for secure wireless communications, even for resource-constrained devices.

3.7 RPL and Security

Routing protocols are a core component of conventional networks, and this also applies to 6LoWPAN networks. RPL is an optimized IPv6 routing protocol designed by IETF especially for Low power and Lossy Networks (LLNs) and is primarily used by 6LoWPAN networks. RPL is a distance-vector routing protocol, and its mapping topology is based on a Destination-Oriented Directed Acyclic Graph (DODAG) structure. A generic topology authentication scheme called Trust Anchor Interconnection Loop (TRAIL) for RPL has been presented in (Fan, Wang, Zhang & Lin, 2014). TRAIL can prevent the topological inconsistency attacks from spurious nodes by discovering and isolating the forged nodes. A round-trip message has been used by TRAIL to validate upward path integrity to the root node and help the nodes in the tree get genuine rank information. The innovation of TRAIL is that each node in the tree can validate its upward path to the root and detect any fake rank attacks. In the DODAG tree, it is essential for nodes to select their correct parent nodes, since every node except the root must have a parent node. The RPL rank is used to describe a node's position in the tree topology. In the authors present a secure selection scheme to help a child node to choose an authentic parent node. In its selection algorithm, a node's threshold value will be calculated based on average and maximum rank values from its neighbour nodes to exclude spoofing nodes from becoming its parent.

3.8 CoAP and Security

CoAP is a HTTP-like application layer protocol designed for constrained device networks. As there are some special requirements such as group communications in IoT networks, CoAP provides multicast support which HTTP does not have. To better suit the low-bandwidth connections and low-computational-power device environments, the User Datagram Protocol (UDP) protocol is adopted by CoAP. UDP is a simpler, low-latency and connectionless transport layer protocol compared with its counterpart Transmission Control Protocol (TCP). CoAP is a stateless protocol and is based on the client-server architecture model. It uses request/response-style operations to exchange messages between the client and server. Similar to HTTP, CoAP is also based on a representational state transfer (REST) model, where each resource on the server has its own Uniform Resource Identifier (URI), a client can access a resource by making a request to the server, and the request can be one of these four methods: GET, POST, PUT and DELETE

Nowadays, Transport Layer Security (TLS: RFC 5246) is the predominant encryption protocol for HTTP, but the implementation of TLS is overcomplicated for the resource-confined IoT devices. To secure communications, CoAP employs Datagram Transport Layer Security (DTLS: RFC 6347) (Fleisch, 2010) as its security protocol. DTLS offers the same security services that TLS provides. The main difference between TLS and DTLS is that TLS is based on the TCP protocol and DTLS is based on the UDP protocol. The CoAP specification has defined four different security modes. A device can be in one of four security modes: NoSec, PreSharedKey, RawPublicKey and Certificate. Again, IETF standards provide secure mechanisms for secure web-based communications within constrained networks.

3.9 Future IoT Security Directions

As indicated by the above three examples, there is already significant work underway to secure mission-critical IoT applications. A lot of effort has gone into developing IP-compatible secure communications networks which are suitable for resource-constrained devices, and which use state-of-the-art security techniques. However, many of these techniques require careful, unified, system-wide design, and experienced network engineers to design and maintain a secure IoT system. The emphasis of our work is not on this style of "technical" security, but rather it is on the system management aspect of Smart Home security, i.e., how to properly install and maintain the security enabled by these powerful tools

3.10 A Suitable Smart Home Architecture for Security

There have been many different proposals for Smart Home architectures, each of which have particular security issues. Three of the most important and popular architectures are middleware, cloud and gateway architectures. The next sections investigate the security issues and implementation difficulties for these architecture styles (Bauk, Dlabač, & Škurić, 2018).

3.11 Middleware Architectures and Security

Middleware is a software layer that sits between the low-level layer of devices and the high-level application layer. It usually provides a common interface and a standard data exchange structure to abstract the complex and various lower-level details of the hardware. When the middleware receives a request from a higher-layer application, it converts the high-level standardized resources access request to the corresponding device-specific methods. When the device responds back to the application, the middleware processes the low-level methods and data transformations, and then sends the related abstract commands and data back to the application. The application does not need to know the underlying details of the different implementations of the hardware, it can just simply invoke the commands and functions provided by the middleware. Security and privacy protection should be considered at all levels of the middleware, from the lower hardware interaction level to the higher common interface level.

VIRTUS Middleware is a middleware solution based on the open eXtensible Messaging and Presence Protocol (XMPP) protocol. It adopts the Simple Authentication and Security Layer (SASL) protocol for authentication and the Transport Layer Security (TLS) for data security and privacy. Secure Middleware for Embedded Peer-to-Peer systems (SMEPP) (Atzori, Iera & Morabito, 2010) is a middleware focusing on providing peer-to-peer security communication between smart nodes. Before a device can communicate with others, it needs to join a group by providing a valid credential. There are three different security levels, but only level 1 and level 2 take up the security mechanisms. There is no security implementation under level 0. SMEPP implements pre-shared key cryptography under level 1 and public-key cryptography under level 2 for group admission. On the other hand, SMEPP adopts authentication under level 1 and authentication together with encryption approach under level 2 to protect data security.

While middleware has been extensively used in corporate systems with desktop-class machines to manage complex heterogeneous networks, currently proposed IoT middleware solutions require substantial additional complex software layers and cryptographic routines to be implemented on devices which have neither the memory nor the computational power to host them. Apart from the performance problems, another concern for middleware architecture is that the coding defects in middleware inadvertently introduced by developers may potentially pose security threats to the IoT devices. So we reject middleware solutions as presently infeasible for many IoT-class devices.

3.12 Cloud Architectures and Security

Collaboration between devices is an important aspect of IoT. Such interoperable functions require high processing power which most IoT devices are not capable of. To solve the performance problem of IoT devices, researchers have proposed cloud-based solutions for IoT. The cloud has the resources to monitor, collect, store and process data from IoT devices (Adolphs et al. 2015) By analyzing this data, the cloud can trigger actions according to user-defined policies to achieve complex Smart Home control. The cloud-based architecture of IoT is also known as the Cloud of Things (CoT).

The authors in propose an IoT cloud architecture based on the IETF's CoAP protocol . The architecture consists of three decoupled stages which are the network, protocol and business logic stages. Each stage includes an incoming event queue, a thread pool and an event handler that processes the stage logic. The lightweight DTLS is used by this architecture as its security protocol for authentication and communication

A secure scheme for the Home Area Network (HAN) based on cloud computing has been introduced in . A Home Management System (HMS) manages devices and policies, and provides the access point for users. In the paper, the authors implement the HMS functions in the cloud and the HMS interfaces with the cloud services (Fan, Wang, Zhang & Lin, 2014). This scheme employs symmetric key encryption to apply confidentiality between end-to-end communications and each smart object is assigned a unique key.

The cloud-based solution removes the need for a separate home controller and provides a good way for IoT to connect and cooperate; however, it replaces the need for local computation with a need for substantial Internet communication. Due to the resource-limited nature of IoT, large amounts of raw data generated by IoT devices have to be transferred to the cloud without pre-processing; therefore, devices in the home need a high-speed, low-latency, always-on Internet connection, but such always-on high-speed Internet connections are not always available, especially in rural or remote areas. Control latency is increased, especially if the servers are overseas or the network is congested.

All devices must be accessible via the Internet which presents a broad attack surface, and each device needs to have sufficient resources to implement full network security protocols. Denial of service attacks, based on limiting access to the broader Internet, or occasional network outages may cause mission-critical tasks such as home healthcare and physical security systems to fail. Furthermore, because users do not have the full control of their cloud services, they have to trust cloud providers to implement appropriate and sufficient security measures for their data, but it is not always the case. Because cloud-based systems fail without always-on network connectivity, we do not believe that they can provide a secure and available Smart Home system by themselves, and they also expose all network devices to network attacks (Fan, Wang, Zhang & Lin, 2014).

3.13 Gateway Architectures

An IoT gateway is a relatively resource-rich network processor working on the same LAN with the other IoT endpoints. It can not only be a central management point to deal with the coordination of IoT devices, but it can also improve interconnection and interoperability between smart devices from different manufacturers. In addition, it can act as a bridge to connect the local IoT infrastructure to the cloud. Since the gateway has more computing power and resources, high computation and memory-rich tasks can be offloaded from IoT devices to the gateway. In terms of security, the gateway can centralize user authentication and apply access control to guard against unauthorized access or modification of restricted data. It also acts as a firewall to protect the smart devices and privacy from cyber threats, and to reduce the attack surface.

In the authors present an integrated access gateway (IAGW) architecture to support various application nodes through standard interfaces for Smart Home environments. The architecture comprises the ubiquitous sensor networks layer, the network layer and the service layer. IAGW includes a security module to implement the authentication, authorization and encryption. One of the benefits of this architecture is that it has a Quality of Service (QoS) module to prioritize traffic and guarantee resources for mission-critical operations.

A systematic concept called Server-Based Internet-Of-Things Architecture (SBIOTA) is a proposed gateway server to provide an effective, efficient, secure and cooperative integration solution for IoT. This conceptual architecture includes a novel auto-configuration service on the gateway to facilitate the device's deployment and management process so that a device can be plugged into a network and be fully functional on that network with a minimum of manual configuration. Its initial approach is that the authentication and communication between the gateway and devices take place through a separate network port or a short-range antenna physically adjacent to the server. Before connecting the devices to the network, the user needs to place them in physical proximity to the gateway to be authenticated and exchange related information to ensure only legitimate devices are allowed to connect to the network.

4. IoT – IDENTITY PROTECTION

IoT devices collect data about their environment, which includes people. These benefits introduce heavy risk. The data itself does not present the danger, however, its depth does. The highly detailed data collection paints a very clear picture of an individual, giving criminals all the information they need to take advantage of someone.

People may also not be aware of the level of privacy; for example, entertainment devices may gather A/V data, or "watch" a consumer, and share intimate information. The demand and price for this data exacerbates the issue considering the number and diversity of parties interested in sensitive data.

Problems specific to IoT technology lead to many of its privacy issues, which primarily stem from the user's inability to establish and control privacy

4.1 Consent

The traditional model for "notice and consent" within connected systems generally enforces existing privacy protections. It allows users to interact with privacy mechanisms, and set preferences typically through accepting an agreement or limiting actions. Many IoT devices have no such accommodations. Users not only have no control, but they are also not afforded any transparency regarding device activities.

4.2 The Right to be Left Alone

Users have normal expectations for privacy in certain situations. This comes from the commonly accepted idea of public and private spaces; for example, individuals are not surprised by surveillance cameras in commercial spaces (Fleisch, 2010) however, they do not expect them in their personal vehicle. IoT devices challenge these norms people recognize as the "right to be left alone." Even in public spaces, IoT creeps beyond the limits of expected privacy due to its power.

4.3 Indistinguishable Data

IoT deploys in a wide variety of ways. Much of IoT implementation remains group targeted rather than personal. Even if users give IoT devices consent for each action, not every system can reasonably process every set of preferences; for example, small devices in a complex assembly cannot honor the requests of tens of thousands of users they encounter for mere seconds.

4.4 Granularity

Modern big data poses a substantial threat to privacy, but IoT compounds the issue with its scale and intimacy. It goes not only where passive systems cannot, but it collects data everywhere. This supports creation of highly detailed profiles which facilitate discrimination and expose individuals to physical, financial, and reputation harm.

4.5 Comfort

The growth of IoT normalizes it. Users become comfortable with what they perceive as safe technology. IoT also lacks the transparency that warns users in traditional connected systems; consequently, many act without any consideration for the potential consequences (Fleisch, 2010).

REFERENCES

Ackoff, R. L. (1971). Towards a system of systems concepts. *Management Science, 17*(11), 661–671. doi:10.1287/mnsc.17.11.661

Adolphs, P., Bedenbender, H., Dirzus, D., Ehlich, M., Epple, U., Hankel, M., ... Koziolek, H. (2015). *Status report-reference architecture model industrie 4.0 (rami4. 0)*. VDI-Verein Deutscher Ingenieure eV and ZVEI-German Electrical and Electronic Manufacturers Association, Tech. Rep.

Atzori, L., Iera, A., & Morabito, G. (2010). The Internet of Things: A Survey. *Computer Networks*, *54*(15), 2787–2805. doi:10.1016/j.comnet.2010.05.010

Atzori, L., Iera, A., & Morabito, G. (2010). The internet of things: A survey. *Computer Networks*, *54*(15), 2787–2805. doi:10.1016/j.comnet.2010.05.010

Bauk, S., Dlabač, T., & Škurić, M. (2018, February). Internet of Things, high resolution management and new business models. In *2018 23rd International Scientific-Professional Conference on Information Technology (IT)* (pp. 1-4). IEEE. 10.1109/SPIT.2018.8350850

Evans, D. (2011). The internet of things: How the next evolution of the internet is changing everything. *CISCO White Paper, 1*(2011), 1-11.

Evans, D. (2011). *The Internet of Things: How the Next Evolution of the Internet Is Changing Everything*. Cisco. www.cisco.com/web/about/ac79/docs/innov/IoT_IBSG_0411FINAL.pdf

Fan, P. F., Wang, L. L., Zhang, S. Y., & Lin, T. T. (2014). The Research on the Internet of Things Industry Chain for Barriers and Solutions. *Applied Mechanics and Materials*, *441*, 1030–1035. doi:10.4028/www.scientific.net/AMM.441.1030

Fleisch, E. (2010). What is the internet of things? An economic perspective. *Economics, Management, and Financial Markets, 5*(2), 125-157.

Gubbi, J., Buyya, R., Marusic, S., & Palaniswami, M. (2013). Internet of Things (IoT): A vision, architectural elements, and future directions. *Future Generation Computer Systems, 29*(7), 1645-1660.

Howells, R. (2015). *The Business Case for IoT*. SAP. http://scn.sap.com/community/business-trends/blog/2015/06/18/the-business-case-for-iot

Report, S. (2015). *Reference Architecture Model Industrie 4.0 (RAMI4.0), VDI/ VDE Society Measurement and Automatic Control*. www.vdi.de/fileadmin/vdi_de/redakteur_dateien/gma_dateien/5305_Publikation_GMA_Status _Report_ZVEI_Reference_Architecture_Model.pdf

Weyrich, M., & Ebert, C. (2015). Reference architectures for the internet of things. *IEEE Software, 33*(1), 112–116. doi:10.1109/MS.2016.20

Chapter 7
A Review on the Importance of Blockchain and Its Current Applications in IoT Security

Manjula Josephine Bollarapu
Koneru Lakshmaiah Education Foundation, India

Ruth Ramya Kalangi
Koneru Lakshmaiah Education Foundation, India

K. V. S. N. Rama Rao
Koneru Lakshmaiah Education Foundation, India

ABSTRACT

In recent years, blockchain technology has attracted considerable attention. As blockchain is one of the revolutionary technologies that is impacting various industries in the market now with its unique features of decentralization, transparency, and incredible security. Blockchain technology can be used for anything which requires their transactions to be recorded in a secure manner. In this chapter, the authors survey the importance of the blockchain technology and the applications that are being developed on the basis of blockchain technology in area of IoT and security.

DOI: 10.4018/978-1-7998-2414-5.ch007

BLOCKCHAIN IN IOT

Decentralized Framework for IoT Digital Forensics for Efficient Investigation: A Blockchain-based

Jung Hyun Ryuet.al.(2019) proposed 2 outlines the diagram of proposed advanced legal sciences system for IoT condition. The proposed structure is partitioned into three layers: cloud; blockchain; and IoT gadgets. For the most part, in an IoT domain, gadgets speak with the cloud. By 2020, the quantity of IoT gadgets is relied upon to increment to 26 billion . For this situation, it is practically difficult to examine countless IoT gadgets utilizing existing advanced measurable strategies. Figure 2 shows a review of proposed computerized criminological structure for IoT condition in this paper. Each IoT gadget stores information produced during the time spent speaking with different gadgets in the blockchain as an exchange. The IoT condition incorporates every little condition utilizing IoT gadgets: sensors; keen vehicle; savvy building; shrewd industry; brilliant home; brilliant matrix. In these conditions, cybercrime can happen whenever, and legitimate criminological system for it must be built up. In the IoT gadget classification, gadgets have different purposes, administrations, makers, advances, and information types. IoT gadgets send and receivelarge measures of information paying little heed to gadget client's will. For this situation, if the current criminological strategy is applied to every gadget framing an enormous number of connections, the examination turns out to be very difcult. Along these lines, in the proposed structure, the information created during the time spent correspondence of each IoT gadget are put away as an exchange in the blockchain. The computerized scientific agent abuses the put away trustworthiness of squares and the simplifed chain of guardianship process.

Secure Firmware Update for Embedded Devices in an IoT Environment: A Block chain Based

Boohyung Leeet.al.,(2017) In this paper, we center around a safe firmware update issue, which is an essential security challenge for the implanted gadgets in an IoT domain. Another firmware update conspire that uses a blockchain innovation is proposed to safely check a firmware adaptation, approve the accuracy of firmware, and download the most recent firmware for the installed gadgets. In the proposed plot, an inserted gadget demands its firmware update to hubs in a blockchain arrange and gets a reaction to decide if its firmware is modern or not. If not most recent, the implanted gadget downloads the most recent firmware from a distributed firmware sharing system of the hubs. Indeed, even for the situation that the variant of the firmware is upto-date, its respectability, i.e., accuracy of firmware, is checked. The proposed conspire ensures that the inserted gadget's firmware is state-of-the-art while not altered. Assaults focusing on known vulnerabilities on firmware of installed gadgets are in this manner moderated.

Blockchain Mechanisms for IoT Security

MatevžPustišeka(2018) et.al.,present three potential designs for the IoT front-end BC applications. They vary in situating of Ethereumblockchain customers (nearby gadget, remote server) and in situating of key store required for the administration of active exchanges. The functional limitations of these structures, which use the Ethereum arrange for believed exchange trade, are the information volumes, the area and synchronization of the full blockchain hub and the area and the entrance to the Ethereum key store. Consequences of these tests demonstrate that a full Ethereum hub isn't probably going to dependably run on a compelled IoT gadgets. In this manner the design with remote Ethereum customers is by all accounts a feasible methodology, where two sub-alternatives exist and contrast in key store area/the executives. Likewise, we proposed the utilization of designs with an exclusive correspondence between the IoT gadget and remote blockchain customer to additionally diminish the system traffic and improve security. We anticipate that it should have the option to work over low-power, low-bitrate portable innovations, as well. Our exploration explains contrasts in compositional methodologies, yet ultimate conclusion for a specific record convention and front-end application design is at emphatically dependent on the specific planned use case.

Securing Academic Certificates Through Block Chain

One of the incredible promising application of the blockchain innovation is that it can serve as a decentralized, changeless, and completely secure store for a wide range of benefits not just as a currency That is the thing that makes it intriguing likewise for public sector use.A University can safely store its scholarly archives utilizing block chain technology. The accompanying fundamental necessities were set up before the venture of putting the academic certificates on the blockchain starts a) the process should involve no other services or products other than the Bitcoinblockchain, b) the process should allow someone to authenticate a University of Nicosia certificate without having to contact the University of Nicosia, and c) The process should allow someone to complete the process even if the University of Nicosia, or more likely their website, no longer existed. The University of Nicosia is a private university, but this use case is just as relevant for a public university. The process of storing the academic certificates on the blockchain followed these steps Hash of the individual certificates. A hash of an certificate is at the center of the procedure. A hash function is a single function that accepts any arbitary information as input and produces a string with a fixed number of characters .The index document containing the hashes of all the individual declarations is published on the University of Nicosia home page. But if this was all, there would be no use for the blockchain. For the procedure to be genuinely decentralized individuals ought to have the option to find a copy of the index document anywhere on the web and compare it to the index document on the blockchain.

Discover a duplicate of the list record anyplace on the web and contrast it with the list archive on the blockchain. The check procedure is done in two stages; one for confirming the file archive and the second for confirming the specific endorsement: Verifying the file report. Guarantee that a legitimate record report from the University of Nicosia is utilized. The hash of the file archive ought to be equivalent to the hash put away on the blockchain, in the predefined time period. Check the declaration. When the file archive has been checked, a SHA-256 hash of the declaration (in pdf) ought to be contrasted with the hash of a similar authentication recorded in the list report. On the off chance that the hash esteems are comparative, the declaration is real. Obviously, the examination of the hash esteems just ensures the legitimacy of the testament, not that the individual who sent the authentication is equivalent to the individual on the declaration.

That must be approved in different manners. The utilization case above has given one potential utilization of the Bitcoinblockchain innovation for open segment. All associations giving declarations, licenses and so forth could profit by the new innovation, as this utilization case appears. The utilization case from the University of Nicosia has highlighted a few difficulties that ought to be researched more top to bottom so as to show up at a best practice for putting away declarations and licenses on the blockchain. The Bitcoin innovation fits the meaning of an advanced stage and the attributes of a data framework can likewise be found in the innovation, as appeared in table 3. Its scattered and disseminated "possession" is in accordance with the focal trait of an II. Introduced base is another key component in a data framework and indicates specialized and non-specialized components delineating the system impacts deciding the improvement of the foundation . The introduced base for this situation is the authoritative, monetary, and lawful components overseeing the present open help II. The legitimate elements are of exceptional significance, as is likewise examined in a large number of the distributions recorded in area three. Be that as it may, the lawful and regulatoryfactors examined in these papers are for the most part about controlling the cash and the installment framework. The utilization case portrayed above, and comparable employments of Bitcoin, gets away from these concerns since the installment part is only an essential reaction and not simply the objective. That is the situation with all utilization cases having a place with purported "keen agreements" utilization of Bitcoin. The money is utilized uniquely as a token in these cases. A data framework without direct Government control may appear to be unnerving for open part. While considering Bitcoin as an intriguing innovation with regards to eGovernment we have to survey history and be helped to remember the "fight" between worldwide system gauges toward the finish of the 1980s, start of 1990s. Governments had the decision between the controlled OSI convention and the Internet convention, and the greater part of them picked the OSI convention. USA's Government OSI Profile – GOSIP – turned into the standard for some other countries' OSI profiles, for example NOSIP – Norwegian OSI Profile. Web's ascent in prominence made it a true standard that before long invade the OSI convention, not least on the grounds that the OSI norms attempted to convey working and interoperable administrations (in the same place.). Web turned into the national and worldwide standard for worldwide correspondence not as a result of national needs, however notwithstanding them. This is something to hold up under at the top of the priority list while considering an innovation that utilizes the equivalent appropriated model that Internet itself.

In each popular government, the security of a political decision involves national security. The PC security field has for 10 years considered the potential outcomes of electronic democratic frameworks, with the objective of limiting the expense of having a national political decision, while satisfying and expanding the security states of a political race. From the beginning of fairly choosing up-and-comers, the democratic framework has been founded on pen and paper. Supplanting the conventional pen and paper conspire with another political decision framework is basic to restrict misrepresentation and having the democratic procedure recognizable and obvious . Electronic democratic machines have been seen as defective, by the security network, principally dependent on physical security concerns. Anybody with physical access to such machine can undermine the machine, in this way influencing all votes cast on the previously mentioned machine. Coming up next are the jobs and parts recognized for an e-Voting framework.

BLOCK CHAIN FOR EDUCATION

Patrick Ochejaet.al.,(2019), It is a typical practice to give a synopsis of a student's learning accomplishments in type of a transcript or authentication. Be that as it may, point by point data on the profundity of learning and how learning or lessons were directed is absent in the transcript of scores. This work presents the principal pragmatic usage of another stage for monitoring learning accomplishments past transcripts and authentications. This is accomplished by keeping up advanced hashes of learning exercises and overseeing access rights using keen agreements on the blockchain. The blockchain of learning logs (BOLL) is a stage that empower students to move their taking in records starting with one organization then onto the next in a protected and undeniable arrangement. This principally takes care of the chilly beginning issue looked by learning information logical stages when attempting to offer customized understanding to new students. BOLL empowers existing learning information logical stages to get to the taking in logs from different organizations with the authorization of the students as well as establishment who initially have responsibility for logs. The fundamental commitment of this paper is to examine how learning records could be associated across establishments utilizing BOLL. We present a diagram of how the usage has been done, examine asset prerequisites, and look at the focal points BOLL has over other comparative instruments.

Guang Chen et.al(2018)., Blockchain is the center innovation used to make the cryptographic forms of money, as bitcoin. As a major aspect of the fourth modern insurgency since the innovation of steam motor, power, and data innovation, blockchain innovation has been applied in numerous zones, for example, money, legal executive, and trade. The current paper concentrated on its likely instructive applications and investigated how blockchain innovation can be utilized to take care of some training issues. This article previously presented the highlights and points of interest of blockchain innovation following by investigating a portion of the current blockchain applications for training. Some imaginative utilizations of utilizing blockchain innovation were proposed, and the advantages and difficulties of utilizing blockchain innovation for instruction were additionally talked about.

REFERENCES

Anand, Conti, Kaliyar, & Lal. (2019). *TARE: Topology Adaptive Re-kEying scheme for secure group communication in IoT networks*. Springer Science+Business Media, LLC.

Bistarelli, S., Mercanti, I., Santancini, P., & Santini, F. (2019). *End-to-End Voting with Non-Permissioned and Permissioned Ledgers*. Springer Nature B.V. doi:10.100710723-019-09478-y

Chen, G., Xu, B., Lu, M., & Chen, N.-S. (2018). Exploring blockchain technology and its potential applications for education. *Smart Learning Environments*, 5(1), 1–10. doi:10.118640561-017-0050-x

Huh & Seo. (2018). *Blockchain-based mobile fingerprint verification and automatic log-in platform for future computing*. Springer Science+Business Media, LLC.

Karaarslan & Adiguzel. (n.d.). Blockchain Based DNS and PKI Solutions. In *Standards for Major Internet Disrutors: Blockchain, Intents and Related Paradigm*. Academic Press.

Kshetri & Voas. (2018). Blockchain-Enabled E-Voting. *IEEE Software*, 95-99.

Lee, B., & Lee, J.-H. (2017). Blockchain-based secure firmware update for embedded devices in an Internet of Things environment. *The Journal of Supercomputing, 73*(3), pp1152–pp1167. doi:10.100711227-016-1870-0

Li, H., Tian, H., Zhang, F., & He, J. (2019). Blockchain-based searchable symmetric encryption scheme. *Computers & Electrical Engineering, 73*, 32–45. doi:10.1016/j.compeleceng.2018.10.015

Liu, J., Jager, T., Kakvi, S. A., & Warinschi, B. (2018). How to build time-lock encryption. *Designs, Codes and Cryptography, 86*(11), 2549–2586. doi:10.100710623-018-0461-x

Minoli, D., & Occhiogrosso, B. (2018). Blockchain mechanisms for IoT security. *Internet of Things, 1-2*, 1–13. doi:10.1016/j.iot.2018.05.002

Ocheja, P., Flanagan, B., Ueda, H., & Ogata, H. (2019). *Managing lifelong learning records through blockchain*. Research and Practice in Technology Enhanced Learning. doi:10.118641039-019-0097-0

Pustišeka. (2018). Approaches to Front-End IoT Application Development for the Ethereum Blockchain. *Procedia Computer Science, 129*, 410–419.

Ryu, Sharma, Jo, & Park. (2019). *A blockchain-based decentralized efcient investigation framework for IoT digital forensics*. Springer Science+Business Media, LLC.

Shahzad. (2019). Trustworthy Electronic Voting Using Adjusted Blockchain Technology. *IEEE Access: Practical Innovations, Open Solutions, 7*, 24477–24488.

Turkanovic. (2018, January 5). EduCTX: A Blockchain-Based Higher Education Credit Platform. *IEEE Access: Practical Innovations, Open Solutions*, 5112–5127.

Wang, B., Sun, J., He, Y., Pang, D., & Lu, N. (2018). Large-scale Election Based On Blockchain. *Procedia Computer Science, 129*, 234–237. doi:10.1016/j.procs.2018.03.063

Zhou, L., Wang, L., Sun, Y., & Lv, P. (2018). BeeKeeper: A Blockchain-Based IoT System With Secure Storage and Homomorphic Computation. *IEEE Access: Practical Innovations, Open Solutions, 6*, 43472–43488. doi:10.1109/ACCESS.2018.2847632

Chapter 8
Blockchain Technology– Security Booster

Harsha Kundan Patil

iD https://orcid.org/0000-0002-1801-4086

Ashoka Center for Business and Computer Studies, Nashik, India

ABSTRACT

"Blockchain" as the name suggests is the chain of blocks. It is the chunk of digital information (blocks) that are connected through the public databases (Chain). It is nothing but the newer version of file organisation. Blocks store digital information like actual record of any transaction, details of involve entities in the transaction, time stamps, and other metadata of the transactions. Blocks also have unique ids, which are known as hash. Blockchain technology is built using peer-to-peer networking. Anyone who is on network can access the blocks. There is no centralised community to control the blockchain. It is operated by miners, the peoples who lend their computing power to the network to solve the complex computation algorithm problems. These blocks are stored in multiple computers. Due to its distribution and decentralisation, the validation process is broadcast in nature, which provides it "the trusted approach". Blockchain enables security and tamperproof capabilities for storing data and smart contracts. Any tampering of data attempted by a node or user in a block changes the hash of the block. The blockchain technology has the capability to face and provides the solution to fight with the problem of risk and security concern online. In 2008, a mysterious white paper titled "Bitcoin: A Peer to Peer Electronic Cash System", by visionary Satoshi Nakamoto gave birth to the concept of blockchain. The chapter explains the structure of blockchain technology in detail and enlighten the aspects that make blockchain technology the secure concept of today's world.

DOI: 10.4018/978-1-7998-2414-5.ch008

INTRODUCTION

"Blockchain" as the name suggest is the Chain of Blocks. The Chunk of digital information (Blocks) which are connected through the public databases (Chain). It is nothing but the newer version of the File organisation. Blocks stored digital information like actual record of any transaction, details of involve entities in the transaction, timestamps and other metadata of the transactions. Blocks also has unique id which is known as hash.

Blockchain technology is built using peer-to-peer networking. Anyone who is on network can access the blocks. There is no centralised community to control the Blockchain. It is operated by miners; the peoples who lend their computing power to the network to solve the complex computation algorithm problems. These blocks are stored in multiple computers. Figure 1 shows step by step working of Blockchain.

Step1: Whenany online transaction like purchasing through Amazon occurred and successfully completed the details of transaction is recorded.

Step2: The next step is verification. The details of the transaction verified through network of computers. Thousands of computers connected through global network are utilised for verification process. Which involves verification of purchased article details, transactiontimestamp, cost and parties involved in it.

Step3: After transaction details verified it stored in block with digital signatures of involved parties. One block may contain many verified transactions. The block also have the hash key which gives the unique identification to the block. This block is then added to existing chain of block. So in this way the blockchain grows. Once the block is added to blockchain it is publically available for all.

Each computer which is connected to the blockchain network has their own copy of blockchain and whenever new block added on it the copy of each computer is updated. That means all the computers of the blockchain network have the same copy of network and each time whenever any block is access or added the verifications are done by all connected computers. As we know it is easy to hide from one's eye but difficult to hide from all's eyes. This 360 degree verification of public network makes blockchain very secured.

Concept of Blockchain Technology and its Emergence

Blockchain, the underlying technology behind cryptocurrencies has its origin that stem from a problem of verifying timestamp digitally in the late 1980s and early 1990s. In 1990, Haber & Stornetta published a paper titled 'How to Timestamp a digital Document'. In this paper, they proposed to create a hash chain by linking

Figure 1. Blockchain Generation

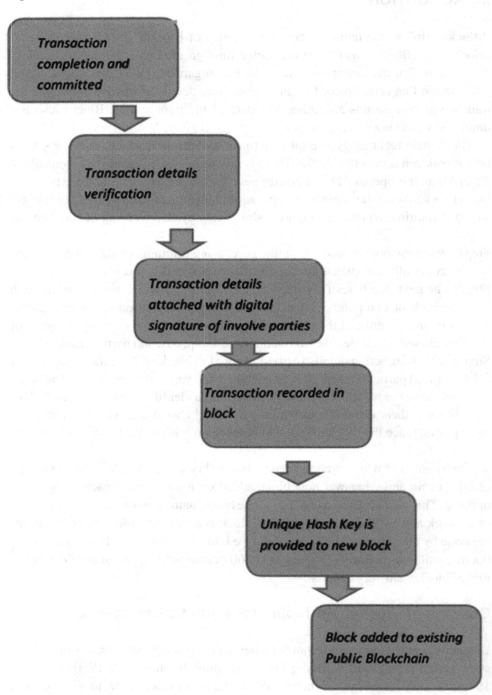

the issued timestamps together so that the documents get prevented from being either forward dated or back dated, (Haber,1990). Then, Wei Dai one of the noted researchers, introduced the concept of b-money which is used to create money through solving computational puzzles and decentralized consensus. But this proposal lacks implementation details (Dai, 1998). A concept called "reusable proofs of work" was introduced by Hal Finney. This concept combined the ideas of both b-money and computationally difficult Hash cash puzzle by Adam Back for the creation of cryptocurrency.

Block chain technology is having the focus of Ecommerce developer due to its quality of exchange of value units without the need of intermediaries (Nakamoto, 2008). It allow us to secure our digital assets like art or digital data from sensors on a marketplace (Draskovic and Saleh, 2017), or allowing property owners to transfer their land without a notary (Kombe et al., 2017). Technology is also get used to address several other scientific problems (Dhillon, 2016; Golem, 2016; Wolf et al., 2016; Breitinger and Gipp, 2017; van Rossum, 2017; Androulaki et al., 2018) like trust problems in the form of malicious behavior in peer-review processes (Stahel and Moore, 2014; Degen, 2016; Dansinger, 2017), lacking quality and redundancy of study designs (Belluz and Hoffman, 2015), and the restriction of free access to scientific publications (Myllylahti, 2014; Teplitskiy et al., 2017; Schiltz, 2018).

Blockchain Concept

As the world requirements more transformation and digitization, everybody is prepared to receive and adapt new technologies (Dorri et. al. 2016). Blockchain, a new troublesome technology was introduced with its very first modern application termed Bitcoin. The term Blockchain is simply well-defined as the chain of blocks containing encrypted material stored on a decentralized distributed network. This developing technology influences various industries amazingly and its application grows numerously. Blockchain, a shared ledger in which all the data are recorded digitally has a common history and is available to all the participants in the network. This eliminates any fraudulent activity or duplication of transactions. Blockchain is a chain of blocks. Each block covers encrypted information and hashed sticks to previous block, making it problematic to retroactively alter without adapting the entire chain. The first block is called genesis block. Every block contains two components Block header and Block Body.

Block Header

The various components present in the block header is version, Hash of previous block, Merkle root, Timestamp, Target, Nonce.

Public Blockchain

It is a decentralized network in which only the transaction information is totally available to the public. In this type of Blockchain, any user can link the network at any time and they can pile, send and receive data at anywhere and at any time. This feature of Public Blockchain network types it call as Permission less network. The participants in this network gets incentivized and rewarded using the token associated with them. Many decentralized consensus devices such as PoW, PoS are used to make decisions.Public Blockchain networks provide self-governance and higher level of security since all the transaction information are present in all the nodes in the network which makes hacking a particular node impossible.

Private Blockchain

Private Blockchain usually called Permissioned Blockchain are exploits within a institute in which the members need consent in order to join the network. Private Blockchains are more centralized and the transactions are private. The originalities that want to collaborate and share data can make use of private blockchains since it offers more efficiency and faster transactions. The code in this type of blockchain is precisely private and hidden which results in eliminating decentralization and disintermediation. Here, the central-in-charge helps to achieve consensus by giving the mining rights to anyone in the network.

Consortium or Federated Blockchain

A hybrid model between public and private Blockchain in which a number of approved users have control over the network. The term consortium is defined as the group of companies or the group of illustrative individuals who come together to make decisions for the best benefit of the whole network. The consortium blockchain allows only a few selected predetermined parties to verify transactions and to participate in the consensus process instead of allowing any user in the network in case of public blockchain and a single organization in case of private blockchain,(Pilkington, 2016).

Security framework:

Generally redundancy of data is the main source and responsible for generate inconsistency issues in data. But this property is well utilised in Blockchain. The inconsistency generated due to redundancy works as indicator for alteration of block data. Whenever any block data changes the hash key automatically changed which recursively generate inconsistency with trailing blocks.

So if anyone wants to edit block data it indirectly required to alter the hash details of all blocks connected to block chain, which may involve to alteration of millions of computers' blockchain which is very complex to handle. The longest blockchain i.e. Maximum users agreed upon blockchain has been the accepted block chain. This technique known as consensus which accept the longest blockchain when multiple copies of blockchain are available.

By storing data across its network, the blockchain eliminates the risks that come with data being held centrally. Blockchain deploy the encryption methods to strengthen the security of data. After user name password the OTP method is also failed to secure the user data. In blockchain the existing methods are exploiting in a way which overall improved the security of blockchain. The combination of public key and private key worked on blockchain for implementing the security policy of blockchain. Anyone who wants to see the block can see it publically but retrieval of data from block is only possible with the help of private key. If any owner forget the private key of his block it will never be accessible to anyone including himself.

Blockchain and IOT: Security Review

In the era of smartness, smart mobile phone, smart infrastructure, smart devices and smart machines are the leaves of tree named IoT. The heavy acceptance and developments in the area of IoT also attracted hackers as vulnerability of digital data increases. The ecosystem of IoT work in decentralised manner (Atzori et.al., 2010). Data is generated and shared throughout the network and not controlled by any specific device. Due to this distributed data approach, data availability and efficiency of connected devices' service become more rapid, well-organized and reasonable. Rather than working with clod computing or other storage solutions nowadays IoT devices are preferring use of distributed database technology through blockchain concept, (Giusto et. al. 2014).

Conferring to various research reports, there are about 5 billion IoT connected devices which is forecast to upsurge up to 50 billion devices by 2022. The IoT devices shows an important role in changing the current world to smart world. As the number of IoT devices continues to proliferate, data and transaction verification, access control all become important (Christidis et al., 2016). Further, the security holes of IoT upsurges due to the collection of data from various devices at one place, controlling remotely of devices by hackers, handling the devices, lack of ability to find compromised nodes, leakage of sensitive data and other activities. It is an arduous task to overcome the security issues faced by IoT devicesThe problems and security issues with IoT devices could be unlocked if IoT devices becomes decentralized.

Many security experts believe that Blockchain could be the silver bullet needed by the IoT devices to solve its issues. Blockchain when integrated with IoT could improve security and distributed processing power of IoT devices and also solves the problem of cloud-based data monopolyFurther, the blockchain is able to track and process the massive flow of data that pours from myriad of IoT devices. Blockchain and IoT is viewed as a perfect match since blockchain could solve many of the issues associated with IoT devices.

Even if many of the matters of IoT devices are resolved by rapidly accelerating Blockchain technology, the convergence of these two blossoming technologies suffer from certain problems. Since the IoT devices are designed to be light weight and have low processing power, the integration of Blockchain in these devices poses a problem. Also, associated with Blockchain is the scalability issue and sky rocketing fees. So, many companies took convergence of these technologies on their many agenda and starts working on it.

(Elsts, Mitskas, and Oikonomou 2018)IOTA, the Blockchainless cryptocurrency for the Internet of Things is especially being designed for the integration of IoT devices with Blockchain technology. It is a quantum resistant Directed Acyclic Graph (DAG) which works on the top of their own ledger called Tangle. In this graph, nodes are the IOTA transactions and the validation corresponds to edges. Each transaction must validate two other transactions before joining the network. For validation, Proof-of-Work mechanism is used. IOTA is designed to provide zero fee transactions and unique verification process which is able to solve the scalability issues of Blockchain.

DAG differs from other blockchain in such a way that DAG works on 'horizontal' scheme and blockchain is based on 'vertical' scheme and also there are no miners and blocks in DAG, hence the name blocklesschain. The nature of graph is acyclic and also flows in a specific direction. The transactions in IOTA is not duplicated and there is no wait time for the blocks to be confirmed which in turns reduces the sky rocketing transaction fees. Even though, IOTA tries to be a perfect solution, there exists communication overhead of integrating IoT devices with IOTA blockchain.

Following features of Blockchain technology makes more efficient for using in IoT also shows in figure2:

Decentralization

As architecture of IoT and Blockchain is very similar, that is the reason that decentralisation concept of blockchain boosted the use of it in IoT. Blockchain provides the solution for IoT for managing the data and working of all connected devices without any third party. So failure of any device in a network of things never results in unavailability of data.

Figure 2. Features of Blockchain, enhancing efficiency of IoT

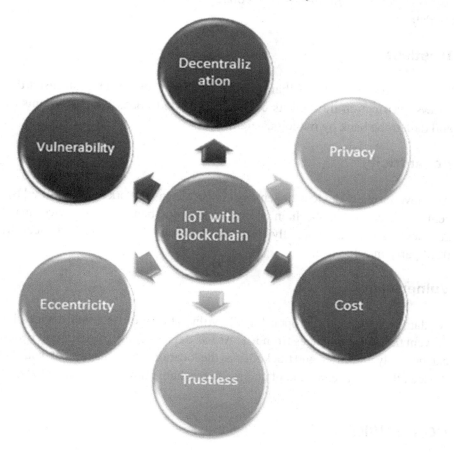

Privacy

Deployment of blockchain networks concepts in IoT, enhance the privacy of individual device data. As devices are connected in internet, any hacker can easily access the device and can manipulate the data, but due to using of Blockchain technology its consensus protocol prevent such alteration of data records.

Cost

Use of Blockchain Database is major reason for making IoT devices more affordable. Due to cost reduction IoT devices and technology has been implemented in many other domain easily. As no third party is required to maintain and verify the data cost is effectively diminishes. The connected nodes itself taking part in validating the data.

Trustless

Trustless concept of blockchain makes IoT more secure. Decentralised database allows verification through its connected smarted nodes which prevents devices and data to be hack by malicious elements.

Eccentricity

As conventionally devices or sensors connected in network are controlled by some central device. But block chain allows the eccentric behaviour of devices in network and devices can automatically responses and interact with other devices without third party interference.

Vulnerability

As data in blockchain is open for all. Vulnerability of data and devices helps to prevent the theft of devices from IoT. As IoT devices connected through Blockchain can be easily identified and tracked as as the location and management data about the device all the time can be kept and made reachable through a distributed database.

CONCLUSION

Decentralisation of authority and data is the biggest feature of the blockchain. The versatile technology behind blockchain gifted the IoT and other network based applications more powerful, efficient and secure. Nowadays researcher and engineers are deploying blockchain in many domain to enhance the data security. Above discussed features of blockchain not only make IoT application powerful but also helps in every area to strengthen the power of applications.

REFERENCES

Ali, M. S., Dolui, K., & Antonelli, F. (2017). IoT data privacy via blockchains and IPFS. In *International Conference on the Internet of Things*. ACM. 10.1145/3131542.3131563

Androulaki, E., Barger, A., Bortnikov, V., Cachin, C., Christidis, K., De Caro, A., ... (2018). Hyperledger fabric: a distributed operating system for permissioned blockchains. In *EuroSys '18 - Proceedings of the Thirteenth EuroSys Conference.* Porto: ACM. 10.1145/3190508.3190538

Antonopoulos, A. M. (2014). *Mastering Bitcoin* (1st ed.). O'Reilly Media.

Atzori, L., Iera, A., & Morabito, G. (2010). The Internet of Things: A survey. *Computer Networks, 54*(15), 2787–2805. doi:10.1016/j.comnet.2010.05.010

Banerjee, M., Lee, J., & Choo, K.-K. R. (2017). *A blockchain future to Internet of Things security: A position paper.* Digital Communications and Networks. doi:10.1016/j.dcan.2017.10.006

Banerjee, M., Lee, J., & Choo, K. K. R. (2018). A Blockchain future for internet of things security: A position paper. *Digit. Commun. Networks, 4*(3), 149–160. doi:10.1016/j.dcan.2017.10.006

Belluz, J., & Hoffman, S. (2015). *The One Chart You Need to Understand Any Health Study.* Vox. Available online at: https://www.vox.com/2015/1/5/7482871/ types-of-study-design

Chollet, Castiaux, Bruneton, & Sainlez. (2013). *Continuous interconnected supply chain using blockchain and internet of things supply chain traceability.* Deloitte Blockchain.

Christidis, K., & Devetsikiotis, M. (2016). Blockchains and Smart Contracts for the Internet of Things. *IEEE Access: Practical Innovations, Open Solutions, 4,* 2292–2303. doi:10.1109/ACCESS.2016.2566339

Conoscenti, M., Torino, D., Vetr, A., Torino, D., & De Martin, J. C. (2016). Blockchain for the Internet of Things: a Systematic Literature Review. *IEEE/ACS 13th International Conference of Computer Systems and Applications (AICCSA).* 10.1109/AICCSA.2016.7945805

Dai, W. (1998). *B-money.* http://www.weidai.com/bmoney.txt

Dhillon, V. (2016). *Blockchain-Enabled Open Science Framework.* O'Reilly Media. Available online at: https://www.oreilly.com/ideas/blockchain-enabled-open-science-framework

Dhillon, V., Metcalf, D., & Hooper, M. (2017). *"Blockchain in science," in Blockchain Enabled Applications* (1st ed.). Apress. doi:10.1007/978-1-4842-3081-7

Dorri, A., Kanhere, S., & Jurdak, R. (2016). *Blockchain in internet of things: challenges and solutions.* arXiv: 1608.05187

Draskovic, D., & Saleh, G. (2017). *Datapace - Decentralized Data Marketplace Based on Blockchain.* Available online at: https://www.datapace.io/datapace_whitepaper.pdf

Elsts, Mitskas, & Oikonomou. (2018). Distributed Ledger Technology and the Internet of Things: A Feasibility Study. In BlockSys, Shenzhen, China.

Giusto, D., Iera, A., Morabito, G., & Atzori, L. (2014). The Internet of Things. In *20th Tyrrhenian Workshop on Digital Communication.* Springer Publishing Company, Incorporated.

Golem. (2016). *The Golem Project - Global Market for Idle Computer Power.* Available online at: https://golem.network/crowdfunding

Gord, M. (2016). *Smart Contracts Described by Nick Szabo 20 Years ago now becoming Reality. Bitcoin Magazine.*

Haber, S., & Stometta, W. S. (1991). How to time stamp a digital documents. Journal of Cryptography, 3(2), 99-111. doi:10.1007/3-540-38424-3_32

Huh, Cho, & Kim. (2017). Managing IoT Devices using Blockchain Platform. *ICACT2017.*

Janowicz, K., Regalia, B., Hitzler, P., Mai, G., Delbecque, S., Fröhlich, M., Martinent, P., & Lazarus, T. (2018). On the prospects of blockchain and distributed ledger technologies for open science and academic publishing. *Semantic Web, 9*(5), 545–555. doi:10.3233/SW-180322

Khan & Salah. (2017). IoT security: Review, blockchain solutions, and open challenges. *Future Generation Computer Systems.*

Kombe, C., Manyilizu, M., & Mvuma, A. (2017). Design of land administration and title registration model based on blockchain technology. *Journal of Information Engineering and Applications, 7,* 8–15.

Liang, X., Zhao, J., Shetty, S., & Li, D. (2017). Towards data assurance and resilience in IoT using blockchain. *Conference Paper.* 10.1109/MILCOM.2017.8170858

Macleod, M. R., Michie, S., Roberts, I., Dirnagl, U., Chalmers, I., Ioannidis, J. P., Salman, R. A.-S., Chan, A.-W., & Glasziou, P. (2014). Biomedical research: Increasing value, reducing waste. *Lancet, 383*(9912), 101–104. doi:10.1016/S0140-6736(13)62329-6 PMID:24411643

Myllylahti, M. (2014). Newspaper paywalls–the hype and the reality. *Digit. Journal.*, *2*(2), 179–194. doi:10.1080/21670811.2013.813214

Nakamoto, S. (2008). *Bitcoin: A. Peer to Peer. Electronic cash system.* https://bitcoin.org/bitcoin.pdf

Pilkington. (2016). Blockchain technology: Principle and applications. *Research Handbook on Digital Transformations.*

Schiltz, M. (2018). Science without publication paywalls: cOAlition S for the realisation of full and immediate open access. *PLoS Medicine, 15*(9), e1002663. doi:10.1371/journal.pmed.1002663 PMID:30178782

Stahel, P. F., & Moore, E. E. (2014). Peer review for biomedical publications: We can improve the system. *BMC Medicine, 12*(1), 179. doi:10.118612916-014-0179-1 PMID:25270270

Swan. (2015). *Blockchain Blue Print for a new economy.* O'Reilly Media.

Teplitskiy, M., Lu, G., & Duede, E. (2017). Amplifying the impact of open access: Wikipedia and the diffusion of science. *Journal of the Association for Information Science and Technology, 68*(9), 2116–2127. doi:10.1002/asi.23687

van Rossum, J. (2017). *Blockchain for Research - Perspectives on a New Paradigm for Scholarly Communication. Technical report.* Digital Science. doi:10.6084/m9.figshare.5607778

Wolf, M., Wiegand, M., & Drichel, A. (2016). *PEvO (Publish and Evaluate Onchain).* Available online at: https://pevo.science/files/pevo_whitepaper.pdf

Wortner, P., Schubotz, M., Breitinger, C., Leible, S., & Gipp, B. (2019). Securing the integrity of time series data in open science projects using blockchain-based trusted timestamping. *Proceedings of the Workshop on Web Archiving and Digital Libraries (WADL '19)*, 1–3.

Zhang, Y., & Wen, J. (2015). *An IoT electric business model based on the protocol of bitcoin. In ICIN.* IEEE.

Zheng, Z., Xie, S., Dai, H., Chen, X., & Wang, H. (2017). *An overview of blockchain technology: Architecture, consensus, and future trends. In Big Data (Big DataCongress).* IEEE International.

Chapter 9
Blockchain Technology:
Limitations and Future Possibilities

Suvarna Sharma
Maulana Azad National Institute of Technology, India

Puneeta Rosmin
Kamla Raja Girls Government Post Graduate College, India

Amit Bhagat
Maulana Azad National Institute of Technology, India

ABSTRACT

Blockchain, as the name suggests, is a linear chain of blocks. It is a digital ledger that holds information on transactions taking place over the web. So every block contains data in the form of coding that is organized in a chronological manner. In 2004, a concept called "reusable proofs of work" was introduced by Hal Finney. In 2009, a mysterious white paper titled "Bitcoin: A Peer to Peer Electronic Cash System," by visionary Satoshi Nakamoto gave birth to the concept of blockchain. This is a survey of blockchain technology that first provides a short introduction of the blockchain, discussing its advantages and followed by possible limitations and their possibilities for the future.

DOI: 10.4018/978-1-7998-2414-5.ch009

1. INTRODUCTION

1.1 Blockchain

There are numerous blockchain definitions by different authors, and as pointed out in (V. L. Lemieux, 2016), there is no single, internationally agreed definition; therefore, it is important to understand the main parts of the blockchain.

Don & Alex Tapscott gave definition of blockchain in 2016, *"The blockchain is an incorruptible digital ledger of economic transactions that can be programmed to record not just financial transactions but virtually everything of value"*.

Blockchain is a new technology, often referred to as the Internet of Value. Blockchain technology is known- how is a chain of "blocks" that incorporate data. It accommodates a continuously growing list of immutable blocks using a distributed database system. Blockchain permits a transparent way of communication and transaction for end-users and providers to connect directly without the need for agents. Blockchain has come to be one of the most talked-about technologies in the IT world. From a mere concept a few years ago, blockchain technology is already being used by companies in large-scale industrial implementations. Despite the technology that the innovation itself is progressive, there are certain boundaries of blockchain that have sprung up. These blockchain restrictions don't make the technology less revolutionary, however, they have raised questions about its effectivity and reliability.

Figure 1. Blockchain Technology

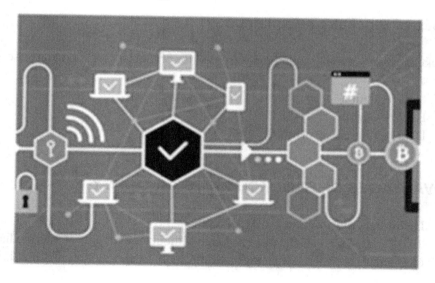

The Blockchain is replicated among the nodes in the Blockchain network. Any node in the network can read the transactions. Figure 2 shows the structure of a Blockchain.

Figure 2. Blockchain

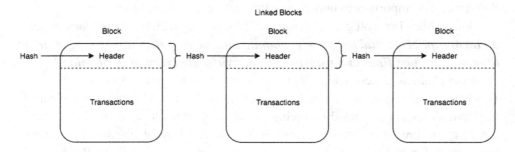

The structure of blockchain technology is represented by a list of blocks with transactions in a particular order. Two vital data structures used in blockchain include:

- **Pointers** — variables that keep information about the location of another variable
- **Linked lists** — a sequence of blocks where each block has specific data and links to the following block with the help of a pointer

Types of Blockchain Explained

Blockchain can serve the following purposes for organizations and enterprises:

- Cost reduction
- History of data
- Data validity & security

ADVANTAGES OF BLOCKCHAIN TECHNOLOGY

- **Disintermediation and trustless trade**
  Two social affairs can make an exchange without the oversight or intermediation of an outcast, solidly decreasing or despite massacring counterparty possibility.

- **Empowered clients**

  Customers are accountable for every one of their information and trades.

- **High-quality information**

  Blockchain information is finished, reliable, convenient, exact, and generally accessible.

- **Process respectability**

  Clients can assume that exchanges will be executed precisely as the convention summons expelling the requirement for a trusted outsider.

- **Transparency and changelessness**

  Any sort of transactions whether modifying or reversal can be shown to customers as all the transactions are permanent, which means they can't be adjusted or erased.

- **Faster Transactions**

  Interbank Transactions can possibly take days for clearing the cheques and demand drafts, particularly outside of working hours. With the use of Blockchain, all interbank transactions are carried out within a short span of time. Customers can use E-Banking, M-Banking, and UPI, etc for any sort of transaction even at home.

- **Lower exchange costs**

  By taking out outsider middle people and overhead expenses for trading resources, blockchains can possibly extraordinarily diminish exchange charges.

1.2 Blockchain Limitations

Blockchain technology has already spread its roots in various industries and domains including asset management, retail, monetary-use cases, digital currencies, e-contracts, decentralized exchanges, and more. However, like every other technology, blockchain isn't perfect. There are certain implementational, operational, and maintenance-related barriers that limit the effectiveness of blockchain technology.

Here are some current issues that clearly point to blockchain limitations:

1. Weak performance

   Being distributed in nature, blockchain technology will always be slower than centralized databases. Whenever a new block gets added to the blockchain, it has to carry out all the processes that a regular database does. However, it also has to carry out additional processes that affect its performance.

2. Signature verification

   Every blockchain transaction must be digitally signed and verified using a public or private key cryptography scheme. This signature verification process is very complex to compute and this consumes time.

3. Redundancy

   In a blockchain network, for every node to be processed, it has to traverse and process every intermediate node independently to reach the target node. In contrast, a centralized database system can process nodes in parallel without any dependencies from the other nodes. Thus, the redundancy involved in blockchain technology affects its performance.

4. Energy and resource consumption

   A blockchain network grows at an unprecedented pace, which will consume heavy resources. Every block in a blockchain network needs to be thoroughly validated and mined by the miners. As the blockchain network grows, the miners need to validate the blocks in a network also needs to be increased. Every miner needs a supercomputer or similarly powerful hardware resources to mine the blockchain. All these entail heavy energy consumption.

5. Security Pitfall

   With the growing number of nodes or blocks in blockchain technology, the vulnerabilities associated with the entire blockchain also increases. Among all the possible security flaws that can affect the blockchain network, there is one unavoidable security flaw. If more than half of the computers working as nodes in a blockchain network validate something then that's considered to be true. Do it follows that if more than half the nodes in a network tell a lie, then the lie will be considered as truth by the entire blockchain network. This is known as the 51 percent attack, which is an unavoidable security flaw in blockchain and its applications and may well be the most serious of all the blockchain limitations.

Figure 3. Blockchain pitfall

6. System failures
    Human error is also a very common means of system failures. This applies
    even to blockchain technology. The blockchain as a whole can be considered
    to be a database, and every block can be considered a storage container, but
    still, the data that goes into the blockchain network is fed by humans. This data
    needs to be of good quality as there is no practical mechanism that monitors
    the data that is being transmitted in a blockchain network. The data stored in
    a blockchain is not inherently trustworthy and can contaminate the data of
    the entire network.

7. Attaining consensus
    In a decentralized technology like blockchain, every transaction made must
    ensure that every block in the blockchain network must reach a common
    consensus. Depending on the network size and the number of blocks or nodes
    involved in a blockchain, the back-and-forth communications involved to attain
    a consensus can consume a considerable amount of time and resources.

8. Limited expandable and storage issues
    As mentioned above, blockchains have consensus mechanisms that make it
    mandatory for every participating node to verify a transaction. This limits the
    number of transactions that can be made in a given time. Although there are
    solutions such as distributed ledger technology (DLT) to increase the number
    of transactions that can be made per second, there has to be a limit on the rate

of transactions made in a blockchain network. Because a blockchain is an immutable distributed chain of blocks, the size of the blockchain grows at a very rapid pace, and this can cause serious storage concerns.

9. Lack of Technical knowledge:
   Despite Blockchain's increasing popularity, still many investors aren't aware of all the technical terms and also there is no proper documentation that helps users to get detailed knowledge. Due to which, investors are unable to ask questions directly or get their doubts resolved.

10. Manual errors:
    Manual errors can lead to outdated log information or even create a mismatching data while entering the data into the database. To make sure the data entered is correct, that data needs to be validated. Due to which, the phrase 'garbage in, garbage out' is used in the context of the blockchain.

11. Unsurpassed energy required:
    The programs that run blockchain have a lot of mathematical calculations that need to be done and which is not at all possible without the heavy energy consumption required by powerful computers.

1.3 Future Possibilities of Blockchain:

Blockchain technology is a growing invention that includes a chain of blocks. A **Blockchain** is a distributed or a **digital ledger**, which is primarily created to record the details of each financial and non-financial transaction. The absolute and permanent data is stored in a distributed database. The entire record is completely transparent which means that anyone who is linking to the network is able to view the transactions. Fundamentally, the **Blockchain technology** is the combination of three technologies, i.e. private key cryptography, P2P network, and the program. **Blockchain technology** has shown its revolution in the field of information registration and distribution which removes the requirement for an intermediary expert to enable digital relationships.

Blockchain technology has provided the most popular product, i.e. Bitcoin which is a type of cryptocurrency and functions as a public ledger for all transactions happening on the network. It has resolved the problem of double-spending, unauthorized spending, and thus increasing security. It also helps to remove the need for an intermediary expert. Since there has been a substantial increase in the number of cyber-attacks recently, **Blockchain technology** helps to attract a varied audience.

The future of Blockchain in Finance Industry:

Blockchain technology has a great future worldwide. An incredible **scope of Blockchain technology** has been observed in the financial field. The financial organizations were not able to sufficiently handle the heavy workload after demonetization and thus brought out the problems of having a centralized specialist for handling the financial transactions. As a result, the RBI is inspiring banks to encourage digitization. They have also released a statement that emphasized the probability of Blockchain to fight faking and the chances of bringing about particular modifications in the working of financial markets, collateral identification, and payment system. Incorporating **Blockchain** with financial transactions gives out amazing benefits, such as a significant amount of time and money that could be saved, including a drastic reduction in time needed for processing and validating transactions. The blockchain functions on a distributed database that makes the operations smoothly, ensuring tight security, and made it safe from cyber-attacks.

Figure 4. Blockchain in Finance Industry

After recognizing the **benefits of Blockchain Technology,** several financial institutions have started spending considerably in this particular field. Blockchain can also help in shortening the flow of black-money and dealing with the extensive money cleaning in the economy because each address used for transactions is stored forever on the databases, making all the transactions provable and responsible. The government is observing **Blockchain** as a way to explore a range of options that may help to apply a fitter control on the nation's economy.

Blockchain Technology is one of the most consistent technologies when it requires to keep track of financial properties. **Blockchain technology** has attracted many companies who want to add the distinct features of it to their security structures. Many studies have been carried out for digital currencies and blockchain technology, which represents that both of these technologies will be continuing to disrupt the world.

Apart from financial industries, blockchain technology also has a bright future in other sectors. Let us have a look at the future **scope of Blockchain technology** in different sectors:

I.   Blockchain in Digital Advertising: Presently, digital advertising faces a lot of challenges like domain fraud, bot traffic, lack of transparency and long payment models, due to the issue like incentives are not affiliated. Because of this the promoters and publishers feel they are dropping the deal. Blockchain has provided a solution to carry transparency to the supply chain as it fetches trust in a trustless environment. Blockchain allows the right companies to succeed, by decreasing the number of bad players in the supply chain. Publishers can also gather a vast percentage of the total advertisement dollars arriving in the ecosystem. The Blockchain technology is still in its beginning; however, this technology should stay here, and all advertisement companies are observing how blockchain will help to enhance their business.

Figure 5. Blockchain in Digital Advertising

II. **Blockchain in Cyber Security:** Though the blockchain is a public ledger, the data is verified and encrypted using innovative cryptography technology. In this manner, the information or data is less likely to be attacked or altered without authorization.

III. **Blockchain will remove the requirement of the third party:** With the help of Blockchain technology, basically, it is possible to impact a varied range of processes and techniques. It eliminates the need for a trusted third party in the transactions. Well, most prominent organizations in the world exist today to function as a trusted third party, for instance, SWIFT, and the Depository Trust Cleaning Company. Corporate chances flourish for companies that can build applied Blockchain technologies aiming for particular transactions, like the mortgage industry. The existing mortgages needed a complicated web of title searches, title insurance, and uncountable minor transaction fees which are required to keep the system running. These systems occur because traditionally, the transfer of land has been a process that requires a significant amount of belief in the old records. The Blockchain technology was going to address all these concerns, and a particular property's ledger consists of a verifiable and validated transactions history, lowering the necessity of institutions to provide risk modification and trust services.

IV. **Governments will provide their digital currencies:** It is confirmed that the paper money at its last phase, but it is also found that the authorized currency is facing severe competition by cryptocurrencies. In 2017, it is observed that the price of Bitcoin has flown which was never seen by any single service or money all around the world. The currency is still one of the most appreciated properties available in the market, and the nation took notice, due to the price of Bitcoin is denied by the basic idea of demand and supply. The need for Bitcoin will again climb at some point, with a fixed limit of twenty-one million units of Bitcoin. Because of this, a few governments will get a chance to create their digital currencies to avoid dropping face to independent and unregulated property and participate in an open market.

V. **Blockchain beyond the world of computing:** In 2017, the world had seen the infinite collection of options in the **use of blockchain technology**. Currently, most of the countries are developing their blockchain strategies to hold the future. Also, it is highly possible that the rest of the advanced European countries will follow suit by accepting the blockchain technology to create a constant financial environment that helps nations on ruins like Greece and Spain. There are specific problems associated with the security of finances, and Blockchain will be used to address these kinds of issues. Blockchain will also be used to generate registries that are used for medical purposes, to manage insurance policies, and to interrupt the model of useless data storage.

VI. **Managing World trade with the help of Blockchain Technology:** Blockchain is valuable to business particularly how it makes it easy for anybody to track the supply chain of everything provided using the technology. It will be outdated to track the numbers, and no company wants to lose a shipment because of human inability. Well, it is easy to register cargo shipments in the Blockchain, this enables the parties involved in the job operation to follow the delivery procedure from point A to B. With the help of Blockchain technology, it is easy for the customs agents to track down the forbidden products like fake medicines, changed food products, false clothes reproduction, fake auto parts, electronic apparatus and other piracy agents which are trying to provide the low-quality goods inside any country without talking about the internal laws.

VII. **Supply chain Management:** With the help of blockchain technology, it is possible to document the transaction in an everlasting distributed record, and supervise the transactions more sturdily and transparently. This also helps to minimize human errors and time delays. It is also used to monitor costs, employment, and releases at each point of the supply chain. But this has a severe effect on understanding and monitoring the actual ecological impacts of products. Not only this the decentralized ledger can also be utilized to check the legitimacy or fair trade status of products by following them from their source.

VIII. **The Blockchain in Forecasting:** The blockchain technology is set to alter the complete methodology for research, consulting, analysis and forecasting. The global distributed prediction markets are created with the help of online platforms.

IX. **Use of Blockchain in the Internet of Things and Networking:** Different companies like Samsung and IBM are utilizing the blockchain technology for a new concept called ADEPT, this will help to create a distributed network of IoT devices. The blockchain technology will remove the requirement for a central location to manage the communication between them; this will function as a public ledger for a massive number of devices. The devices may communicate with each other to upgrade the software, handle the errors and observe energy practice.

X. **Blockchain in cloud storage:** The data on a centralized server is exposed to hacking, loss of data, or human error. With the help of blockchain technology, it is possible to make the cloud storage more protected and robust against hacking.

2. CONCLUSION

Blockchain technology is a conveyed database that records all exchanges that have ever happened in the system. The primary component of blockchain is that it permits untrusted parties to convey between one another without the need of a confided in third party. Blockchain technology, where each exchange is entered into an open record that is transparent to all, is a decentralized domain for exchanges, (S. Nakamoto, 2019). The purpose of Blockchain is to give privacy, security, security, and straightforwardness to each of its customers. In conclusion, blockchain technology appears to not just improve assignments in current ventures, yet additionally hold the possibility to alter frameworks that follow along of the historical backdrop of antiquities through a boundlessly improved, straightforward record framework. In this chapter, we conduct an analysis in which we show how open science can benefit from this technology and its properties.

REFERENCES

Finney, H. (2004). *Reusable proofs of work (rpow).* http://web. archive. org/ web/20071222072154/http://rpow.net/

Lemieux, V. L. (2016). *Blockchain technology for recordkeeping: Help or hype.* Unpublished report. Available: https://www.researchgate.net/profile/Victoria_ Lemieux

Nakamoto, S. (2019). *Bitcoin: A peer-to-peer electronic cash system.* Manubot.

Tapscott & Tapscott. (2016). *Blockchain Revolution: How the Technology Behind Bitcoin Is Changing Money, Business, and the World.* Penguin Random House.

Chapter 10
Blockchain Technology for the Internet of Things Applications in Apparel Supply Chain Management

Kamalendu Pal

https://orcid.org/0000-0001-7158-6481

City, University of London, UK

ABSTRACT

Adoption of the internet of things (IoT) and blockchain technology opens new opportunities of business process automation in apparel supply chain management. The IoT technology helps to capture real-time information from different aspects of garment manufacturing activities by using radio frequency identification (RFID) tags and sensors. Blockchain technology is an emerging concept of computing that enable the decentralized and immutable storage of business transactions. In combination with IoT, blockchain technology can enable a broad range of application scenarios to enhance business value and trust. This chapter presents some of the blockchain-based IoT technology applications in apparel business processes. Moreover, the chapter provides a classification of threat models, which are considered by blockchain protocols in IoT networks. Finally, the chapter provides a taxonomy and a side-by-side comparison of the state-of-the-art methods towards secure and privacy-preserving blockchain technologies concerning the blockchain model, specific security goals, performance, and limitations.

DOI: 10.4018/978-1-7998-2414-5.ch010

INTRODUCTION

Apparel (i.e. textile and clothing) industry is an integral part of the world economy and society (Pal & Ul-Haque, 2020) (Pal, 2020). In recent decades, global apparel manufacturing businesses are inclined to worldwide activities due to the economic advantage of the globalization of product design and development (Pal, 2020a). In a typical textile and clothing supply chain is the sequence of organizations – their facilities, functions, and activities – that involved in producing and developing a product or service. The sequence begins with raw materials purchase from selective suppliers and products are made at one or more manufacturing plants (Pal, 2019). Then these products are moved to intermediate collection points (e.g., warehouse, distribution centers) to store temporarily to move to next stage of supply chain and ultimately deliver the products to intermediate-users or retailers or customers (Pal, 2017) (Pal, 2019). The path from supplier to the customer can include several intermediaries – such as wholesalers, warehouse, and retailers, depending on the products and markets. Also, global apparel supply chains becoming increasingly heterogeneous and complicated due to a growing need for inter-organizational and intra-organizational connectedness, which is enabled by advances in modern technologies and tightly coupled business processes. Hence, information has been an important strategic asset in apparel business operational management. The apparel business networks are also using the information systems to monitor the supply chain activities ((Pal & Ul-Haque, 2020).

As a result, many global textile and clothing businesses are investing in new information and communication technology (ICT) to harness the smooth information sharing ability in supply chain operations (Pal & Ul-Haque, 2020). With the recent progress in Radio Frequency Identification (RFID) technology, low-cost wireless sensor hardwires, and world wide web technologies, the Internet of Things (IoT) advance has attracted attention in connecting global apparel business activities and sharing operational business information. These technologies promise to reshape the modus operandi of modern supply chains through enhanced data collection as well as information sharing and analysis between collaborating supply chain stakeholders. In this way, IoT technology supports the capability to connect and integrate both digital and physical business world. The process is quite simple: (i) collect data from real-world objects, (ii) communicate and aggregate those data into information, and (iii) present clear results to systems or users so that decisions can be made or object behaviour adapted.

Different research groups analysed IoT technology deployment-related issues in SCM and logistics (Atzori et al., 2018) (Gubbi et al., 2013). Particularly, a group of researchers reviewed the energy management in smart factories and concluded that IoT powered manufacturing can improve supply chain competitiveness through more effective tracking of the flow of materials, and leading to improvements in the effectiveness and efficiencies of important business processes (Shrouf et al., 2014). The other important characteristics of IoT-based systems (e.g. sharing precise and timely information related to production, quality assurance, distribution, and logistics) are also reported in the context of multi-party supply chains (Chen et al., 2014) (Cui, 2018) (Yan-e, 2011). Also, the use of IoT applications inside the production plant can increase the visibility of parts and processes, and by extension, using IoT devices along the supply chain can help to boost productivity, reduce operational costs, and enhance customer satisfaction (Deloitte, 2017).

Despite the increasing applicability of IoT applications in supply chains, there are many challenges for the use of this technology. For example, IoT-related technical issues experienced when operating at the ecosystem level, such as security, authenticity, confidentiality, and privacy of all stakeholders (Tzounis et al., 2017). Academics and practitioners consider privacy and security issues are mainly related to the vulnerability of IoT system applications. Existing security solutions are not well suited because current IoT devices may consume huge amounts of energy and often these devices need substantial information processing overhead (Dorri et al., 2017). Besides, problems such as physical tampering, hacking, and data theft might increase trust-related issues within apparel network information exchange business partners (Kshetri, 2017). Therefore IoT applications must be secure against external security attacks, in the perception layer, secure the aggregation of data in the network layer and offer particular protections that only authorized entities can access and change data in the application layer.

Moreover, most of the IoT devices are limited in power, data processing capability, and memory resources due to their small sizes and low inherent design cost. Academics and practitioners are urging to design IoT devices and their protocols in a way to design to be resource-efficient and meanwhile perform real-time data processing (Pal, 2020), keep connectivity and protect the security and privacy of the transmit data using IoT data communication network. Besides, IoT data reliability can be achieved by using distributed information processing methods which execute a verification process among all its participants to ensure that data remain immutable and untampered. Considering these technical issues and realizing the basic characteristics of today's blockchain technology now offers several potential solutions to address known disadvantages related to IoT applications in apparel business networks.

A blockchain is a distributed network for orchestrating transactions, value, and assets between peers, without the assistance of intermediaries. It is also commonly referred to as a 'ledger' that records transactions. The blockchain technology helps to record transactions or any digital interaction that is designed to be secure, transparent, highly resistance to outages, auditable, and efficient. These characteristics provide impetus to blockchain-based IoT architecture for secure data processing in a distributed environment. In order words, IoT-based information systems to improve their IoT networked infrastructure to blockchain complimented technology. It is a distributed ledger which managed by a peer-to-peer (P2P) network to provides internode communication and verifying new blocks. Once data is recorded in the blockchain, it cannot be modified without modification of all subsequent blocks and that needs a consensus of the network majority. A convergence of IoT and blockchain technologies can lead to a verifiable, secure, and robust mechanism of storing and managing data processed by smart connected devices. This network of connected devices will be able to interact with their environment and make decisions without any human intervention. However, integrating blockchain technology in IoT-based information systems will enhance security, data privacy, and reliability of IoT devices, it creates a new set of challenges.

This chapter presents how apparel businesses can leverage IoT applications in combination with blockchain technology to streamline their apparel business supply chains business information. When combined, these enabling technologies will help global textile and clothing companies to overcome problems related to data acquisition and integrity, address security challenges, and reduce information asymmetry. This chapter will demonstrate areas of disadvantages towards safety and privacy in blockchain technology. The rest of this chapter is organized as follows. Section 2 presents an introduction of IoT and its applications in apparel industry. It includes IoT applications in apparel supply chain management, and drawbacks of IoT applications in apparel supply chain. Section 3 describes blockchain technology in apparel supply chain management applications. Section 4 explains blockchain applications for the IoT. Section 5 describes the background related security and privacy for enterprise computing and research challenges. Then Section 6 reviews some of the threat models for blockchain technology. Finally, Section 7 concludes the chapter by discussing relevant research issues.

INTERNET OF THINGS AND ITS APPLICATIONS IN APPAREL INDUSTRY

The idea of the IoT was first created in 1999 by Kevin Ashton (Keertikumar et al., 2015). The IoT technology has been used in apparel industries for different business process automation purpose. Sensing Enterprise (SE) is an attribute of an enterprise or a network that allows it to react to business stimuli originating on the Internet. This area of computing has come into focus recently on the enterprise automation, and there are handful of evidences of the successful use of this technology in supply chain operations. IoT based information system aims to improve organizational communication and collaboration activities. In recent decades, World Wide Web technologies are getting prominence for business use and the number of Internet-based IoT services are increasing rapidly for supply chain communities. These services, which human users can access using devices. The main form of communication is human-to-human. IoT attempts to not only have humans communicating through the Internet but also have objects or devices. These things are to be able to exchange information by themselves over the Internet, and new forms of Internet communication would be formed: human-to-things and things-to-things. In this way, IoT refers to an information network that connects sensors on or in physical objects (*'things'*) ranging from consumer goods, pallets of goods to everyday tools, and industrial machinery.

Simplistically, the IoT technology is characterized by three types of visions:

1. **Things Oriented Vision**: This vision is supported by the fact that this technology can track anything using sensors. The advancement and convergence of micro-electronical systems technology, wireless communications and digital electronics has resulted in the development of miniature devices having the ability to sense, compute and communicate wirelessly in an effective way. The basic philosophy is uniquely identifying an object using specifications of Electronic Product Code (EPC). It is important to note that future of 'Things Oriented Vision' will depend upon sensor technology evolution for accurate sensing (without any error) and its capabilities to fulfil the "thing" oriented other issues.
2. **Internet Oriented Vision**: This vision is based upon the need to make smart objects which are connected. To take full advantage of the available Internet technology, there is a need to deploy large-scale, platform-independent, wireless sensor network infrastructure that includes data management and processing, actuation, and analytics. Cloud computing promises high reliability, scalability, and autonomy to provide ubiquitous access, dynamic resource discovery and composability required for the next generation Internet of Things applications.
3. **Semantic Oriented Vision**: This vision is powered by the fact that the number of sensors which are used in the apparel industry is huge and the data that these IoT infrastructures collect is massive. Thus, the industry needs to process this data in a meaningful way to form value-added services using semantic technologies (e.g. ontology, knowledge-based reasoning), which are efficient, secure, scalable, and market-oriented computing.

In this way, the IoT application builds on three pillars, related to the ability of smart objects to (i) be identifiable (anything identifies itself), (ii) to communicate (anything communicates), and (iii) to interact (anything interacts) – either among themselves, building networks of interconnected objects, or with end-users or other entities in the network.

Furthermore, cloud computing and the more recent concept of fog computing (i.e., a decentralized computing structure, extending the concept of cloud computing through the local performance of computation, storage and communication through so-called 'edge devices') provides computing resources and scalability to connect, store and analyse IoT data (often labelled as big data) received from connected devices and sources including WSNs, global positioning systems (GPS), GPRS, and geographic information systems (GIS). The analysis of IoT data can assist firms to sense and then respond to situations in real-time and may lead to automation or value-creating predictive analytics capabilities (Tzounis et al., 2017). Moreover, through the connection of a heterogeneous set of hardware devices, (e.g., sensors) IoT streamlines critical business processes through the capture of data, such as the identification of human operators and environmental variables (e.g., temperature, humidity, vibration, air currents). IoT devices are often deployed to sense the physical world, communicate over a wireless signal and to actuate based on predefined conditions.

According to Barreto et al. (Barreto et al., 2017), the three distinguishing features of IoT are context, omnipresence and optimization. The context describes the capability of IoT to provide real-time monitoring, to interact, and to enable instant response to specific situations that are controlled. Omnipresence lies in the pervasiveness of the technology and its broad applicability, while optimization refers to the specific functionalities and characteristics each physical object has (Witkowski et al., 2017). These features pave the way for novel and innovative IoT use cases among exchange partners within both simple and complex supply chains and open new business opportunities.

IoT Applications in Apparel Supply Chain Management

The application of IoT promises significant improvements in supply chain performance and operational efficiency. The benefits result primarily from real-time information exchange, which can reduce time wastage caused by the bullwhip effect (Wang et al., 2008) (Zhou, 2012). Moreover, IoT can help to revolutionize supply chains by improving operational efficiencies and creating revenue opportunities. Three of the areas that can benefit from IoT deployment include (1) inventory management and warehouse operations, (2) production and manufacturing operations, and (3) transportation operations (See Table 1). For example, smart forklifts and racks, and novel usage of *smart glasses* (i.e. wearable devices equipped with sensors and camera technologies to locate objects in the warehouse), monitoring cameras, and other intelligent warehouse management software.

Also, in warehouse operations – reusable assets (e.g. inventory storage totes and pallets) can be attached with IoT enabled tags or devices that help in guiding and directing the warehouse pickers to their storage locations. In this way, IoT technologies not only help to automate the operational activities in the warehouses, but they reduce human intervention (and error) linked with manual storage management. This advantage results from using industrial-grade RFID-tags and RFID-readers that send a radio signal to identify correctly tag-embedded on pallets, totes, or the product cartons leading to a reduction in the time spent in collecting, recording, and retrieving business operational data.

IoT technologies are also used in apparel production and manufacturing activities. Apparel manufacturing processes consist of spinning and knitting. Spinning is the conversion of fibers into yarn, while knitting is a process of making fabric by intermeshing a series of loops of one or more yarn. It generally contains three major phases, i.e., producing raw materials, processing materials, and making clothes. Industrial machines with embedded sensors can be monitored in real-time and controlled by smart instruments, such as microcomputers, microcontrollers, microprocessors, and intelligent sensors. IoT-based solutions can enhance operational control over the processing capacity, set-up time, and throughput. Therefore, IoT-based technologies usage can lead to more efficient machine utilization, reduction of bottlenecks in production and can help in optimizing production planning and scheduling at varying levels within an apparel business. As a result, this enhanced insight into key manufacturing processes will enable stronger collaboration and value co-creation with suppliers as well as improved machine-to-machine and machine-to-human interaction.

Moreover, when it comes to transportation activities in apparel supply chain management, IoT-based technology can also provide potential advantages. For example, a GPS (Global Positioning System) helps to position vehicles (e.g. trucks) from remote distribution centers and to optimize both routing and delivery time. In a greater extent, GPS, RFID technology, and attached sensors increase the in-transit visibility by precisely localizing vehicles on public roads or at shipping terminals through large scale mapping, traffic data collection and analysis. The data gathered from these IoT devices will help to improve the forecasting of delivery times, fleet availability, and routing efficiency (Waller & Fawcett, 2013). Moreover, these devices can be used for enhancing the sharing of under-utilized resources among vehicles in the parking space or on the road (Barreto et al., 2017).

Table 1. IoT Levers in Apparel Supply Chain Business

Inventory Management and Warehouse Operations	
Enablers	**Processes**
• Smart racks • Smart glasses • Monitoring cameras • Smart forklifts • Smart warehouse management system (SWMS)	• Route optimization, elimination of in-process collisions • Fast, cost-efficient, and flexible operations • Better handling of items that are hard to reach (i.e., items that are difficult to detect on the shelf or racks) • Real-time visibility of inventory levels • Avoidance of stockouts • Agility and fast responsiveness to inadequacies (e.g., misplacement of items) • Workspace monitoring (e.g., for security purposes) • Stock keeping units (e.g., pallets) recognition • Simultaneous threat detection and scanning for imperfections
Production and Manufacturing Operations	
Enablers	**Processes**
Embedded machine sensors Machine analytics	• Real-time condition monitoring • Predictive maintenance: Detection of physical stress levels, pileups, and prevention of failures • Improved measurement of throughput, setup-time, and overall productivity • Enhancement of both machine-to-machine and machine-to-human interactions
Transportation Operations	
Enablers	**Processes**
GPRS sensors RFID tags Routers GPS satellites	• Continuous visibility of products along the supply chain • Real-time shipment tracking • Remote sensing (e.g., temperature, humidity, vibrations) • Improve activity bottlenecks and outdoor traffic, transport mobility, road, and driver safety • Maximizing fuel efficiency and optimize routing strategies

Drawbacks and Threats of IoT Applications in Apparel Supply Chain

Apparel manufacturing process consists of spinning and knitting. Spinning is the conversion of fibers into yarn, while knitting is a process of making fabric by intermeshing a series of loops of one or more yarn. The use of IoT-based applications in the apparel supply chain has proved to be effective in operational efficiency. The IoT technology addresses different apparel manufacturing chain challenges including the growing business need to improve supply chain information transparency and improve the integrity of production data and the identity of products (i.e., the right products, at the right time, in the right place, incorrect quantity, and at the right price). In this way, as IoT systems generate massive volumes of data across the apparel network business environment, and this data often resides in silos, which are often the potential for security and privacy-related risks.

There are different types of IoT security issues need to be addressed and these include IoT device trust, access control, data integrity, physical tampering, and user privacy. An IoT technology deployment survey concluded that 70 percentage of IoT devices are vulnerable due to encryption-related issues, unprotected interfaces, and inappropriate authorization (Lee & Lee, 2015). In highlighting different privacy and security issues, a group of researchers (Cam-Winget et al., 2016) comment on the recent system security solutions are insufficient due to scalability issues in processing and analyzing data generated from huge networks of heterogeneous IoT-based devices and the need to fulfil real-time requirements. Proper security and privacy approaches are considered unusable to IoT-based information system environment due to their dynamic topology and distributed nature. In addition, the current Internet architecture with its server-based computing platform might not be able to deal with an enormous number of devices and vast amounts of data because individual servers may pose a single point of failure for cyber-attacks and physical damage. For example, IoT devices are at risk from DDoS attacks, data theft, and remote hijacking. Also, Marjani and colleagues (Marjani et al., 2017) argue that some IoT-based applications lack a service level agreement (SLA) to safeguard 'Personally Identifiable Information' (PII) demanded by privacy laws. Therefore, it can have a negative influence on data integrity. Hence, system security may suffer in privacy protection for both individuals and enterprises (Suresh et al., 2014).

Moreover, apparel supply chain business partners may have concerns regarding the physical security and confidentiality of product information as it moves along the enterprise value chain. Even though IoT-based information system helps supply chain exchange partners to validate and verify the authenticity of items in the supply chain; there are still some concerns about the vulnerability of IoT devices to counterfeiting, cloning, and fraudulent practices, such as unauthorized access, tampering, and manipulation of content. For example, if RFID tags are compromised, it may be possible to bypass security measures and to introduce new vulnerabilities during automatic verification processes (Kumar & Iyengar, 2017). In addition, the manual retrieval and storage of information regarding unique tag identities in a centralized database enables the reproducing or forging of this information at any time (Lin et al., 2017). Hence, it is difficult to identify counterfeit products accompanied by misleading provenance histories (Hua et al., 2018).

At the end, centralized systems may pose a disadvantage for IoT-based system deployments in the apparel manufacturing business for traceability operations. The existence of centralized business organizations may lead to mistrust, which may curb the futuristic enhancement of supply chains (Tse et al., 2017). A centralized approach for data storing and processing can lead to several business risks and operational problems related to data integrity, security, and privacy. For example, cloud-based solutions for monitoring IoT data may be subject to manipulation and privacy legislation issues that arise when exporting substantial amounts of confidential and highly sensitive information to external services in other jurisdictions (Khetri, 2017) (Kamilaris et al., 2019). Moreover, these solutions may create obscurity and enhance information asymmetry between supply chain exchange partners. An additional factor is that centralized information systems act as a black box, and the collaborating business nodes do not know how their data is stored, managed, utilized, and secured (Galvez et al., 2018). Blockchain technology can help to alleviate several of these problems.

BLOCKCHAIN TECHNOLOGY IN APPAREL BUSINESS

Since the innovation of Bitcoin, a digital cryptocurrency, in 2008 (Nakamoto, 2008), blockchain technology has positioned itself in the focal point of interest among a diverse range of researchers and practitioners. Blockchain is a decentralized ledger that stores all transactions that have been made on top of a peer-to-peer (P2P) network in a secure, verifiable, and transparent way. The main advantage of blockchain over the existing technologies is that it enables the two parties to make transactions over the Internet securely without the interference of any intermediary party. The omission of the third party can reduce the processing cost while improving the security and efficiency of transactions.

Due to the considerable amount of benefits that blockchain can bring in information processing, this technology is expanding its applicability to new territories such as supply chain management, and logistics management. Today, blockchain also stands as a gatekeeper in the emerging "trust economy", in which the global apparel supply chain operates to serve its suppliers and customers. The efficiency of a global apparel supply chain relies on trust between the different stakeholders and the interaction between blockchain and IoT technologies can assist in increasing the traceability and reliability of information along with the business network. To achieve this strategic objective, the IoT technology should be integrated with enterprise resource planning (ERP) and point of sales (POS) systems of apparel business to be able to share and monitor real-time information at each stage, as shown in Figure 1.

Globally, blockchain technology offers a way to record transactions or any digital interaction that is designed to be secure, transparent, highly resistant to outages, auditable, and efficient. In other words, the blockchain technology has introduced an effective solution to the IoT based information systems security. A blockchain enhance IoT devices to send data for inclusion in a shared transaction repository with the tamper-resistant record and enables business partners to access and supply

Figure 1. RFID tagging level at different stages in the apparel manufacturing network

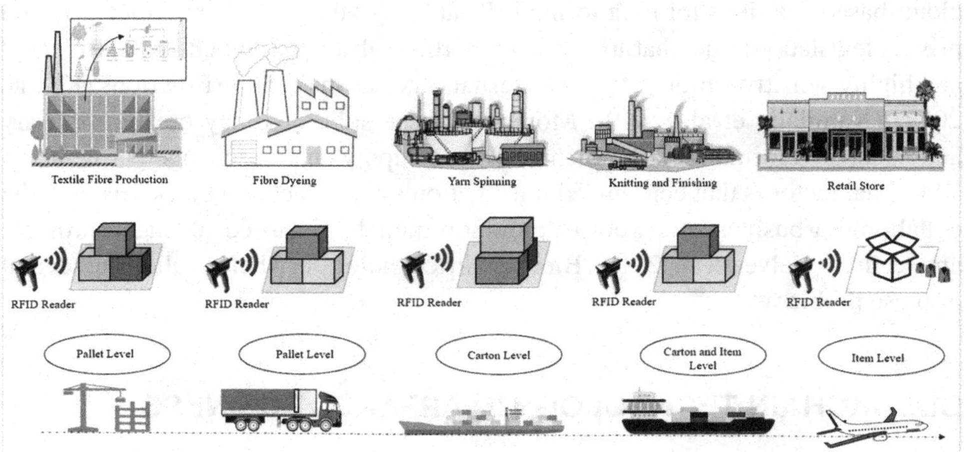

IoT data without the intervention of central control and management, which creates a digital fusion.

Therefore, blockchain is now a vital and important technology for different enterprise applications in the apparel business. In simple, a '*blockchain*' is a particular type of data structure used in some distributed manner (known as '*distributed ledger*' - DL) which stores and transmits data in packages called '*blocks*' that are connected in a digital '*chain*'. The idea of distributed ledger originated from the concept of '*shared ledger*'. A shared ledger can be a single ledge with *layered permissions* or a distributed ledger, which consists of multiple ledgers maintained by a distributed network of nodes (or *business activities*). Distributed Ledger Technology (DLT) refers to a novel and fast-evolving approach to recording and sharing data across multiple data stores (or ledgers). This technology allows for transactions and data to be recorded, shared, and synchronized across a distributed network of different network participants. Blockchains employ '*cryptographic*' and algorithmic methods to record and synchronize data across a network in an '*immutable manner*'. A simple diagrammatic representation of blockchain is shown in Figure 2.

A blockchain is a linked list in a true sense, as each block stores the hash of the previous block in its chain. Each block also digitally signs its contents by storing the hash of its contents inside the block. These hashes provide cryptographic integrity, as any adversary intending to modify a block needs to also modify all the previous blocks in a chain, which makes the attack cryptographically infeasible. A key design strategy is to construct a Merkle tree (Katz & Lindell, 2007) to efficiently store and verify the hashes. Thus, each block only stores the root of the Merkle tree, as, given the root, it is easy to verify the immutability.

Figure 2. Basic blockchain representations

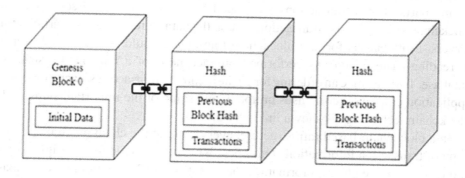

Figure 3. Design steps of a decentralized blockchain application

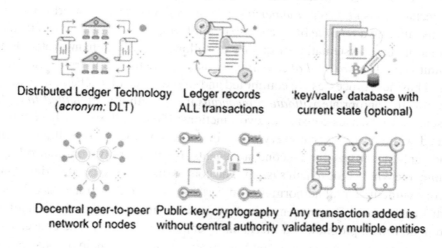

DLs are categorized as *'permissioned'* or *'permissionless'*, depending on whether network participants (nodes) need permission from any entity to make changes to the ledger. Also, DLs are classified as *'public'* or *'private'* depending on whether the ledgers can be accessed by anyone or only by the participating nodes in the network. *'Public Key Cryptography* (PKC)' techniques are often used in blockchain technology-based implementation. PKC is an asymmetric encryption scheme that uses two sets of keys: a public key that is widely disseminated and a private key that is only known to the owner. PKC can be used to create digital signatures and is used in a wide array of applications, such as *'HyperText Transmission Protocols'* (HTTPs) used in the Internet operation, for authentication in critical applications and also in chip-based payment cards.

Transactions in a blockchain system are identical to their traditional database counterparts. These transactions are issued by the clients to the servers of the blockchain system. These transactions act on the data stored on all the participating servers. In its vanilla form, a blockchain transaction could be visualized as a set of reading/write operations performed on each node of a replicated distributed database. To determine an ordering for all the incoming transactions, each blockchain application employs a consensus protocol, and some of the important steps in the blockchain technology is shown in Figure 3.

In a blockchain-based infrastructure, every node of the chain maintains a local copy of transaction information. This copy, which is identical to the original copy and updated in the global information sheet as it is distributed within the database with well-built constancy support. In this database, once data is entered within the blockchain ledger, then no one is capable to change this data in the future and this mechanism is known as *tamperproof*. However, a systematic effort is required towards building a *reliable* blockchain-based information infrastructure. The main features of these systematic efforts are as follows: (i) Blockchain Protocols for Commitment: The *protocol of commitment* makes sure that valid transaction from apparel business processes are committed and stored in the blockchain information storage with appropriate *validation mechanism* and within a *stipulated time*; (ii) Consensus: Consensus consists of two functions: First, it allows blockchain to be updated while ensuring that every block in the chain is valid as well as keeping participants incentivized and second, it prevents any single entity from controlling or crashing the whole blockchain system. The consensus aim is to create a distributed network without central authorities with participants who do not necessarily need to trust each other. The consensus is an essential part of blockchain technology. Each node runs a programmed mechanism, called a consensus. The consensus is the process by which nodes agree on how to update the blockchain because of a set of transactions. Achieving consensus ensures most of the nodes in the network have validated the same set of transactions; (iii) Security: Safety is an important aspect of the blockchain-based transaction processes. All the data within the blockchain ecosystem needs to be secured, and tamper-proof. This ensures that there are no malicious nodes within the blockchain-based enterprise ecosystem; (iv) Privacy and Authenticity: Privacy in blockchain enables the client/user to perform transactions without leaking its identification information in the network; and (v) Smart Contracts: In 1994, Nick Szabo (Szabo, 1994) presented the basic concept of a smart contract. It is a self-executable code that runs on the blockchain to facilitate, perform, and enforce the terms of an agreement. Thus, smart contracts guarantee low transaction fees, high-speed, precision, efficiency, and transparency, compared to traditional systems that require a trusted third party to enforce and execute the terms of an agreement.

In recent years, the blockchain technology ushering a huge range of industrial applications and many comparable information exchange schemes have been developed for different types of industrial business process automation purpose.

BLOCKCHAIN APPLICATIONS FOR THE IoT

The blockchain technology is used in different application areas in SCM. Some of these applications are described in this section.

Applications in Supply Chain

Academics and practitioners identified industrial business processes, particularly supply chain and logistics management, are important areas for deploying IoT based information system applications (Atkore et al., 2018) (Gubbi et al., 2013). IoT based industrial information systems can enhance the competitiveness of enterprise through more effective tracking of the flow of raw materials, leading to improve the effectiveness and efficiencies of business processes (Shroud et al., 2014). In the context of globalized business practice, with multiple collaborating-partners based supply chains, IoT-based applications enhance to facilitate the sharing of more precise and timely information relevant to production, quality control, distribution and logistics (Chen et al., 2014). However, researchers expressed their concern regarding standalone IoT-based applications along with global supply chain management (Pal, 2020). The main concerns were raised on the issues of standalone IoT systems security and privacy.

Different hybrid information system architectures (e.g. IoT with blockchain, cloud based IoT and blockchain technology) have been proposed by the research community. A blockchain enhances IoT-based applications tamper-resistant characteristics. In recent years, different blockchain-based information management systems have been reported by researchers. For example, IBM has developed a new blockchain-based service that is designed to track high-value items through complex supply chains in a secure cloud-based application system (Kim, 2016). Another exemplary industrial application is a fine-wine Provence-tracking service, known as the Chai Wine vault, developed by London-based Company Ever ledger (Finextra, 2016) in business-partnership with fine-wine expert Maureen Downey. An innovative anti-counterfeit application, called Block Verify, is designed and deployed for tracking anti-counterfeit products (Hulse apple, 2015) to create a sustainable business world. A start-up company from Finland (i.e. Kouvola) in partnership with IBM, developed a smart tendering application for the supply chain management. The reported application is built on an automatic blockchain-based smart contract (Banker, 2016). Another blockchain-based smart contract, called SmartLog, the application was launched by Kouvola in recent years (AhIman, 2016).

In recent decades, due to globalization manufacturing supply chain networks are going through an evolutionary change through continued digitization of its business practices. These global manufacturing chains are evolving into value-creating networks where the value chain itself turns into an important source of competitive advantage. At the same time, developments are in progress to integrate blockchain technology with other innovative technological solutions (e.g. IoT-based applications, cloud-based solutions, and fog computing-based automation), leading to novel structures of modern manufacturing supply chains, new types partnerships, holistic mechanisms of collaboration and value-enhancing applications for the global business.

Applications in Vehicles Management

The IoT-based Vehicles (or Transport) management is an emerging application area where the convergence of IoT on blockchain technologies are playing a significant role. This type of application permits the integration of vehicles into the new era of the IoT to establish smart communication between vehicles and heterogeneous networks such as vehicle-to-vehicle, vehicle-to-road, vehicle-to-human, and vehicle-to-everything. In recent years, researchers are trying to use blockchain technology to internet-of-vehicle (IoV) applications. Using decentralized security model, a group of researchers (Huang et al., 2018) designed a blockchain ecosystem model, known as LNSC (Lighting Network and Smart Contract), for electric vehicle and charging pile management. The LNSC model uses elliptic curve cryptography to calculate hash functions of electric vehicles and charging piles. To avoid the location tracking in the IoV, a group of researchers (Dorri et al., 2017) proposed a decentralized privacy-preserving architecture, where overlay nodes manage the blockchain. Also, the hash of the backup storage is stored in the blockchain.

Lei and fellow researchers (Lei et al., 2017) reported a research project that uses a blockchain-based dynamic key management for vehicular communication systems. This system is based on a decentralized blockchain structure, and the third-party authorities are removed, and the key transfer processes are verified and authenticated by the security manager network. In this way, with the rapid development of IoT and embedded technologies, drivers can access various services. However, these services are vulnerable to potential attacks such as replay, impersonation and session key disclosure attacks because they are provided through public channels. Many traditional cryptographic algorithms such as RSA also are suitable for vehicular networks because a vehicle is equipped with resource-constrained sensors.

Applications on the Internet of Things Devices Management

In IoT, devices management relates to security solutions for the physical devices, embedded software, and residing data on the devices. Internet of Things (IoT) comprises "Things" (or IoT devices) which have remote sensing and / or actuating capabilities and can exchange data with other connected devices and applications (directly or indirectly). IoT devices can collect data and process the data either locally or send to centralized servers or cloud-based application back-ends for processing. A recent on-demand model of manufacturing that is leveraging IoT technologies is called Cloud-Based Manufacturing (CBM); and it enables ubiquitous, convenient, on-demand network access to a shared pool of configurable manufacturing resources that can be rapidly provisioned and released with minimal management effort or service provider interaction.

But attackers seek to exfiltrate the data of IoT devices by using the malicious codes in malware, especially on the open-source Android platform. Gu et al., (Gu et al., 2018) introduced a malware detection system based on the consortium blockchain, named CB-MDEE, which is composed of detecting consortium chain by test members and public chain by users. The CB-MDEE system uses a soft-computing based comparison technique and more than one marking functions to minimise the false-positive rate and improve the identification ability of malware variants. A research group (Lee et al., 2017) uses a firmware update scheme based on the blockchain technology, to safeguard the embedded devices in the IoT system.

Applications in Internet of Things Access Management

Access control is a mechanism in computer security that regulates access to the system resources. The current access control systems face many problems, such as the presence of the third-party, inefficiency, and lack of privacy. These problems can be addressed by blockchain, the technology that received major attention in recent years and has many potentials. Jemel and other researchers (Jemel & Serhrouchni, 2017) report a couple of problems in centralized access control systems. As there is a third party, which has access to the data, the risk of privacy leakage exists. Also, a central party is in charge to control the access, so the risk of a single point of failure also exists. This study presents an access control mechanism with a temporal dimension to solve these problems and adapts a blockchain-based solution for verifying access permissions. Attribute-based Encryption method (Sahai & Waters, 2005) also has some problems such as privacy leakage from the private key generator (PKG) (Hur & Noh, 2011) and a single point of failure as mentioned before. Wang and colleagues (Wang, et al.,2018) introduce a framework for data sharing and access control to address this problem by implementing decentralized storage.

Based on the data management and the type of applications, blockchain can be classified either as private (permission) or public (permissionless). Both classes are decentralized and provide a certain level of immunity against faulty or malicious users for blockchain technology. The main differences between private and public blockchains lie in the execution of the consensus protocol, the maintenance of the ledger, and the authorization mechanism to join the distributed network.

Recently, there is a huge amount of investment from the industries, as well as a significant interest from academia to solve major research challenges in blockchain technologies. For example, the consensus protocols are the major building blocks of the blockchain technologies, thus, the threats targeting the consensus protocols become a significant research issue in the blockchain.

BLOCKCHAIN SECURITY AND PRIVACY ISSUES

Blockchain technology offers an approach to storing information, executing transactions, performing functions, and establishing trust is a secure computing without centralized authority in a networked environment. From data management point of view, a blockchain is a distributed database, which logs an evolving list of transaction records by organizing them into a hierarchical chain of blocks. From security perspective, the blockchain is created and maintained using a peer-to-peer overlay network and secured through intelligent and decentralized utilization of cryptographic techniques. Many consider blockchain as a technology breakthrough for cryptography and cybersecurity, with use cases ranging from globally deployed procurement systems in textile and clothing industries, to smart contracts, to global product transportation management over the Internet of Things, and so forth. Although blockchain has received growing interest in the academia and industry in the recent years, the security and privacy of blockchains continue to be at the center of the debate when deploying blockchain in different industrial applications.

Key Security Risk Areas of Blockchain

The main areas of security on blockchain technology are: (i) Ledger, (ii) Consensus Mechanism, (iii) Networking Infrastructure, (iv) Identity Access Management, and (v) Cryptography. A diagrammatic representation is shown these risk areas in Figure 4.

Ledger: The ledger is used to register all transactions and changes in the status of the data. The ledger is distributed by smart design and shared between the blockchain participating nodes. Two challenging problems (or hazards) generally threaten the applicability of the ledger technology in blockchain applications:

(a) unauthorized entry into the ledger; and (b) unauthorized (or improper, or illegal) operations on recorded ledger data.

Consensus Mechanism: A consensus mechanism is a protocol (i.e. set of rules) to ensure that all the participants in the blockchain network are complying with the agreed rules for day-to-day operations. It makes sure that the transactions originate from a legitimate source by having every participant consent to the state of the distributed ledger. The public blockchain is a decentralized technology, and no centralized authority is in place to regulate the required act. Therefore, the network requires authorizations from the network participants for the verification and authentication of any activities that occur in the blockchain network. The whole process is done based on the consensus of the network participants, and it makes the blockchain a trustless, secure, and reliable technology for digital transactions. Distinct consensus mechanisms follow different principles, which enables the network participants to comply with those rules. Several consensus mechanisms have been introduced considering the requirements of secure digital transactions. However, proof of work (PoW), proof of stake (PoS), and delegated proof of stake (DPoS) are the few consensus protocols used by the industries. In this way, the blockchain relies on the distributed consensus mechanism to establish mutual trust. However, the consensus mechanism itself has vulnerability, which can be exploited by attackers to control the entire blockchain. Although a few approaches, e.g., (Muhammad et al., 2018), have been introduced in blockchains to deter and prevent attacks, due to the inherent characteristics of openness, the PoW-based permissionless blockchain networks may not be completely secure.

Network Infrastructure: The network infrastructure is required for both blockchain and Distributed Ledger Technology (DLT). The network infrastructure threats can be detected in the case of nodes being stopped by malicious attacker by using good anticipatory mechanisms. In August 2016, nearly 120,000 Bitcoin (over US $60mn at the time) were stolen from Bitfinex (Nagaraj & Maguire, 2017). Based in Hong Kong, Bitfinex is one of the world's largest digital and cryptocurrency exchanges. The incident exploited security vulnerabilities within individual organizations. The blockchain network itself remained fully functional and operated as envisioned. The incident may have been prevented had there been a detailed end-to-end review of security, using scenarios, meaning there would have been a higher chance of identifying risks up front and being able to mitigate them at that point.

Identity Access Management: Privacy in blockchain enables the client/user to perform transactions without leaking its identification information in the network. The blockchain transparency compromises data privacy even though there is no direct relationship between transactions and individuals. They can

Figure 4. Various Security Risk Areas of Blockchain

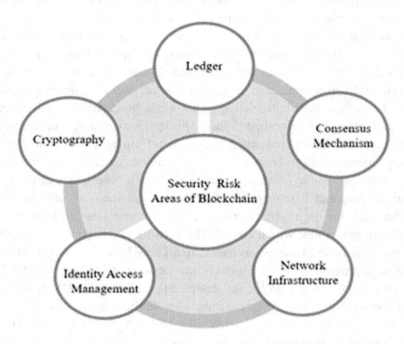

reveal the user identity by checking, auditing, and tracing each transaction from the system's very first transaction. Also, blockchain technology uses numerous techniques to achieve the highest level of privacy and authenticity for transactions. As information is coming from different users within the blockchain industrial ecosystem, the infrastructure needs to ensure every user privacy and authenticity. Blockchain-based information system often employs a combination of public and private key to securely encrypt and decrypt data.

Cryptography: The records on a blockchain are secured through cryptography. Network participants have their own private keys that are assigned to the transactions they make and act as a personal digital signature. If a record is altered, the signature will become invalid and the peer network will know right away that something has happened. However, there could be software bugs and glitches in cryptography coding. These could include anything from coding mistakes by developers, poor implementations of an underlying flaw in the cryptography routines. Even experienced programmers can make a mistake in putting together tried and tested cryptographic tools so that they are not secure. Hackers can take advantages of this weakness.

Safety is an important aspect of the blockchain-based transaction processes. All the data within the blockchain ecosystem needs to be secured, and tamper-proof. This ensures that there are no malicious nodes within the blockchain-based enterprise ecosystem. This is because, as mentioned earlier, the data inserted into a public ledger or inside the blockchain is now distributed to individual users and everyone maintains their local copy of the blockchain. In that local copy, that individual cannot tamper but upgrade the data and retransmit the data within the network. But for the transaction to be validated, the other nodes should be convinced that the broadcasted information is not malicious, and the system security is ensured.

THREAT MODELS FOR BLOCKCHAIN

This section explains the threat models that are considered by the blockchain protocols in IoT networks. Threat agents are mostly malicious users whose intention is to steal assets, break functionalities, or disrupt services. However, threat agents might also be inadvertent entities, such as developers of smart contacts who unintentionally create bugs and designers of blockchain applications who make mistakes in the design or ignore some issues.

Threats facilitate various attacks on assets. Threats arise from vulnerabilities at the network, in smart contracts, from consensus protocol deviations or violations of consensus protocol assumptions, or application-specific vulnerabilities. Countermeasures protect owners from threats. They involve various security and safety solutions and tools, incentives, reputation techniques, best practices, and so on. Risks are caused by threats and their agents and may lead to a loss of monetary assets, a loss of privacy, a loss of reputation, service malfunctions, and disruptions of services and applications (i.e., availability issues).

The owners of the blockchain-based information systems wish to minimize the risk caused by threats that arise from threat agents. This section presents five types of attacks: *identity-based attacks*, *manipulation-based attacks*, *cryptanalytic attacks*, *reputation-based attacks*, and *service-based attacks*. A diagrammatic representation of these attacks is shown in Figure 5.

Identity-Based Attacks

The emergence of DLT based upon a blockchain data structure, has given rise to new approaches to identity management that aim to upend dominant approaches to providing and consuming digital identities. These new approaches to identity management (IdM) propose to enhance decentralization, transparency and user control in transactions that involve identity information. In identity-based attacks, the attacker forge identity to masquerade as authorized user, to get access to the system and manipulate it. Again, identity-based attacks can be broadly classified into four different types, and they are namely: Key attack, Replay attack, Impersonation attack, and Sybil attack.

Key attack: In blockchain technology, certificates and identities are validated and protected in Hyperledger Fabric by asymmetric cryptography. How each participant chooses to store and protect their private key is up to them. There are a wide range of wallets and management methods available as there is no cohesive management scheme required by Hyperledger Fabric. An outside attacker obtaining private key(s) could lead to any number of attacks. In this section an example has been used where the attack is defined in the context of a system combining electric vehicles and charging piles, as follows: "If the private key of an electric vehicle that has been used for longtime leaks, the attacker can impersonate this electric vehicle to deceive others" (Huang et al., 2018). To deal with this attack, LNSC (Lightning Network and Smart Contract) protocol (Huang et al., 2018) provides a mutual authentication mechanism between the electric vehicles and charging piles. To this end, it employs the elliptic curve encryption to calculate the hash functions, and hence it ensures resiliency against the key leakage attack.

Replay attack: A replay attack is usually a scheme that is utilized during a fork of a blockchain. For example, an attacker might copy an existing transaction and then attempt to resubmit it to the blockchain as if it were a new transaction. A hacker may also attempt to resubmit the transaction if a hacker has your digital signature and because your original transaction was valid. If the attacker succeeds in resubmitting this rogue transaction, they will receive the wallet transactions twice. This attack aims to spoof the identities of two parties, intercept their data packets, and relay them to their destinations without modification. To resist this attack, LNSC (Huang et al., 2018) uses the idea of elliptic curve encryption to calculate the hash functions. On the other hand, BSein (blockchain-based system for secure mutual authentication) (Lin et al., 2018) uses a fresh one-time public/private key pair, which is generated for each request, to encrypt the message and compute the Message Authentication Code (MAC). In this way, the replay attack can be detected.

Impersonation attack: An adversary tries to masquerade as a legitimate user to perform unauthorized operations. As presented in Table II, three methods are proposed to protect against this attack. The idea of elliptic curve encryption to calculate the hash functions is proposed by LNSC protocol (Huang et al., 2018). Wang et al. (Wang et al., 2018) propose a distributed incentive-based cooperation mechanism, which protects the user's privacy as well as a transaction verification method of the node cooperation. The mechanism hides the user's privacy information within a group and ensures their protection from the impersonation attack. BSein (Lin et al., 2018), on the other hand, uses the idea of attribute-based signatures, i.e., only legitimate terminals can generate a valid signature, and hence any impersonation attempt will be detected when its corresponding authentication operation fails.

Sybil attack: A sybil attack is when an attacker creates multiple accounts on a blockchain to deceive the other blockchain participants. This behaviour is like folks who troll on social media by creating multiple accounts to accomplish their silly behaviour. A sybil attack could be quite like a phishing attack where an imposter pretends to be someone such as your boss asking you for your network password. Preventing sybil attacks is considered straightforward in the sense that you need to pay attention to who your wallet funds are being sent to. These types of attacks should not be an issue on a permissioned blockchain since the members are clearly identified and wallets are not normally used. Under this attack, an adversary creates many fake identities. By performing many interactions in the network, the adversary can gain a large influence within the community, i.e, increasing/decreasing the reputation of some agents. TrustChain (i.e. capable of creating trusted transactions among strangers without central control) (Otte et al., 2017) addresses this issue by creating an immutable chain of temporally ordered interactions for each agent. It computes the trustworthiness of agents in an online community with Sybil-resistance by using prior transactions as input. It ensures that agents who use resources from the community also contribute back.

Manipulation-based Attacks

They involve unauthorized access and tamper of data. In this category, four attacks are classified, namely: False data injection attack, Tampering attack, Overlay attack, and Modification attack

False data injection attack: This attack aims to compromise the data integrity of the control system to make it take wrong control decisions. Liang et al. (Liang et al., 2018) consider the meter node as a private blockchain network. Also, the interactions among the nodes are based on a consensus mechanism, which consists of executing a distributed voting algorithm. Each node can verify the integrity of the received data. The latter is considered correct when a positive agreement is reached.

Tampering attack: The adversary may tamper the bitcoin transactions of the bitcoin addresses, amounts and other information after signing. To prevent this attack, Wang et al. (Wang et al., 2017) use a public-key cryptosystem that is compatible with the existing Bitcoin system. They propose adding the homomorphic Paillier encryption system to cover the plaintext amounts in transactions, and the encrypted amounts will be checked by the Commitment Proof.

Overlay attack: It means that the attacker adds a forgery encrypted amount to the original encrypted amount under the receiver's public key. In (Wang et al., 2017), this attack is detected as every transaction is embedded with a timestamp to mark its uniqueness. Different inputs under the same trader can be distinguished and linked to the different transactions, and hence resistance against the overlay attack is ensured.

Modification attack: It consists in modifying the broadcast transaction or the response message. To deal with this attack, LNSC (Huang et al., 2018) uses the idea of elliptic curve encryption to calculate the hash functions. BSeIN (Lin et al., 2018), on the other hand, employs the attribute signature and the MAC.

Man-in-the-middle attack: An attacker by spoofing the identities of two parties can secretly relay and even modify the communication between these parties, which believe they are communicating directly, but in fact, the whole conversation is under the control of the attacker. To resist this attack, BSeIn (Lin et al., 2018) provides secure mutual authentication. In (Huang et al., 2018), LNSC provides mutual authentication by using elliptic curve encryption (Kumanduri & Romero, 1998) (Washington, 2008) to calculate the hash functions.

Cryptanalytic Attacks

They aim to break the cryptographic algorithm and expose its keys. In (Yin et al., 2018) the quantum attack is investigated in the blockchain. This attack is designed to solve the elliptic curve digital logarithm, i.e., derive the private key from the elliptic curve public key. In this way, an adversary can sign unauthorized transactions and forge the valid signature of users. To deal with this issue, Yin et al. (Yin et al., 2018) use the idea of lattice-based signature scheme., which allows deriving many sub-private keys from the seed in the deterministic wallet of blockchain.

Reputation-based Attacks

An agent manipulates his reputation by changing it to a positive one. In this category, we can find the following attacks, namely: Hiding Blocks attack, and Whitewashing attack.

Hiding Blocks attack: Under this attack, an agent-only exposes transactions that have a positive impact on his reputation and hides the ones with a negative reputation. In (Otte et al., 2017), an immutable chain of temporally ordered interactions for each agent. Since each record has a sequence number, any agent in the network can request specific records of others. The requested agents cannot refuse to provide their records. Otherwise, other agents will stop interacting with them.

Figure 5. Classification of threat models for blockchain

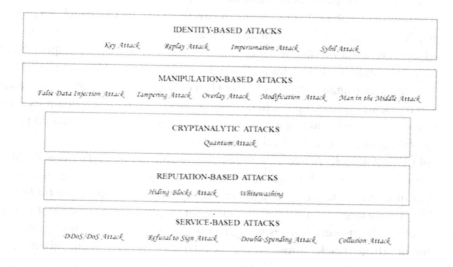

Whitewashing: When an agent has a negative reputation, it can get rid of its identity and make a new one. There is no way to prevent this behaviour. However, it is suggested in (Otte et a., 2017) to give lower priorities to the agents of new identities when applying the allocation policy.

Service-based Attacks

They aim either to make the service unavailable or make it behave differently from its specifications. Under this category, we can find the following attacks:

DDoS/DoS attack: A distributed denial-of-service (DDOS) attack is an extremely common type of a network attack against a website, a network node, or even a membership service provider. This DDOS attack is essentially initiated by many multiples (possibly thousands) of remote nodes, and then coordination is used to start their attacks. Essentially, a DDOS attack occurs when multiple systems flood a network resource with what are known as connection requests, messages, or other types of communication packets. The goal of this type of attack is to slow down or crash the system. The concentrated attack and subsequent shut down of the system results in a "denial of service" for legitimate users. Denial of Service (DoS) and DDoS are common security problems. DoS attacks on connectivity of consensus nodes may result in a loss of consensus power, thus preventing consensus nodes from being rewarded. For validating nodes, this attack leads to a disruption of some blockchain dependent services. It involves sending a huge number of requests to cause the failure of the blockchain system. The idea of distributed SDN architecture is proposed by DistBlockNet protocol in (Sharma et al., 2017). CoinParty (Ziegeldorf et al., 2018) proposes the idea of decentralized mixing service. Liu et al. (Liu et al., 2018) employ a ring-based signature with the Elliptic Curve Digital Signature Algorithm (ECDSA). The resilience against DoS in BSeIn (Lin et al., 2018) is achieved by limiting the block size, checking the maximum number of attribute signatures for the transaction input, and using '*multi-receivers*' encryption technique to provide confidentiality for authorized participants.

Refusal to Sign attack: A malicious agent can decide to not sign a transaction that is not in his favour. Although preventing this attack is not possible, punishment measures can be taken against the refusal agents. It is proposed in (Otte Et al., 2017) to not interact with the malicious agent or split the transactions into smaller amounts. If an agent refuses to sign a transaction, the interaction is aborted.

Double-spending attack: It means that the attackers spend the same bitcoin twice to acquire extra amounts. In (Wang et al., 2017), the Timestamp and the Proof-of-Work mechanism is used. In (Aitzhan & Svetinovic, 2016), a multi-signature transaction is employed, where a minimum number of keys must sign a transaction before spending tokens.

Collusion Attack: Nodes can collide with each other and behave selfishly to maximize their profit. In (He et al., 2018), an incentive mechanism and pricing strategy are proposed to thwart selfish behaviours.

CONCLUSION

Today's textile and clothing supply chain face significant volatility, uncertainty and complexity imposed by a dynamic business environment. Changes in customer buying pattern – the demand for a lower price, higher service levels, mobile commerce and so on – necessitate customer intelligence and varying fulfilment models. These have introduced significant stress on apparel manufacturing supply chain networks, compelling clothing businesses to revisit their supply chain design strategies. It includes the deployment of appropriate information systems that enhance supply chain execution. In such scenarios, enterprise information systems architecture plays a very important role.

This chapter explains and summarizes some of the main issues of apparel manufacturing supply chain management system. IoT is a smart worldwide network of interconnected objects, which through unique address schemes can interact with each other and cooperate with their neighbors to reach common goals. The data obtained from the IoT applications along apparel business processes can make operational decision-making much easier. However, standalone IoT application systems face security and privacy-related problems.

Existing security solutions are not necessarily suited for IoT due to high energy consumption and processing overhead. With rapid growth in the number of connected IoT device, many obstacles arise that may slow down the adoption of the IoT across different apparel business processes automation. Firstly, the market for IoT devices and platforms is fragmented, with many standards and many vendors. Secondly, there are concerns about interoperability, as the solution implemented often tend to create new data silos. IoT device data often stored in the cloud securely, but they are not protected against compromised integrity devices or tampering at the source. In contrast, the blockchain is an emerging technology that can help with IoT systems resiliency. The blockchain build trust between IoT devices and reducing the risk of tampering with cryptographic techniques.

Security and business organizational issues tend to enhance the need to build an apparel manufacturing supply chain management system leveraging blockchain ledger technology. Regardless of the particularities of the specific textile manufacturing supply chain-related application, blockchain can offer a wide range of advantages. By registering and documenting a product's (e.g. cotton, fiber, textile cloths) lifecycle across the manufacturing supply chain nodes increases the transparency and the trust of the participating business partners.

Finally, the chapter tries to emphasize the security and privacy related issues of blockchain-based technology deployment. Then the chapter concludes by presenting five different types of threat models, namely - identity-based attacks, manipulation-based attacks, cryptanalytic attacks, reputation-based attacks, and service-based attacks in the context of blockchain technology.

The idea of a permissioned blockchain presents many hopeful solutions to development and integration of smart apparel supply chain operations. In practice however many more efforts need to be conducted to security of permissioned blockchains before they can be a realistic implementation. In the future the current research moves on to a more in-depth approach to permissioned blockchain security, whether an analytical or experimental analysis. The attack surface of the membership service provider (MSP) needs to be analyzed comparatively and rigorous proofs need to be built to numerically quantify the threats that accompany permissioned blockchain. Further work is encouraged in comparative analysis of key management systems to find a best fit system for permissioned blockchain. In addition, there still exist several challenging research areas, such as resiliency against combined attacks, dynamic and adaptable security framework, compliance with GDPR (General Data Protection Regulation), and energy-efficient mining related issues.

On 25 May 2018, the GDPR became enforceable in the European Union (EU) region. This has a paradoxical effect on blockchain data in general and should be strongly considered when implement any blockchain identity solution within the EU region. In this way, enforcing data privacy and protecting user data is no longer optional in Europe. However, it should be noted that the text of the GDPR documentation is void of both technical and non-technical implementation details necessary to achieve GDPR compliance. This constitutes a significant research gap that this research aims to fill in the future.

REFERENCES

AhIman, R. (2016). *Finish city partners with IBM to validate blockchain application in logistics.* https://cointelegraph.com/news/finish-city-partners-with-ibm-to-validate-blockchain-application-in-logistics

Aitzhan, N. Z., & Svetinovic, D. (2016). Security and Privacy in Decentralized Energy Trading through Multi-signatures, Blockchain and Anonymous Messaging Streams. *IEEE Transaction on Dependable and Secure Computing*, 1.

Atzori, L., Iera, A., & Morabito, G. (2018). The Internet of Things: A survey. *Computer Networks*, 54(15), 2787–2805. doi:10.1016/j.comnet.2010.05.010

Banker, S. (2016). *Will blockchain technology revolutionize supply chain applications?* https://logisticsviewpoints.com/2016/06/20/will-block-chain-technology-revolutionize-supply -chain-applications/

Barreto, L., Amaral, A., & Pereira, T. (2017). Industry 4.0 implications in logistics: An overview. *Procedia Manufacturing*, *2017*(13), 1245–1252. doi:10.1016/j.promfg.2017.09.045

Cam-Winget, N., Sadeghi, A.-R., & Jin, Y. (2016). INVITED: Can IoT be Secured: Emerging Challenges in Connecting the Unconnected. *Proceedings of the 53rd Annual Design Automation Conference (DAC '16)*. 10.1145/2744769.2905004

Chen, R., Guo, J., & Bao, F. (2014). Trust management for service composition in SOA-based IoT systems. *Proceedings of the 2014 IEEE Wireless Communications and Networking Conference (WCNC)*, 3444–3449. 10.1109/WCNC.2014.6953138

Cui, Y. (2018). Supply Chain Innovation with IoT. In Multi-Criteria Methods and Techniques Applied to Supply Chain Management. Intech Open. doi:10.5772/intechopen.74155

Deloitte. (2017). *Digital Procurement: New Capabilities from Disruptive Technologies*. Deloitte Development LLC.

Dorri, A., Kanhere, S. S., Jurdak, R., & Gauravaram, P. (2017). Blockchain for IoT security and privacy: The case study of a smart home. *Proceedings of the 2017 IEEE International Conference on Pervasive Computing and Communications Workshops (PerCom Workshops)*.

Finextra. (2016). *Everledger secures the first bottle of wine on the blockchain*. https://www.finextra.com/pressaritcle/67381/everledger-secures-the-first-bottle-of-wine-on-the-blockchain

Galvez, J. F., Mejuto, J. C., & Gandara, J. S. (2018). Future challenges on the use of blockchain for food traceability analysis. *Trends in Analytical Chemistry, 107*, 222–232. doi:10.1016/j.trac.2018.08.011

Garg, S., Gentry, C., Halevi, S., Sahai, A., & Waters, W. (2013). *Attribute-Based Encryption for Circuits from Multilinear Maps*. Academic Press. doi:10.1007/978-3-642-40084-1_27

Gu, J., Sum, B., Du, X., Wang, J., Zhuang, Y., & Wang, Z. (2018). Consortium Blockchain-Based Malware Detection in Mobile Devices. *IEEE Access: Practical Innovations, Open Solutions, 6*, 12118–12128. doi:10.1109/ACCESS.2018.2805783

Gubbi, J., Buyya, R., Marusic, S., & Palaniswami, M. (2013). Internet of Things (IoT): A vision, architectural elements, and future directions. *Future Generation Computer Systems, 29*(7), 1645–1660. doi:10.1016/j.future.2013.01.010

He, Y., Li, H., Cheng, X., Liu, Y., Yang, C., & Sun, L. (2018). A Blockchain based Truthful Incentive Mechanism for Distributed P2P Applications. *IEEE Access: Practical Innovations, Open Solutions, 6*, 1–1. doi:10.1109/ACCESS.2018.2821705

Hua, J., Wang, X., Kang, M., Wang, H., & Wang, F. (2018). Blockchain based Provenance for Agricultural Products: A Distributed Platform with Duplicated and Shared Bookkeeping. *Proceedings of the IEEE Intelligent Vehicles Symposium (IV)*. 10.1109/IVS.2018.8500647

Huang, X., Xu, C., Wang, P., & Liu, H. (2018). LNSC: A security model for electric vehicle and charging pile management based on blockchain ecosystem. *IEEE Access: Practical Innovations, Open Solutions*, 6, 13565–13574. doi:10.1109/ACCESS.2018.2812176

Hulse Apple, C. (2015). *Block Verify uses blockchains to end counterfeiting and making world more honest.* https://cointelegraph.com/news/block-verify-uses-blockchains-to-end-counterfeiting-and-make-world-more-honest

Hur, J., & Noh, D. K. (2011). Attribute-based access control with efficient revocation in data outsourcing systems. *IEEE Transactions on Parallel and Distributed Systems*, 22(7), 1214–1221. doi:10.1109/TPDS.2010.203

Jemel, M., & Serhrouchni, A. (2017). Decentralized access control mechanism with temporal dimension based on blockchain. In *2017 IEEE 14th International Conference on e-Business Engineering (ICEBE)*. IEEE.

Kamilaris, A., Fonts, A., & Prenafeta-Boldv, F. X. (2019). The rise of blockchain technology in agriculture and food supply chain. *Trends in Food Science & Technology*, 91, 640–652. doi:10.1016/j.tifs.2019.07.034

Katz, J., & Lindell, Y. (2007). *Digital Signature Schemes. In Introduction to Modern Cryptography*. Chapman & Hall/ CBC Press. doi:10.1201/9781420010756

Keertikumar, M., Shubham, M., & Banakar, R. M. (2015). Evolution of IoT in smart vehicles: An overview. *Proceedings of the International Conference on Green Computing and Internet of Things (ICGCIoT)*, 804–809. 10.1109/ICGCIoT.2015.7380573

Kim, N. (2016, July). IBM pushes blockchain into the supply chain. *Wall Street Journal*.

Kshetri, N. (2017). Can Blockchain Strengthen the Internet of Things? *IEEE IT Professional*, 19(4), 68–72. doi:10.1109/MITP.2017.3051335

Kumanduri, R., & Romero, C. (1998). *Number Theory with Computer Applications*. Prentice Hall.

Kumar, M. V., & Iyengar, N. C. S. N. (2017). A Framework for blockchain technology in rice supply chain management. *Advanced Science and Technology Letters*, 146, 125–130. doi:10.14257/astl.2017.146.22

Lee, B., & Lee, J. H. (2017). Blockchain-based secure firmware update for embedded devices in an Internet of Things environment. *The Journal of Supercomputing*, 73(3), 1152–1167. doi:10.100711227-016-1870-0

Lee, I., & Lee, K. (2015). The Internet of Things (IoT): Applications, investments, and challenges for enterprises. *Business Horizons, 58*(4), 431–440. doi:10.1016/j. bushor.2015.03.008

Liang, G., Weller, S. R., Luo, F., Zhao, J., & Dong, Z. Y. (2018). Distributed Blockchain-Based Data Protection Framework for Modern Power Systems against Cyber Attacks. *IEEE Transactions on Smart Grid*, 1–1.

Lin, C., He, D., Huang, X., Choo, K. K. R., & Vasilakos, A. V. (2018). Bsein: A blockchain-based secure mutual authentication with fine-grained access control system for industry 4.0. *Journal of Network and Computer Applications, 116*, 42–52. doi:10.1016/j.jnca.2018.05.005

Lin, I. C., Shin, H., Liu, J. C., & Jie, Y. X. (2017). Food traceability system using blockchain. *Proceedings of the 79th IASTEM International Conference*.

Liu, Y., Liu, X., Tang, C., Wang, J., & Zhang, L. (2018). Unlinkable Coin Mixing Scheme for Transaction Privacy Enhancement of Bitcoin. *IEEE Access: Practical Innovations, Open Solutions, 6*, 23261–23270. doi:10.1109/ACCESS.2018.2827163

Mahjabin, T., Xiao, Y., Sun, G., & Jiang, W. (2017). A survey of distributed denial-of-service attack, prevention, and mitigation techniques. *International Journal of Distributed Sensor Networks, 13*(12), 155014771774146. doi:10.1177/1550147717741463

Muhammad, S., Aziz, M., Charles, K., Kevin, H., & Laurent, N. (2018). Countering double spending in next-generation blockchains. IEEE ICC 2018.

Nakamoto, S. (2008). Bitcoin: A Peer-to-Peer Electronoic Cash Aystem, 2008.

Nagaraj, K., & Maguire, E. (2017). *Securing the Chain*. KPMG International. https://assets.kpmg.com/content/dam/kpmg/xx/pdf/2017/05/securing-the-chain.pdf

Otte, P., de Vos, M., & Pouwelse, J. (2017, Sept.). TrustChain: A Sybil-resistant scalable blockchain. *Future Generation Computer Systems*.

Paillisse, J., Subira, J., Lopez, L., Rodriguez-Natal, A., Ermagan, V., Maino, F., & Cabellos, A. (2019). *Distributed Access Control with Blockchain*. Academic Press.

Pal, K. (2017). Supply Chain Coordination Based on Web Services. In H. K. Chan, N. Subramanian, & M. D. Abdulrahman (Eds.), *Supply Chain Management in the Big Data Era* (pp. 137–171). IGI Global Publication. doi:10.4018/978-1-5225-0956-1.ch009

Pal, K. (2019). Algorithmic Solutions for RFID Tag Anti-Collision Problem in Supply Chain Management. *Procedia Computer Science*, 929-934.

Pal, K. (2020). Information Sharing for Manufacturing Supply Chain Management Based on Blockchain Technology. In Cross-industry Use of Blockchain Technology and Opportunities for the Future. IGI Global.

Pal, K. (2020a). Ontology-Assisted Enterprise Information Systems Integration in Manufacturing Supply Chain. In Handbook of Research on Developments and Trends in Industrial and Material Engineering. IGI Global.

Pal, K., & Ul-Haque, A. (2020). Internet of Things and Blockchain Technology in Apparel ManufacturingSupply Chain Data Management. *Proceeding of 11th International Conference on Ambient Systems, Networks and Technologies (ANT-2020).*

Rejeb, A. (2018). Blockchain Potential in Tilapia Supply Chain in Ghana. *Acta Tech. Jaurinensis*, *11*(2), 104–118. doi:10.14513/actatechjaur.v11.n2.462

Sahai, A., & Waters, B. (2005). Fuzzy identity-based encryption. In *Annual International Conference on the Theory and Applications of Cryptographic Techniques*. Springer.

Sharma, P. K., Singh, S., Jeong, Y. S., & Park, J. H. (2017). DistBlockNet: A Distributed Blockchains-Based Secure SDN Architecture for IoT Networks. *IEEE Communication Management*, *55*(9), 78–85. doi:10.1109/MCOM.2017.1700041

Shrouf, F., Ordieres, J., & Miragliotta, G. (2014). Smart factories in Industry 4.0: A review of the concept and of energy management approached in production based on the Internet of Things paradigm. *Proceedings of the IEEE International Conference on Industrial Engineering and Engineering Management*, 679–701. 10.1109/IEEM.2014.7058728

Szabo, N. (1994). *Smart Contracts*. Available online: https://archive.is/zQ1p8

Tse, D., Zhang, B., Yang, Y., Cheng, C., & My, H. (2017). Blockchain application in food supply information security. *Proceedings of the IEEE International Conference on Industrial Engineering and Engineering Management (IEEM 2017)*, 1357–1361. 10.1109/IEEM.2017.8290114

Tzounis, A., Katsoulas, N., Bartzanas, T., & Kittas, C. (2017). Internet of things in agriculture, recent advances and future challenges. *Biosystems Engineering*, *164*, 31–48. doi:10.1016/j.biosystemseng.2017.09.007

Waller, M. A., & Fawcett, S. E. (2013). Data science, predictive analytics, and big data: A revolution that will transform supply chain design and management. *Journal of Business Logistics, 34*(2), 77–84. doi:10.1111/jbl.12010

Wang, Q., Qin, B., Hu, J., & Xiao, F. (2017, Sept.). Preserving transaction privacy in bitcoin. *Future Generation Computer Systems.*

Wang, S., Zhang, Y., & Zhang, Y. (2018). A blockchain-based framework for data sharing with fine-grained access control in decentralized storage systems. *IEEE Access: Practical Innovations, Open Solutions, 6*, 38437–38450. doi:10.1109/ACCESS.2018.2851611

Wang, S. J., Liu, S. F., & Wang, W. L. (2008). The simulated impact of RFID-enabled supply chain on pull-based inventory replenishment in TFT-LCD industry. *International Journal of Production Economics, 112*(2), 570–586. doi:10.1016/j.ijpe.2007.05.002

Washington, L. C. (2008). *Elliptic Curves: Number Theory and Cryptography* (2nd ed.). Chapman & Hall/CRC. doi:10.1201/9781420071474

Witkowski, K. (2017). Internet of Things, Big Data, Industry 4.0 - Innovative Solutions in Logistics and Supply Chains Management. *Procedia Engineering, 2017*(182), 763–769. doi:10.1016/j.proeng.2017.03.197

Yan-e, D. (2011). Design of intelligent agriculture management information system based on IoT. *Proceedings of the 2011 Fourth International Conference on Intelligent Computation Technology and Automation, 1*, 1045–1049. 10.1109/ICICTA.2011.262

Yin, W., Wen, Q., Li, W., Zhang, H., & Jin, Z. (2018). An Anti-Quantum Transaction Authentication Approach in Blockchain. *IEEE Access: Practical Innovations, Open Solutions, 6*, 5393–5401. doi:10.1109/ACCESS.2017.2788411

Zhou, Z. (2012). Applying RFID to reduce bullwhip effect in a FMCG supply chain. In *Proceedings of the Advances in Computational Environment Science* (pp. 193-199). Springer.

Ziegeldorf, J. H., Matzutt, R., Henze, M., Grossmann, F., & Wehrle, K. (2018). Secure and anonymous decentralized Bitcoin mixing. *Future Generation Computer Systems, 80*, 448–466. doi:10.1016/j.future.2016.05.018

KEY TERMS AND DEFINITIONS

Block: A block is a data structure used to communicate incremental changes to the local state of a node. It consists of a list of transactions, a reference to a previous block and a nonce.

Blockchain: In simple, a blockchain is just a data structure that can be shared by different users using computing data communication network (e.g. peer-to-peer or P2P). Blockchain is a distributed data structure comprising a chain of blocks. It can act as a global ledger that maintains records of all transactions on a blockchain network. The transactions are time stamped and bundled into blocks where each block is identified by its *cryptographic hash*.

Blockchain Headers: The block header is dependent on the combination of messages in the block. It lists the transaction(s), the time at which the list was made, and a reference back to the hash of the most recent block.

Cryptography: Cryptography is the science of keeping communications private. It is the study of methods of sending messages in disguised form so that only the intended recipients can remove the disguise and read the message. Blockchain's transactions achieve validity, trust, and finality based on cryptographic proofs and underlying mathematical computations between various trading partners.

Decentralized Computing Infrastructure: These computing infrastructures feature computing nodes that can make independent processing and computational decisions irrespective of what other peer computing nodes may decide.

Hashing: Software causes the block header to be "hashed". Hashing is the process by which a grouping of digital data is converted into a single number, called a hash. The number is unique (effectively a "digital fingerprint" of the source data) and the source data cannot be reverse engineered and recovered from it.

Immutability: This term refers to the fact that blockchain transactions cannot be deleted or altered.

Internet of Things (IoT): The internet of things (IoT), also called the internet of everything or the Industrial Internet, is now technology paradigm envisioned as a global network of machines and devices capable of interacting with each other. The IoT is recognized as one of the most important areas of future technology and is gaining vast attention from a wide range of industries.

Provenance: In a blockchain ledger, provenance is a way to trace the origin of every transaction such that there is no dispute about the origin and sequence of the transactions in the ledger.

Smart Contract: Smart contracts are made from software coding and can self-perform autonomously. Depending on a range of factors, they may sometimes amount to binding contracts in the legal sense or otherwise affect legal relationships between parties.

Supply Chain Management: A supply chain consists of a network of *key business processes* and facilities, involving end users and suppliers that provide products, services, and information. In this chain management, improving the efficiency of the overall chain is an influential factor; and it needs at least four important strategic issues to be considered: supply chain network design, capacity planning, risk assessment and management, and performances monitoring and measurement.

Time-Stamped: A time stamp is associated with each block and this allows all participants to know when a transaction recorded by a blockchain occurred. This is likely to be particularly useful when it is necessary to prove transacting history (for example – legal or regulatory reasons).

Transparency: In a fully permissionless blockchain, all messages (including – when consensus has been reached – when they have been included on a blockchain as blocks) sent by participants are visible to all other participants.

Warehouse: A warehouse can also be called storage area and it is a commercial building where raw materials or goods are stored by suppliers, exporters, manufacturers, or wholesalers, they are constructed and equipped with tools according to special standards depending on the purpose of their use.

Chapter 11
IoT and Blockchain in Indian Perspective

Dipti Chauhan
Department of Computer Science and Engineering, Prestige Institute of Engineering Management and Research, Indore, India

Jay Kumar Jain
Department of Information Technology, Sagar Institute of Research and Technology, Bhopal, India

ABSTRACT

Internet of things (IoT) is a collection of smart equipment that creates a smart world. It has not just changed the way we interact with important devices but has also enhanced the potential of these devices. A major limitation of IoT is that it relies on centralized communication models. Traditional IoT solutions require high infrastructure and maintenance costs, which result in scalability problems. Moreover, the vulnerability of cloud servers and their failure can affect the IoT system. There is still no one platform that connects all devices. The peer-to-peer communication model instead of the standard server/client one can be the sustainable solution the IoT industry is looking for. The major challenge with the peer-to-peer networks is security. This is where the use of blockchain in IoT can help the IoT industry scale up in a sustainable way. Indeed, blockchain and IoT together can handle a portion of IoT's greatest difficulties. The main objective of this chapter is to provide an overview of IoT and Blockchain in Indian perspectives.

DOI: 10.4018/978-1-7998-2414-5.ch011

INTRODUCTION

The quick development in scaling down, gadgets and remote correspondence advances have added to remarkable advances in our society. This has brought about an expansion in the quantity of appropriate electronic gadgets for some zones, a decrease in their creation costs and a change in perspective from this present reality into the advanced world. Therefore, the manner by which we associate with one another and with the outside world has changed, utilizing current innovation to pick up a superior comprehension of the world. Díaz, M. et al. (2016), The Internet of Things (IoT) has developed as a lot of advancements from Wireless Sensors Networks (WSN) to Radio Frequency Identification (RFID) that give the capacities to detect, actuate with and communicate over the Internet.

These days, an IoT device can be an electronic device from a wearable to an equipment improvement stage and the scope of uses where it very well may be utilized incorporate numerous territories of the general public. According Rivera, J. et al. (2014), The IoT assumes a focal role in transforming flow current cities into smart cities, electrical grids into smart grids and houses into smart homes, and many more. As indicated by different research reports, the number of connected devices is predicted to reach anywhere from 20 to 50 billion by 2020 mainly due to the vast number of devices that IoT can put on the scene. Regularly, these IoT devices are constrained in register, stockpiling, and system limit, and in this manner they are more defenceless against assaults than other endpoint gadgets, for example, cell phones, tablets, or PCs.

The possibility of the internet of things (IoT) was created in parallel to Wireless Sensor Networks (WSNs). The term internet of things was contrived by Ashton, K. (2009). There is no one of a kind definition accessible for the Internet of Things that is adequate by the world network of clients. Actually, there are a wide range of gatherings including academicians, specialists, experts, trend-setters, designers and corporate individuals that have characterized the term. What the majority of the definitions share for all intents and purposes is the possibility that the principal form of the Internet was about information made by individuals, while the following adaptation is about information made by things.

The Internet of Things is a rising worldview in the IT field. The expression "Internet of Things" which is additionally without further ado understood as IoT is produced using the two well known words for example the first is "Internet" and the second is "Things". The Internet is a worldwide arrangement of interconnected PCs that utilizes the standard Internet convention suite (TCP/IP) to serve billions of clients around the world. It is a system of systems that comprises a large number of private, open, scholastic, business, and government systems, of neighbourhood to worldwide extension, that are connected by a wide exhibit of electronic, remote and optical systems administration innovations by Nunberg, G. (2012).

According to Evangelos A, K. et al. (2011), while going to the Things that can be any article or individual which can be recognizable by this present reality. Everyday objects incorporate not just electronic devices we experience and utilize day by day and innovatively propelled items, for example, hardware and equipments, yet "things" that we don't do typically consider as electronic by any stretch of the imagination, for example, nourishment, clothing; and furniture; materials, parts and gear, stock and concentrated things; tourist spots, landmarks and masterpieces and all the variety of business, culture and advancement.

Blockchain is another engineering that reforms the Internet and replaces the regular brought together customer server plan. Blockchain stores information on a chain of hubs. It is a common open record on which the whole decentralized appropriated distributed system depends. Every hub has a duplicate of the record. At the point when an exchange is mentioned, every hub gets the exchange solicitation message, refreshes its very own duplicate of the record and passes the message to the close-by hubs. Every exchange is carefully marked to demonstrate that it is substantial. On the off chance that a message is encoded with a particular open key, just the proprietor of the matched private key will probably decode and peruse the message. On the other way, in the event that you scramble a message with your private key, just the matched open key can be utilized to decode it. An advanced mark keeps the exchange from being modified by anybody, when it has been agreed upon. As referenced above, blockchain isn't utilized for cryptographic forms of money. We see money related organizations, governments, electrical organizations and numerous different enterprises jumping on the pontoon.

BLOCK CHAIN

The primary work on a cryptographically verified chain of squares was portrayed in 1991 by Stuart Haber and W. Scott Stornetta. They needed to actualize a framework where archive timestamps couldn't be messed with. In 1992, Bayer, Haber and Stornetta consolidated Merkle trees to the structure, which improved its proficiency by permitting a few record declarations to be gathered into one square. The first blockchain was conceptualized by an individual (or gathering of individuals) known as Satoshi Nakamoto in 2008. Nakamoto improved the plan in a significant manner utilizing a Hashcash-like strategy to add squares to the chain without expecting them to be marked by a confidant in gathering. The structure was executed the next year by Nakamoto as a center segment of the digital currency bitcoin, where it fills in as the open record for all exchanges on the system. The words square and chain were utilized independently in Satoshi Nakamoto's unique paper, however were in the end promoted as a solitary word, blockchain, by 2016. The term blockchain 2.0 alludes to new uses of the conveyed blockchain database, first rising in 2014.

A blockchain is a decentralized, appropriated and open computerized record that is utilized to record exchanges crosswise over numerous systems so that any included record can't be changed retroactively, without the adjustment of every single ensuing block. This enables the members to confirm and review exchanges freely and generally reasonably. A blockchain database is overseen independently utilizing a shared system and an appropriated timestamping server. They are confirmed by mass joint effort controlled by aggregate personal circumstances. Such a design encourages a powerful work process where members' vulnerability in regards to information security is minimal. This blockchain-based trade of significant worth can be finished snappier, more secure and less expensive than with customary frameworks. On the other hand, a blockchain is an open conveyed record that can record exchanges between at least two gatherings proficiently and in an irrefutable and perpetual way.

Figure 1. Blockchain nodes overview

Every node maintains a local copy of the global data-sheet. The system ensures consistency among the local copies:

- The local copies at every node are identical.
- The local copies are always updated based on the global information.

Distributed Ledger: A distributed ledger can be characterized as a database that is consensually shared and synchronized across networks spread across multiple sites, institutions or geographies.

A distributed ledger can be portrayed as a record of any exchanges or contracts kept up in decentralized structure crosswise over various areas and individuals, wiping out the need of a focal specialist to keep a check against control. All the information on it is securely and accurately stored using cryptography and can be accessed using keys and cryptographic signatures. Once the information is stored, it becomes an immutable database and is governed by the rules of the network. While centralized ledgers are prone to cyber-attack, distributed ledgers are inherently harder to attack because all the distributed copies need to be attacked simultaneously for an attack to be successful. Further, these records are impervious to malicious changes by a single party.

Figure 2. Distributed Ledger/ Public Ledger

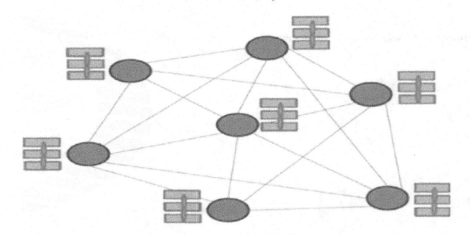

Different aspects for Blockchain:

1. Protocols for commitment: Ensure that every valid transaction from the clients are committed and included in the blockchain within a finite time.
2. Consensus: Ensure that the local copies are consistent and updated.
3. Security: The data needs to be tamper-proof as the clients may act maliciously or can be compromised.

4.   Privacy and Authenticity: The data (or transactions) belong to various clients; privacy and authenticity needs to be ensured.

BlockChain Architecture

Following is a simplified structure of a blockchain;

Figure 3. Simplified structure of blocks in a blockchain

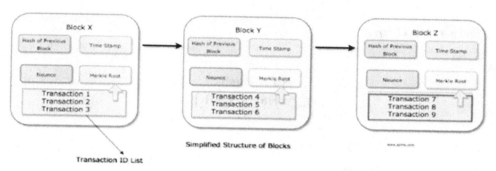

Each block in a simplifiedblockchain architecture must contain the undermentioned components:

1.   **Hash of previous block:** Each block in a block chain architecture is connected to its previous block by the means of cryptographically hashed functions. It ensures that tampering with the blockchain becomes extremely difficult and unlikely. For a malicious node (or group of nodes), altering the blockchain would require altering the hash content of all the previous blocks of the targeted block. Examples of such hashing functions include SHA256, RIPEMD160 etc.

2.   **Time Stamp:** Each block contains a timestamp of when it was added to the blockchain. The Time stamp ensures transparency and integrity in the distributed ledger and makes it easier for auditing of the blockchain.

3.   **Nonce:** Nonce refers to a random series of an array of numbers which is used for adding a block to the blockchain by means of PoW (proof of work), in a permission less blockchain model. The number of zeroes required at the beginning of the nonce determines the difficulty level of adding a block to the blockchain. The only way to determine the nonce value to add the block in the chain is by brute force method.

4. Merkle Root: A Merkle tree structure (also known as a hash tree), consists of a tree data structure, in which all the leaf nodes contain the hash of the data elements, and all non-leaf nodes contain the hash of its children nodes. Any change in any data element gets reflected in the hash of the consecutive nodes and ultimately in the tree root node. This ensures that the data elements contained in the block do not get tampered with and maintain their integrity and remain consistent. The merkel root is also used for constructing the block hash.

Figure 4. Merkle tree

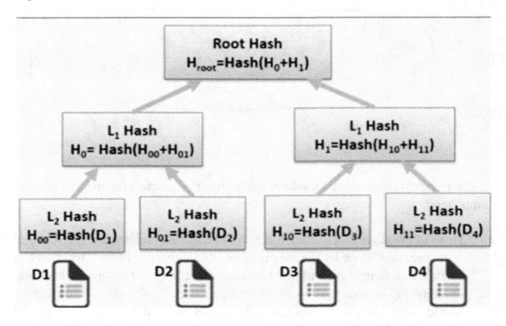

APPLICATIONS DOMAINS OF BLOCKCHAIN

1. **Supply chain management**: Blockchain can be used to track the movement of goods, their origin, quantity and so forth. This achieves another degree of straightforwardness to B2B ecosystems - disentangling procedures, for example, possession move, creation process confirmation and installments.
2. **Smart contracts:** With smart contracts, agreements can be automatically validated, signed and enforced through a blockchain construct. This wipes out the requirement for mediators and hence spares the organization time and cash.

3. **Digital Voting:** Using the blockchain, a voter could check that her or his vote was successfully transmitted while remaining anonymous to the rest of the world. In 2014, Liberal Alliance, a political party in Denmark, turned into the principal association to utilize blockchain to cast a ballot.
4. **Stock trade:** Since blockchain systems approve and settle exchanges so rapidly, it could dispense with the multi day hold up time financial specialists experience when selling stock(s) and looking for access to their assets with the end goal of reinvestment or withdrawal.
5. **Correspondent Banking:** The worldwide installments division is mistake inclined, exorbitant, and open to tax evasion. It takes days if not longer for cash to cross the world. The blockchain is as of now giving arrangements to settlement organizations, for example, Abra, Align Commerce and Bitspark that offer end-to-end blockchain controlled settlement administrations.
6. **Permissioned Blockchain:** In a permissioned blockchain model, the clients need not be completely anonymous, rather, they are either pseudo-anonymous or known to each other. In permissioned blockchain, a certificate authority provides e-certs (x.509 for public certs in hyperledger composer) and membership service providers manage membership for the blockchain. Permissioned blockchains maintain an access control layer to allow certain actions to be performed only by certain identifiable participants.

RELATED WORK

IoT has the ability to make homes and our life more intelligent. These innovative advancements provide convenience in everyday activities, vitality proficiency, security, and solace by Ning, H. et al. (2012). Adding insight capacities to different situations like homes could give expanded life quality to the debilitated and older, for instance. A significant part of the consideration in research has rotated around remote innovations that are strong of remote information control, detecting, and move, for example, cell systems, RFID, Wi-Fi, and Bluetooth, which have been utilized to implant knowledge into the earth.

Kranz, M. et al. (2009), led an examination concerning a Bluetooth-based framework that uses smart-phones sans Internet controllability, in which physical connection of devices to Bluetooth sub-controllers was done, trailed by the smart phone's control by means of inherent network with Bluetooth. Constraints in the scope of tasks for the framework, in any case, implied that it couldn't adapt to versatility, in this way could be controlled uniquely inside the device's region. Scientists have additionally made endeavors to give remote access and system interoperability to control machines and gadgets in the home using home gateways, which has seen the introduction of Wi-Fi based frameworks that utilization web servers dependent on PCs that oversee connected devices in the home.

Karimi, K., et al. (2013), contended that the world is entering a time of IoT figuring innovation with incredible potential to empower the correspondence between machines, machines and foundation, and machines and nature. His examination shows the IoT as an all-inclusive worldwide neural network dependent on cloud innovation that will plague all parts of human life, which will be established on insight given by embedded processing. The correspondence and association of smart machines with other machines, environments, infrastructures and objects will bring about the age of massive data volumes that will be prepared into activities that can control and order items to make lives more secure and simpler.

Jankowski, S. et al. (2014), appointed an examination report into the IoT, which reasoned that the IoT wave of registering would be bigger than the past two figuring waves; the fixed Internet wave and the mobile wave. The report sets that the IoT will prompt the formation of new innovation victors and losers, which will be founded on the capacity of organizations to adjust to an undeniably incorporated and interconnected world. The direction of technology adoption and improvement will be tilted by the S-E-N-S-E structure proposed by the report; sensing, efficient, networked, specialized, and everywhere.

Evans, D. (2011), found that IoT has achieved the point where a large number of sensors and unique systems must incorporate and interoperate under common standards, recommending that such an effort needs the academia, standards organizations, governments, and businesses to work in pairs. The report additionally thinks about what must occur for IoT to pick up acknowledgment by the more extensive open, investigating the impacts of service providers delivering applications that increase the value of the lives of individuals. In finishing the report, the analyst investigates the significance of offering some benefit in human terms, instead of simply being representative of technological advancement.

Porter, M. E. et al. (2014), The Parametric Technology Corporation (PTC) investigated the IoT in connection to the assembling business, concentrating its rise and impacts nearby parallel development of other empowering innovations and market powers. In the report, the development of purely physical items into complex frameworks that consolidate computerized user interfaces, programming, sensors, and processors is examined in connection to increase of item capacities and worth creation. What's more, the report additionally surveys how the effect of IoT has changed manufacturer's capacity to make worth and trade it with customers, particularly as the IoT shifts separation and worth sources towards administration, the cloud, and programming, accordingly making new models of business.

Miorandi, D. et al. (2012). allude to IoT as a general term that includes the whole degree to which the web and the Internet have infested the physical domain, where spatially deployed devices are broadly distributed and embedded into physical objects for their identification proof through improved activation/detecting abilities. The IoT idea imagines a world where physical and digitalized entities will all be connected, offering access to another age of services and applications utilizing relevant and appropriate ICT frameworks.

Tan, L. et al. (2010, August), contend that all objects in the future will have one of a kind highlights for distinguishing proof that can be interconnected to make the IoT. Correspondence, accordingly, will move from being exclusively between people to correspondence among people and things, which will change life, as we probably know it through the development of ubiquitous communications and computing era. RFID and other detecting advancements utilized for significant recognizable proof reasons for existing are generally held as a foundation of the coming IoT period.

Murthy, D. N. et al. (2015), gave the reason to portray how the recently rising "Internet of Things" (IoT) will give phenomenal chances to enter innovation and robotization into all that we do, and simultaneously, give an enormous playing field to organizations to create more current plans of action to catch piece of the overall industry. The data accessible on the Internet today is for the most part obliged by the quantity of clients producing the substance. Web clients have developed from a few thousand a couple of years back to 2.8 billion out of 2014 and are evaluated to develop to 6.5 billion out of 2020.

Queiroz, M. M. et al. (2019), suggested a solution for changing and renovating the connections between all individuals from logistics and supply chain systems. They have proposed means to connect this hole, quite by understanding the individual blockchain appropriation conduct in the coordinations and store network field in India and the USA. Drawing on the rising writing on blockchain, store network and system hypothesis, just as on innovation acknowledgment models (TAMs), have been built up and a model dependent on a somewhat modified form of the traditional bound together hypothesis of acknowledgment and utilization of innovation (UTAUT). The model being created was then assessed utilizing the Partial least squares auxiliary condition demonstrating (PLS-SEM). As the model was in the long run bolstered, the outcomes acquired uncovered the presence of unmistakable reception practices between India-based and USA-based experts. In parallel, the discoveries show up as a valuable commitment to and an indication of advancement for the writing on IT reception, SCM, and blockchain.

Pappalardo, G. et al. (2018), explored Bitcoin system watching exchanges communicated into the system during seven days from 04/05/2016 and afterward observing their consideration into the blockchain during the accompanying seven months. Their study revealed that 42% of the exchanges are as yet excluded in the Blockchain after 1 h from their appearance and 20% of the exchanges are as yet excluded in the Blockchain following 30 days, in this manner uncovering an incredible wastefulness in the Bitcoin framework. In any case, we see that the vast majority of these "overlooked" exchanges have low qualities and as far as moving the framework is less wasteful with 93% of the exchanges worth being incorporated into the Blockchain inside 3 h and 98.8% inside multi day. The way that a sizable part of exchanges isn't handled conveniently throws genuine questions on the ease of use of the BitcoinBlockchain for dependable time-stepping purposes.

The Internet of Things in the INDIA

Government activities, supporting conditions, good living standards for everyday comforts and expanding endorsement of smart applications assumes the fundamental jobs in the development of the market. As indicated by the report of COMSNETS by Kumaran, V. (2015), the Government considered putting resources into IoT for developing approximately 100 Smart cities and its estimated proposed cost is Rs.7060 crores. Although according to Indians requirement, IoT products are useful in each domain and various organizations have invested their resources in lots of sector and this percentage is increase day by day Dhote S., (2017), however center around Smart Water Management, Smart Environment, Healthcare, Smart Agriculture, Smart Waste Management, Smart Safety, Smart Supply Chain, and so forth yet as per the Indian economy factor moderateness to a billion populace is troublesome. Supporting conditions and Indian Infrastructure like power supply, poor contamination, extraordinary temperatures, high level of humidity and residue, No spotless and poor telecom inclusion. The accompanying table: 1 shows IoT Market in Global and in India.

Table 1. IoT Market in Global and in India

S.No.	IoT Global	IoT India
1.	The global IoT market will risefrom 15.4 billion devices in 2015 to 30.7 billion devices in 2020 and 75.4 billion in 2025.	By 2020 IoT showcase in India is relied upon to develop to $ 15 billion with 2.7 billion units from current $ 5.6 billion and 200 million associated units.
2.	During 2016-2021,Global costs on IoT based products and services by activities are anticipated to reach $120 billion-$253 billion achieving a 16% CAGR.	During 2015 – 2020, IoT showcase in India is expected more than 28% to develop at a CAGR and business is relied upon to reach $300 billion by 2020.
3.	IoT will increase $10 to $15 trillion to global GDP in the next 20 years.	The Indian government's objective is to generate an IoT production in India of $ 15 billion by 2020.
4.	In 2020 robotized driving and IoT empower vehicles will be expanded internationally.	In India, the utility area and oil division gradually reach the top 5 segments like Electronics and telecom, Both are revenue generation sectors.

Table 2. IoT Applications – Examples for Different Industries

Industry	Equipments	Interface	Solution or service	Analytics	Outcome
Consumer goods and retail	Sensors that can capture end-user and inventory context: for example, RFID, location sensors, cameras, robots with sensors, specialized devices	Suggestions and recommendations from user devices Targeted advertisements on the end-user's mobile device	Accurate real-time knowledge of the consumer's context (presence, location, preferences, and soon) Monitoring of supply chain inventory	Context-aided realtime user profiling Analytics to extract context from raw sensor data Entire gamut of supply chain analytics enhanced with real-time data	Creation of novel value-added applications for the consumer, like alerts on expiry dates, avatars to check products virtually, and so on Targeted advertising
Manufacturing	Supervisory control and data acquisition (SCADA) systems / Programmable Logic Controllers (PLCs), Controllers or Gateway, Cameras, IoT devices mounted on asset, IoT devices embedded in machines	Mainly on central Consoles, Can connect to experts on their mobile terminals for remote consultation	Remote monitoring and diagnostics, Production line Automation, Equipment handling and Diagnostics through sensors located on the production Floor, Remote expert diagnostics in case of failures	Anomaly detection in equipment usage and functioning, Predictive maintenance Automatic quality monitoring in production line	Reduced field support costs, lower breakdowns, improved operational efficiency, Optimal scheduling of production lines, Anomaly detection and emission detection, Improved quality and lower energy costs
Healthcare	Wearable and personal medical devices, Mobile phones	Remote consultation on medical super specialist mobile terminals with the aid of clinical decision support systems	Remote expert doctor consultation/ monitoring, Chronic disease Management, Elderly care Wellness and fitness programs	Anomaly detection in recorded medical data, Historical correlation	Lower cost of care, Improved patient outcomes, Real-time disease management, Improved quality of life for patients

continues on following page

Table 2. Continued

Industry	Equipments	Interface	Solution or service	Analytics	Outcome
Insurance	Sensors that depict the condition/ usage of the insured entity	Mobile apps - value-added usage based applications, that calculate premiums based on driver behaviour and usage	Collection of user data (like condition of home devices for home insurance, driving habits for car insurance) Prediction of Property damage Remote inspection and assessment of damage and accidents	Usage pattern detection Anomaly detection Automated assessments	Creation of newer Insurance models such as dynamic premium pricing based on condition of property, premium pricing based on usage, and so on
Transportation	On-board vehicle gateway devices RFID tags Sensors	Real-time alerts to drivers/ operators Dashboards / control panels in command and control centers, Public displays / Signage, Web based queries and reports	Real-time vehicle tracking and optimization for logistics and public transportation systems, Asset management and tracking	Visualization, prediction, optimization, and decision support systems for associated transportation systems	Improved service Levels, Lower costs and lower carbon footprint
Utilities (energy, water, gas)	Energy, water, or gas meters	Can be accessed on any internet connected device	Real-time collection of usage data, Demand-supply Prediction, Load balancing, Dynamic tariff generation.	Historical usage analysis, usage prediction, demand-supply prediction	Consumers connected to these smart networks have seen significant cost and resource savings [12].
Agriculture	Location Sensors, GPS integrated circuits	Technologies are used in precision agriculture, providing data that helps farmers monitor and optimize crops	providing data that helps farmers monitor and optimize crops, as well as adapt to changing environmental factors	Yield Monitoring, Yield Mapping, Topography and Boundaries	Provide actionable data to be processed and implemented as need be to optimize crop.

The Application of IoT in Different Industries

The Internet of Things will empower associations in each industry to offer new services or generally change their plans of action. Table 2 provides a glimpse of the new business models that 'cyber-physical systems' can enable in various industries.

TECHNOLOGY CHALLENGES IN IOT

As you apparatus in the mood for propelling sensor based administrations, there are still some handy difficulties you may experience.

1. Device administration: The quantity of sensors, gateways and devices will be very enormous and they will be spread over huge land areas – regularly in remote, out of reach or potentially private areas. Guaranteeing that devices are totally automated and remotely manageable is a challenge.
2. Device diversity and interoperability: Take the case of a power arrange in a city, which is sensor empowered, and should be checked constantly in close ongoing. The age, transmission, and dispersion works in such a mind boggling system require various sorts of sensor gadgets from various merchants. The same number of merchants don't bolster any principles in their items, there are certain to be interoperability issues.
3. Integration of data from various sources: As you convey an IoT application, you will get floods of information from various sources, for example, sensors, logical information from cell phone data, and interpersonal organization feeds and other web assets. Note that the semantics of the information must be a piece of the information itself and not bolted up inside the application rationale in various application storehouses.
4. Scale, data volume, and performance: Prepare your business to deal with the scale, data volume, and speed of IoT applications. As the number of devices and users scale, so will the measure of information that should be ingested, put away, and broken down. You will have a Big Data issue on your hands, and standard designs and stages might be deficient. Additionally, where stringent continuous execution is required, system and application level latencies might be an issue.
5. Flexibility and development of applications: You will observe sensors and devices advancing with as good as ever capacities. This will bring about formation of new investigation procedures and calculations, and new use cases and plans of action. You should rapidly create applications with negligible exertion. You will require ecosystems and stages that empower and continue this.

6. Data security: A good piece of information gathered from devices will be touchy individual information that must be shielded from unapproved get to and utilized uniquely for the particular reason for which the client has enabled that information to be gathered. Clients must be given essential devices that empower them to characterize the approaches for offering their own information to approved people and applications.

7. Another test, however not a technical one, is that you should work with various partners. IoT works in a perplexing environment, and an end-to-end IoT application contacts a few innovations, building exercises, and different elements. Your development as a community oriented player ends up critical, as you have to work with various kinds of elements and associations, for example, silicon chipset sellers, inserted sheets and gadget merchants.

IoT platform suppliers, correspondence specialist co-ops, framework integrators, application designers, industry partnerships just as specialty innovation organizations and new businesses.

Research Directions

In this transformational technology, innovation never ceases. There are many areas where research is underway at TCSInnovation Labs, and is ready to deal with the challenges discussed in this paper. Specific areas of research include:

a) Scalability in networking, storage and computation to handle exponential growth of data volume from sensors

b) Security of the 'data-at-flight' and 'data-at-rest' without compromising on scalability

c) Preservation of privacy of the user data and properly balancing between privacy and utility

d) Interoperability among myriad sensor data sources (physical communication level, network level, data syntax level, and data semantics level)

e) Rich analytics and visualization (generic, sensor-specific, and domain-specific) provided in real-time, as required

CONCLUSION

Just as the internet has transformed businesses and lifestyles in the last twenty years, IoT will disrupt your organization's relationship with its stakeholders. While it is complex, and poses some risks and is still evolving, many pioneers have started adopting this technology. An innovation rationalist stage that empowers device management, application of the board, and sensor information the board with investigation will kick off your commitment with digital physical frameworks. This can help you innovate new processes and initiatives to increase your organization's business performance, and create customer delight with new products and services. Problematic advances consistently produce extraordinary debate, changing the innovation without satisfactorily ensuring its activity or applying it to situations where the expense does not repay the improvement are dangers into which one can fall effectively. In this way, the advantages of applying blockchain to the IoT ought to be broken down cautiously and taken with alert. In this chapter we have given an examination of the fundamental difficulties that blockchain and IoT must address with the goal for them to effectively cooperate. We have also recognized the key focuses where blockchain innovation can help improve IoT applications. It is quite possible that blockchain will reform the IoT. The mix of these two advances ought to be tended to, considering the difficulties recognized in this chapter. The selection of guidelines is vital to the incorporation of blockchain and the IoT as a component of government frameworks. This selection would accelerate the communication between residents, governments and organizations. Agreement will likewise assume a key job in the incorporation of the IoT as a feature of the mining procedures and conveying significantly more blockchain.

REFERENCES

Ashton, K. (2009). That 'internet of things' thing. *RFID Journal, 22*(7), 97-114.

Dhote, S. (2017). *Internet of Things (IoT)*. Market in India.

Díaz, M., Martín, C., & Rubio, B. (2016). State-of-the-art, challenges, and open issues in the integration of Internet of things and cloud computing. *Journal of Network and Computer Applications, 67*, 99–117. doi:10.1016/j.jnca.2016.01.010

Evangelos A, K., Nikolaos D, T., & Anthony C, B. (2011). Integrating RFIDs and smart objects into a Unified Internet of Things architecture. *Advances in Internet of Things*.

Evans, D. (2011). The internet of things: How the next evolution of the internet is changing everything. *CISCO White Paper, 1*(2011), 1-11.

Jankowski, S., Covello, J., Bellini, H., Ritchie, J., & Costa, D. (2014). *The Internet of Things: Making sense of the next mega-trend*. Goldman Sachs.

Karimi, K., & Atkinson, G. (2013). *What the Internet of Things (IoT) needs to become a reality*. White Paper, FreeScale and ARM.

Kranz, M., Holleis, P., & Schmidt, A. (2009). Embedded interaction: Interacting with the internet of things. *IEEE Internet Computing*, *14*(2), 46–53. doi:10.1109/MIC.2009.141

Kumaran, V. (2015). *IoT-Challenges and Opportunities in Indian Market*. IESA COMSNETS.

Miorandi, D., Sicari, S., De Pellegrini, F., & Chlamtac, I. (2012). Internet of things: Vision, applications and research challenges. *Ad Hoc Networks*, *10*(7), 1497–1516. doi:10.1016/j.adhoc.2012.02.016

Murthy, D. N., & Kumar, B. V. (2015). Internet of things (IoT): Is IoT a disruptive technology or a disruptive business model? *Indian Journal of Marketing*, *45*(8), 18–27. doi:10.17010/ijom/2015/v45/i8/79915

Ning, H., & Hu, S. (2012). Technology classification, industry, and education for Future Internet of Things. *International Journal of Communication Systems*, *25*(9), 1230–1241. doi:10.1002/dac.2373

Nunberg, G. (2012). *The advent of the internet*. Academic Press.

Pappalardo, G., Di Matteo, T., Caldarelli, G., & Aste, T. (2018). Blockchain inefficiency in the bitcoin peers network. *EPJ Data Science*, *7*(1), 30. doi:10.1140/epjds13688-018-0159-3

Porter, M. E., & Heppelmann, J. E. (2014). How smart, connected products are transforming competition. *Harvard Business Review*, *92*(11), 64–88.

Queiroz, M. M., & Wamba, S. F. (2019). Blockchain adoption challenges in supply chain: An empirical investigation of the main drivers in India and the USA. *International Journal of Information Management*, *46*, 70–82. doi:10.1016/j.ijinfomgt.2018.11.021

Rivera, J., & van der Meulen, R. (2014). *Forecast alert: Internet of things—endpoints and associated services*. Technical Rreport.

Tan, L., & Wang, N. (2010, August). Future internet: The internet of things. In *2010 3rd international conference on advanced computer theory and engineering (ICACTE)* (Vol. 5, pp. V5-376). IEEE.

Chapter 12
Integrate Hybrid Cloud Computing Server With Automated Remote Monitoring for Blockchain as a Service

Rohit Sansiya
https://orcid.org/0000-0001-7707-0603
Maulana Azad National Institute of Technology, India

Pushpendra Kumar
Central University of Jharkhand, India

Ramjeevan Singh Thakur
Maulana Azad National Institute of Technology, India

Abdulhai Mohammadi
Maulana Azad National Institute of Technology, India

ABSTRACT

Blockchain is also used for bitcoin transactions as a technology for accumulating data files in the cloud for key distribution and file manipulation in distributed fashion. It is a service of cloud that manages elasticity of compute cloud, storage, and technology of network security (i.e., secure solution to store and share information by offering a distributed ledger service). In distributed systems, abandoned events are much more frequent than centralized system. This concept causes a number of issues including data reliability, high economical cost, and information system security. In this chapter, the authors present a new framework in blockchain to supervise the cloud server for administration of blockchain, which is verified the transaction reliability in peer-to-peer networks for sharing of data files in centralized manner. Each transaction can be generated keys for server authentication to verify all the connected members for monitoring the web server.

DOI: 10.4018/978-1-7998-2414-5.ch012

1. INTRODUCTION

In the twentieth century, there exists a collaboration between cloud computing and service oriented structure in diverse areas such as financial sector, ICT computational environment and computational clouds. It can be successfully utilized in a blockchain network. It has recently been accessed on a distributed ledger. Distributed ledger is an individual ledger. All Nodes of distributed ledger have some level of access to that ledger and agree to a protocol and its application sometimes called achieving consensus. It determines the "true state" of the ledger at any point in time. Distributed ledger could be very useful as an industry collaboration tool. Database of a distributed ledger that exists over various areas or among various participants (Belin, O.). However, decentralized distributed ledger eradicates the demand for a centralized authority to authenticate transactions (The World Bank, 2018). Each and every file in a given time stamped of distributed ledger is a unique cryptographic signature. Every participant of the distributed ledger can observe all of the records. In spite of confound acronyms for instance DLT in financial and fintech groups i.e. Distributed Ledger Technology is reordering the business who like to affect their online transactions turning on decentralized views of blockchain as a service (BaaS) (Reiff, N., 2020). Distributed ledgers for instance blockchain are exceptionally helpful for financial transactions. They reduce the functional inefficiencies. Blockchain is a distinct type of distributed ledger. It outlines the record transactions or digital interactions and brings much-needed transparency, competency and affixed security to organizations. It means that there are no central servers for cloud file storage by providing solutions based approach. Blockchain-as-a-Service (BaaS) is the third-party modeling of cloud-based networks management for organizations in blockchain applications. Blockchain applications go far over cryptocurrency and bitcoin. With its capability to originate further transparency and fairness while also saving businesses time and money, the technology is affecting a classification of sectors in methods that area from how agreements are imposed to make government effort further profitability. There is a broad area of blockchain applications for example cryptocurrency, financial, public services, healthcare domain, risk management, and so on. Blockchain-as-a-service (BaaS) is cloud-based infrastructure management third-party services for companies establishment and working blockchain applications (Gaurav, A. B., et.al, 2020). It roles such as a web host. It runs the backend operation for an app. Blockchain-as-a-service (BaaS) may be the impulse that guides the extensive assumption of blockchain technology. Blockchain services utilize the hybrid cloud server to indurate the security of cloud service. In Blockchain as a service prevents the pieces attacks in the service of blockchain. The transactions are being validated by the cloud server when a numerical problem is solved (Singh, S., & Singh, N., 2016). The blockchain transactions process is being implemented by the blockchain network for obtaining a distributed database system independently that records transactional data or other information. It is quickly uncovered that, alongside as long as the infrastructure for cryptocurrencies and blockchain stands to convey commercial advantages in respect of cost and competence. Blockchain also has an appearing part in improving transaction transparency which can be a barbed issue. Blockchain delivers an unchangeable distributed documentation tracking system. In other words, where documentation is meant to transact blockchain can make sure that all participants have the same access for the same information. In other terms, no participant can change records. Everyone is sure that documents are accurate and secure. Many applications that essentially secure storage for data that is not centralized can advantage from storing data on the blockchain. The distributed type of blockchain implies that all parties are uniformly noticed as there is a "single source of truth" (Rosic, A., 2017). As a outcome, contracts are polished more accurately. It allows conclusion and payment to happen without detainment. Blockchain elasticity and its correlated technologies impart itself to several applications that are yet to be invented. Another disadvantage of blockchain application is that at once data has been attached to the blockchain. It is very thorny to reform it. While lucidity is one of the advantages of blockchain. It is not always good to transfer the blockchain data or code i.e. often very seeking and often calls for a hard fork, where one chain is derelicted and a new one is taken up. Especially blockchain applications that make use of "Proof of Work", are particularly incompetent (John Rampton,The Economist). Since mining is mainly competitive and there is exactly one winner every single ten minutes, the effort of every other miner is squandered. As miners are frequently making an effort to enlarge their computational power, so they have a vast chance for searching a valid block hash. The resources used by the Bitcoin network has enlarged remarkably. In recent years, it consumes extra energy than many countries currently, for instance Denmark, Ireland, and Nigeria (Bauerle, N., 2017). It has a slower process in blockchain that slows down when there are too many users on the network. Due to their consensus method blockchain are harder to scale. It consumes too much high energy. Blockchain can't go back as data is immutable. Due to how they operate blockchains are sometimes inefficient. Users have to maintain their own wallets or else they can lose access. Blockchain implementation is a costly process. It still has a long way to go before. It matures and gets standardized. Blockchain doesn't offer interoperability as of now. It's hard to integrate into a legacy system. There are various risks and security challenges that should be observed (Ahram, T. et al., 2017; Chanti, S., 2020). The similar process for the blockchain transactions involves integrating hybrid cloud servers and authorizing the use of blockchain services. We present in this chapter a blockchain architecture, which can be easily combined with large-scale centralized computational environments. We briefly discuss the concept of integration of blockchain with cloud platforms in order to improve the security of data storage as well as resources. Every blockchain transaction is connected among nodes and verified to security against attacks. Cloud computing has been required blockchain services due to its consistency and accessibility. Because it allows the infrastructure to scale in a consistent way which has a bigger focus on scaling the service and Integration of the two technologies can ensure consistent performance and security. it bears chances for enhancing accessibility to many information resources which are locked either in proprietary or inaccessible desktop applications as the access to information in the Cloud is done mostly by web interfaces. The essence of our approach is to trade a small amount of latency and transaction overhead for a potentially large amount of economic utility. Blockchain as a service is using automated remote monitoring on the cloud. It connected with the blockchain network for testing blockchain applications. That makes it advantageous for them to place their IT systems on an interconnected platform, with dense, globally distributed blockchain provider ecosystems for transferring their data between the many blockchain provider ledgers and their legacy IT systems." Every blockchain transaction is an immense responsibility of data and user management in both environments.

2. OVERVIEW OF BLOCKCHAIN TECHNOLOGY

1) Blockchain is the first peer-to-peer decentralized service that record all actual data. Each block is linked with the previous block with a cryptographic hash. Block size of a bitcoin is restricted to 1 MB. While a blockchain transactions, which is composed of the data files in order to keep the transaction in blockchain as a service. Bitcoin became renowned progressively and was recognized as a valid cryptocurrency after captivating and authentic system of operational assets on the cyberspace. For Instance, blockchain transactions can trade-off digital currency securely in blockchain network for data storage. Blockchain is a decentralized technology for the hash value across an organization network. Thus the exchange between size of block in network and security of blocks has been a resilient challenge. The Bitcoin network is prohibited to a levy of minimum transactions in seconds, which is unable to deal with vast amount of high frequency business. However, huge blocks means massive storage space and moderate dissemination in the blockchain network. In a blockchain module under the development of integrated cloud server which impart a pictorial illustrating the figure (1) functional representation of Blockchain-as-a-Service.

Figure 1. Blockchain as a service

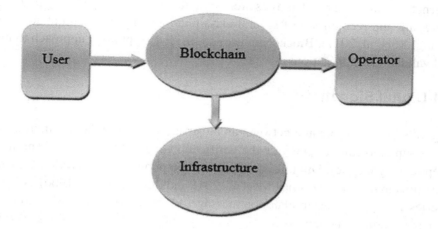

It is known to be a testing work for integrating server with the blockchain cloud, or a way to support added blockchain applications. It is explicit that blockchain as a service focuses to facilitate and accessible in cloud. Whether to blockchain as a service will play a role in more applications is not clear yet. Then we exploit blockchain technology as a trading patterns between users who need cloud service for storing the data files and users who supply all the storage space. The blockchain services needs decentralized control the system for maintaining information. It can be implemented with blockchain services in cloud platform that the service provider is granted to access the data files for the services only. A decentralized blockchain network of cloud storage has been initiated with numerous edges in addition the storage based on the data centers. It is similar to conventional rectification, centralized system of cloud storage resistance client-side encryption process will work for blockchain as a service.

It is near to the subsequent alternative and focus on centralized requirements.

3. SYSTEM OVERVIEW

Blockchain technologies also engage to impart framework for integrating hybrid cloud server for remote monitoring challenge in financial sector of developing nations. It will be allowed them to generate private, public and group based Blockchain technology very rapidly. Blockchain application in de-centralization system with world wide centralized platforms. Centralized system management of hybrid cloud computing assist the consortium for auto scaling the framework based on their entail.

To decrease the amount and effort, centralized cloud server could be the foremost alternative. But once the data files are accumulated and keep centrally planned for surveying and recognition of several classifications of threats and attack models (Liang, X. et. al, 2017). Blockchain uses a lopsided cryptology approach to justify and validate the transactions.

3.1 Digital Signature

Digital signature is a game between an adversary and a simulator. Simulator runs the set-up algorithm to generate the verification key to the adversary and it gives keeps the signing key. Digital signature based on public key encryption is used in a deceitful environment (Kumar, M. et al., 2018 and Bernstein, A. J. 1966). Adversary queries are signing the simulator on messages of its choice and receives in return a proper signature generated using the secret signing key. The transactions of digitally signed are transmit throughout the entire network (Kirkman, S., 2018). To dispense validity, Integrity and non-repudiation to electronic data files. Digital Signature of a person thus differ from record to record consequently verifying authenticity of each and every term of that a document.

3.2 Remote Monitoring

Remote monitoring of the blockchain is the identical, incorporate framework of multi-layer cloud for load balancing of blockchain transactions in centralized maner. This perspective is too straightforward to simplify, and it interpret directly in traditional centralized transaction systems, every transaction entails to be uphold during the central trusted agency. Here the steps are doing in an encompass-

- Reclaim the rear block
- If this is a contemporary block, hold it and recall this was the endmost block we've seen
- If this is a block we handled before, halt for x seconds.
- Reduplication

Mostly the prevailing research on cloud services coalition for SLA supervision for all elaborated of utilizing blockchain as a services. It can either attack is maintain in secured way or the retrieve control structure the monitoring system remotely. The cloud is compulsory to ask about an authorization to execute an activity, like drifting the data to acquire (Keenan, T. P., 2017).

3.3 Benefits of Decentralized Blockchain Services

Since the centralized system is not so much as determining capacity securing the network in the blockchain systems. Decentralization in cloud computing plays an immense job in the execution of the peer-to-peer blockchain networking services impart on the cloud network in the service of cloud storage.

This network is very secure and validated on the basic of blockchain technology (Xu, R., et al., 2018). Blockchain creates a decentralized and distributed storage marketplace, in adequate to the deficiency of remote monitoring server storage. Monitoring the blockchain transactions as an intruder might intuit constructive information of any organizations. Adoption of a hybrid cloud approach where decentralized energy maintain data both on the public and private cloud. The decentralized blockchain network is an contemporary conception absolutely in cloud computing.

3.4 Integration Hybrid Cloud Service for Blockchain Transactions

The foremost intent of this solution is to perceive how blockchain transaction works and how it can be coherent with prevailing combine applications in blockchain transactions. Blockchain transactions are on the frontier of the flattering an unruly technology. There is an intense market for system incorporation beyond blockchains and prevailing bequest and ERP technology is incorporating blockchain solutions turn into manufacture willing with pursuit systems, extant reinforce service. In this proposed work, we pursue for integrating blockchain transactions in the hybrid cloud server. It is unsophisticated and thoroughly decentralized blockchain (Xu, R. et al., 2018). There have also been resembles to integrate access control with some cryptographic antique, such as accredit-based encryption. As a consequence, when exploiting these answers to support your data files to confined steer. It can affix an extent of conviction to the reliability of an organizations data. From the intimate point of view, blockchain technology has no ascendancy across a centralized database structure. They both can use enlightened encryption algorithms. Besides, centralized databases can be disconnected from the network thoroughly. Thus, the constricted instruction is necessary to acquire all requisite encoding data files, encryption to send data files to the cloud server in the blockchain transactions (Bendiab, K., et al., 2018).

4. IMPLEMENTATION

In this section, we first describe the setup of the whole system, and then discuss the implementation of integration hybrid cloud server with remote monitoring for blockchain as a service that will be illustrated as follows.

4.1. System Setup

In the following figure 2, a transaction modifies the state of one or more entities. Each entity maintains a ledger containing an ordered list of transactions. All correct entities agree on the same ordering of transactions. Hundreds to thousands of entities; thousands of transactions/sec. Secrecy of data and metadata about transactions. Set of entities, transaction processing logic can evolve Interoperability, checkpointing, etc. Adapted from decentralized cryptocurrencies: Bitcoin, Ethereum etc.

Figure 2. An append-only log

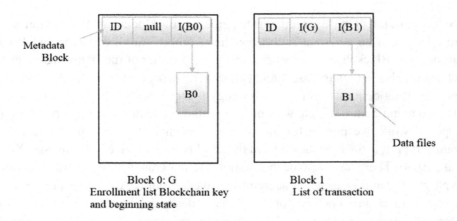

Every pair of correct members share a consistent approval prefix even if the BSP is malicious and even if any number of members are malicious. Relies on semantics of an approval transaction: ("memi", hash, len, sig). A simple protocol for members to agree on a single, consistent ledger. It does not require any explicit peer-to-peer coordination and Approval transactions can be sent anytime. Approval transactions are small: <256 bytes. The protocol is mostly stateless: all the state is kept on the ledger. It requires participation from everyone: each member must periodically send its approval transaction. Each member node must validate all transactions. No confidentiality for transactions. With assumptions about the network, we have other mechanisms for members to suspect potential liveness and fairness violations. Two relaxations by adapting ideas from replicated state machines:

- Assume only a threshold number of nodes to be faulty (i.e., $f < n/3$)
- Prevent members from equivocating (via enclaves)

4.2. Steps 1-8

Step 1: This incorporates immutable storage, electronic signatures and encryption. Information in any format can be kept in the blockchain approximately. It can make public-private keys set and used also for generating and to verifying digital signatures. According to figure 3, Merkle-tree used to ensure well behaved programs under certain assumptions (Perugini, S. 2018 & amp; Romero Laorden, D. et. al.,2016).

Figure 3. Merkle tree for data auditing

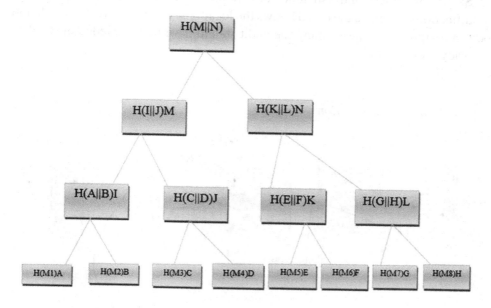

The size of the proof is O ($l*\log n$), where n = number of data blocks and l is the number of challenge queries. Without retrieving data allows to verify the Client i.e. verifier that the CPS still possesses the client's original data. The client (verifier) runs an efficient data audit proof.

Step2: The sender writes hash values for data files over the record. User encrypted records by using public key of receiver and render the encrypted key into the record (Sukhodolskiy, I. et al., 2018 and Wang, K., Kulkarni, 2015). Depending upon the test-cases, it require to select the decentralized consensus problem that makes the extreme knowledge. Pre-processing for erasure codes as follows:

- An (n,f,d)Σ elimination code over finite alphabet Σ is a fault mark key that comprise of
- Enc: Σf?Σn An algorithm for encoding
- Dec: Σn?Σf decoding algorithm d is the least interval (Hamming span between any of the two code expression is at most d) of the key.
- An (n,f,d) elimination key can endure up to d-1 removal.
- If d=n-f + 1, we designate the code an utmost interval distinguishable key.
- For an utmost interval distinguishable key, the initial information can be restore from anyone f out of n tokens of the key term.

Step3: All blocks and authenticators are uploaded to the cloud server. When modifications are made the cloud knows the locations. Because verification should be fast. A third party performing the audit should have no knowledge of the data (Privacy preserving).

Figure 4. Bitcoin Transaction

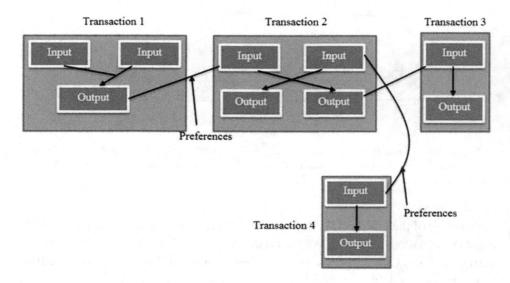

According to fig. 4, the sender can be verified that the transaction is exactly be indicated by the receiver throughout control the block. After each and every transaction, the preference only confirms the bitcoin transaction.

Step4. At this step is whether the nodes will pass on the cloud server for integrating with the blockchain services or both. In sending blockchain transaction process to be performed in this process.

Step 5-6: The number of miners does not affect the transactions. It can be revoked. The blockchain transaction is asserted in cloud server for the blockchain transactions. Some transactions is yet to be inevitable with numerous input were decentralized Transaction-based Ledger. All peers should agree on a sequence of transactions. The most successful use of transactions is a decentralized bitcoin with a peer-to-peer system.

Step 7: Each and every submission of blockchain stub which creates for authenticating record of data files. Automatic contracts, triggered when certain conditions are met. Blockchain Transactions are placed in blocks, which are linked by SHA 256 hashes. Transaction on bitcoin, and analyzing whether the system is safe or not for use. Where the cost of centralized server is generally a preceding output of centralized blockchain transactions.

Step 8: The clarity of unstructured robust network in present transformations. Working of nodes all at once with small solidarity. The mere blockchain transaction is to be well informed of all about the transactions. It only keep these acceptance that associated to his concern.

5. ANALYSIS

In this segment, we will study the preferred implementation in according to implementation and security.

5.1 Storage of Hybrid Cloud Server

Efficient Data Sharing by user dispersed in multi location will provide large increases in random performance and endurance. It has unique I/O access signature. At a later time, the hybrid cloud server can demonstrate their storage after the transaction. Hash key length of data files is (920 # n u) 32 bytes. We suppose that the length of storage disk is 1 TB that can be stored more than 500 million acceptance documents (Wang, S., Zhang, Y., & Zhang, Y. 2018). The disclosure of the blockchain application has allowed us to associate with storage capacity, bandwidth, CPU power, etc. (Zhang, Y., Wu, S., Jin, B., & Du, J., 2017). For instance, that 1TB storage disk on each and every node is adequate.

5.2 Security

"With the emergence of cloud computing, a hybrid cloud server may be appropriate for users who would like to stabilize data security with scalable processing of the data files" (Khadilkar, V. et al., 2011). Data may still need to be on the cloud. In the enlarging solutions of cloud computing security of remote monitoring to recognize the obstacle and the perspective. It can be verified reliably and are very problematic to be hindered (Shih, W. C, et al., 2010 & Park, S. J. 2009).

6. CONCLUSION

In this work, we intended the service oriented decentralized provenance that supports complete transactions is done. An invalid transaction for making payments are not going to accept and never acquire a block. Integrating hybrid cloud service for manipulating a blockchain as a service model in centralized way. The client can concentrate on task and the functionality of blockchain of their disturbing about representation related concern. Transaction data which have been going on and know that The transaction is done. Privacy of data is a growing concern that discourages sharing of data. We have to express to the future work for enhancing scenario.

REFERENCES

Ahram, T., Sargolzaei, A., Sargolzaei, S., Daniels, J., & Amaba, B. (2017). Blockchain technology innovations. In 2017 IEEE Technology & Engineering Management Conference (TEMSCON) (pp. 137-141). IEEE. doi:10.1109/TEMSCON.2017.7998367

Barenji, A. V., Guo, H., Tian, Z., Li, Z., Wang, W. M., & Huang, G. Q. (2019). Blockchain-Based Cloud Manufacturing: Decentralization. *Transdisciplinary Engineering Methods for Social Innovation of Industry 4.0.*, 1003 – 1011. doi:10.3233/978-1-61499-898-3-1003

Bauerle, N. (2017). *What is Blockchain Technology? Blockchain 101.* https://www.coindesk.com/learn/blockchain-101/what-is-blockchain-technology

Belin, O. (n.d.). *The Difference Between Blockchain & Distributed Ledger Technology.* https://tradeix.com/distributed-ledger-technology/

Bendiab, K., Kolokotronis, N., Shiaeles, S., & Boucherkha, S. (2018). WiP: A novel blockchain-based trust model for cloud identity management. In *2018 IEEE 16th Intl Conf on Dependable, Autonomic and Secure Computing, 16th Intl Conf on Pervasive Intelligence and Computing, 4th Intl Conf on Big Data Intelligence and Computing and Cyber Science and Technology Congress (DASC/PiCom/DataCom/CyberSciTech)* (pp. 724-729). IEEE. 10.1109/DASC/PiCom/DataCom/CyberSciTec.2018.00126

Bendiab, K., Kolokotronis, N., Shiaeles, S., & Boucherkha, S. (2018). WiP: A novel blockchain-based trust model for cloud identity management. In *2018 IEEE 16th Intl Conf on Dependable, Autonomic and Secure Computing, 16th Intl Conf on Pervasive Intelligence and Computing, 4th Intl Conf on Big Data Intelligence and Computing and Cyber Science and Technology Congress (DASC/PiCom/DataCom/CyberSciTech)* (pp. 724-729). IEEE. 10.1109/DASC/PiCom/DataCom/CyberSciTec.2018.00126

Bernstein, A. J. (1966). Analysis of programs for parallel processing. *IEEE Transactions on Electronic Computers*, EC-15(5), 757–763. doi:10.1109/PGEC.1966.264565

Biswas, R., Das, S. K., Harvey, D., & Oliker, L. (1999). Portable parallel programming for the dynamic load balancing of unstructured grid applications. In *Proceedings 13th International Parallel Processing Symposium and 10th Symposium on Parallel and Distributed Processing. IPPS/SPDP 1999* (pp. 338-342). IEEE. 10.1109/IPPS.1999.760497

Blockchain & Distributed Ledger Technology (DLT). (2018). The World Bank. https://www.worldbank.org/en/topic/financialsector/brief/blockchain-dlt

Chanti, S., Anwar, T., Chithralekha, T., & Uma, V. (2020). Global Naming and Storage System Using Blockchain. In *Transforming Businesses With Bitcoin Mining and Blockchain Applications* (pp. 146–165). IGI Global. doi:10.4018/978-1-7998-0186-3.ch008

Do, H. G., & Ng, W. K. (2017). Blockchain-based system for secure data storage with private keyword search. In *2017 IEEE World Congress on Services (SERVICES)* (pp. 90-93). IEEE. 10.1109/SERVICES.2017.23

Eldredge, M., Hughes, T. J., Ferencz, R. M., Rifai, S. M., Raefsky, A., & Herndon, B. (1997). High-performance parallel computing in industry. *Parallel Computing*, 23(9), 1217–1233. doi:10.1016/S0167-8191(97)00049-5

Gaurav, A. B., Kumar, P., Kumar, V., & Thakur, R. S. (2020). Conceptual Insights in Blockchain Technology: Security and Applications. In Transforming Businesses With Bitcoin Mining and Blockchain Applications (pp. 221-233). IGI Global.

Keenan, T. P. (2017). Alice in Blockchains: Surprising Security Pitfalls in PoW and PoSBlockchain Systems. In *2017 15th Annual Conference on Privacy, Security and Trust (PST)* (pp. 400-4002). IEEE.

Khadilkar, V., Kantarcioglu, M., Thuraisingham, B., & Mehrotra, S. (2011). *Secure data processing in a hybrid cloud.* arXiv preprint arXiv:1105-1982

Kirkman, S. (2018). A data movement policy framework for improving trust in the cloud using smart contracts and blockchains. In *2018 IEEE International Conference on Cloud Engineering (IC2E)* (pp. 270-273). IEEE. 10.1109/IC2E.2018.00054

Kumar, M., Singh, A. K., & Kumar, T. S. (2018). Secure Log Storage Using Blockchain and Cloud Infrastructure. In *2018 9th International Conference on Computing, Communication and Networking Technologies (ICCCNT)* (pp. 1-4). IEEE. 10.1109/ICCCNT.2018.8494085

Li, C., & Hains, G. (2011). A simple bridging model for high-performance computing. In *2011 International Conference on High Performance Computing & Simulation* (pp. 249-256). IEEE. 10.1109/HPCSim.2011.5999831

Li, J., Liu, Z., Chen, L., Chen, P., & Wu, J. (2017). Blockchain-based security architecture for distributed cloud storage. In *2017 IEEE International Symposium on Parallel and Distributed Processing with Applications and 2017 IEEE International Conference on Ubiquitous Computing and Communications (ISPA/IUCC)* (pp. 408-411). IEEE. 10.1109/ISPA/IUCC.2017.00065

Liang, X., Shetty, S., Tosh, D., Kamhoua, C., Kwiat, K., & Njilla, L. (2017). Provchain: A blockchain-based data provenance architecture in cloud environment with enhanced privacy and availability. In *Proceedings of the 17th IEEE/ACM international symposium on cluster, cloud and grid computing* (pp. 468-477). IEEE Press. 10.1109/CCGRID.2017.8

Maggs, B. M., Matheson, L. R., & Tarjan, R. E. (1995). Models of parallel computation: A survey and synthesis. In *Proceedings of the Twenty-Eighth Annual Hawaii International Conference on System Sciences* (Vol. 2, pp. 61-70). IEEE. 10.1109/HICSS.1995.375476

Park, S. J. (2009). An Analysis of GPU Parallel Computing. In *2009 DoD High Performance Computing Modernization Program Users Group Conference,* (pp. 365-369). IEEE. doi: 10.1109/HPCMP-UGC.2009.59

Perugini, S. (2018). The design of an emerging/multi-paradigm programming languages course. *Journal of Computing Sciences in Colleges, 34*(1), 52–59.

Rampton, J. (n.d.). *5 applications for blockchain in your business*. The Economist. https://execed.economist.com/blog/industry-trends/5-applications-blockchain-your-business

Reiff, N. (2020). Blockchain Explained. *Investopedia*. https://www.investopedia.com/terms/b/blockchain.asp

Romero-Laorden, D., Villazón-Terrazas, J., Martinez-Graullera, O., Ibanez, A., Parrilla, M., & Penas, M. S. (2016). Analysis of parallel computing strategies to accelerate ultrasound imaging processes. *IEEE Transactions on Parallel and Distributed Systems*, 27(12), 3429–3440. doi:10.1109/TPDS.2016.2544312

Rosic, A. (2017). *17 Blockchain Applications That Are Transforming Society*. Blockgeeks. https://blockgeeks.com/guides/blockchain-applications/

Shih, W. C., Tseng, S. S., & Yang, C. T. (2010). Performance study of parallel programming on cloud computing environments using mapreduce. In *2010 International Conference on Information Science and Applications* (pp. 1-8). IEEE. 10.1109/ICISA.2010.5480515

Singh, S., & Singh, N. (2016). Blockchain: Future of financial and cyber security. In *2016 2nd International Conference on Contemporary Computing and Informatics (IC3I)* (pp. 463-467). IEEE.

Sukhodolskiy, I., & Zapechnikov, S. (2018). A blockchain-based access control system for cloud storage. In *2018 IEEE Conference of Russian Young Researchers in Electrical and Electronic Engineering (EIConRus)* (pp. 1575-1578). IEEE. 10.1109/EIConRus.2018.8317400

Wang, K., Kulkarni, A., Lang, M., Arnold, D., & Raicu, I. (2015). Exploring the design tradeoffs for extreme-scale high-performance computing system software. *IEEE Transactions on Parallel and Distributed Systems*, 27(4), 1070–1084. doi:10.1109/TPDS.2015.2430852

Wang, S., Zhang, Y., & Zhang, Y. (2018). A blockchain-based framework for data sharing with fine-grained access control in decentralized storage systems. *IEEE Access: Practical Innovations, Open Solutions*, 6, 38437–38450. doi:10.1109/ACCESS.2018.2851611

Xu, R., Chen, Y., Blasch, E., & Chen, G. (2018). Blendcac: A blockchain-enabled decentralized capability-based access control for iots. In *2018 IEEE International Conference on Internet of Things (iThings) and IEEE Green Computing and Communications (GreenCom) and IEEE Cyber, Physical and Social Computing (CPSCom) and IEEE Smart Data (SmartData)* (pp. 1027-1034). IEEE. 10.1109/Cybermatics_2018.2018.00191

Zhang, Y., Wu, S., Jin, B., & Du, J. (2017). A blockchain-based process provenance for cloud forensics. In *2017 3rd IEEE International Conference on Computer and Communications (ICCC)* (pp. 2470-2473). IEEE. 10.1109/CompComm.2017.8322979

Zheng, Z., Xie, S., Dai, H., Chen, X., & Wang, H. (2017). An overview of blockchain technology: Architecture, consensus, and future trends. In *2017 IEEE International Congress on Big Data (BigData Congress)* (pp. 557-564). IEEE. 10.1109/BigDataCongress.2017.85

KEY TERMS AND DEFINITIONS

Bitcoin: Bitcoin is a cryptocurrency, a form of electronic cash. A purely peer-to-peer version of electronic cash would allow online payments to be sent directly from one party to another without going through a financial institution.

Block: A block is a container data structure which contain series of transactions. Each transaction within a block is digitally signed and encrypted and verified by the peer node of blockchain network.

Blockchain: The Blockchain is a decentralized computation and information sharing platform that enables multiple authoritative domains, who don't trust each other, to cooperate, coordinate and collaborate in a rational decision-making process.

Cloud Computing: This is the on-demand obtainability of computing resources, particularly computing power and data storage, devoid of direct active management by the user.

Cryptocurrency: Cryptocurrency is a mechanism designed to work for the online secure payments system using cryptography.

Compilation of References

Abdul-Ghani, H. A., Konstantas, D., & Mahyoub, M. (2018). A comprehensive IoT attacks survey based on a building-blocked reference model. *International Journal of Advanced Computer Science and Applications*, 355-373.

Ackoff, R. L. (1971). Towards a system of systems concepts. *Management Science, 17*(11), 661–671. doi:10.1287/mnsc.17.11.661

Adolphs, P., Bedenbender, H., Dirzus, D., Ehlich, M., Epple, U., Hankel, M., ... Koziolek, H. (2015). *Status report-reference architecture model industrie 4.0 (rami4. 0)*. VDI-Verein Deutscher Ingenieure eV and ZVEI-German Electrical and Electronic Manufacturers Association, Tech. Rep.

Agrawal, R., Verma, P., Sonanis, R., Goel, U., De, A., Kondaveeti, S. A., & Shekhar, S. (2018, April). Continuous security in IoT using blockchain. In *2018 IEEE International Conference on Acoustics, Speech and Signal Processing (ICASSP)* (pp. 6423-6427). IEEE. 10.1109/ICASSP.2018.8462513

AhIman, R. (2016). *Finish city partners with IBM to validate blockchain application in logistics.* https://cointelegraph.com/news/finish-city-partners-with-ibm-to-validate-blockchain-application-in-logistics

Ahram, T., Sargolzaei, A., Sargolzaei, S., Daniels, J., & Amaba, B. (2017). Blockchain technology innovations. In 2017 IEEE Technology & Engineering Management Conference (TEMSCON) (pp. 137-141). IEEE. doi:10.1109/TEMSCON.2017.7998367

Ahram, T., Sargolzaei, A., Sargolzaei, S., Daniels, J., & Amaba, B. (2017, June). Blockchain technology innovations. In 2017 IEEE Technology & Engineering Management Conference (TEMSCON) (pp. 137-141). IEEE. doi:10.1109/TEMSCON.2017.7998367

Aitzhan, N. Z., & Svetinovic, D. (2016). Security and Privacy in Decentralized Energy Trading through Multi-signatures, Blockchain and Anonymous Messaging Streams. *IEEE Transaction on Dependable and Secure Computing*, 1.

Ali, M. S., Dolui, K., & Antonelli, F. (2017). IoT data privacy via blockchains and IPFS. In *International Conference on the Internet of Things*. ACM. 10.1145/3131542.3131563

Alketbi, A., Nasir, Q., & Talib, M. A. (2018, February). Blockchain for government services— Use cases, security benefits and challenges. In 2018 15th Learning and Technology Conference (L&T) (pp. 112-119). IEEE.

Alphand, O., Amoretti, M., Claeys, T., Dall'Asta, S., Duda, A., Ferrari, G., . . . Zanichelli, F. (2018, April). IoTChain: A blockchain security architecture for the Internet of Things. In 2018 IEEE Wireless Communications and Networking Conference (WCNC) (pp. 1-6). IEEE. doi:10.1109/WCNC.2018.8377385

Anand, Conti, Kaliyar, & Lal. (2019). *TARE: Topology Adaptive Re-kEying scheme for secure group communication in IoT networks.* Springer Science+Business Media, LLC.

Anchor, B. I. S. T. (2019). Taraxa White Paper.

Androulaki, E., Barger, A., Bortnikov, V., Cachin, C., Christidis, K., De Caro, A., ... (2018). Hyperledger fabric: a distributed operating system for permissioned blockchains. In *EuroSys '18 - Proceedings of the Thirteenth EuroSys Conference.* Porto: ACM. 10.1145/3190508.3190538

Antonopoulos, A. M. (2014). *Mastering Bitcoin* (1st ed.). O'Reilly Media.

Anwar, H. (2018). *Consensus Algorithms: The Root Of The Blockchain Technology.* Retrieved from https://101blockchains.com/consensus-algorithms-blockchain

Apostolaki, M., Zohar, A., & Vanbever, L. (2017, May). Hijacking bitcoin: Routing attacks on cryptocurrencies. In 2017 IEEE Symposium on Security and Privacy (SP) (pp. 375-392). IEEE. doi:10.1109/SP.2017.29

Ashton, K. (2009). That 'internet of things' thing. *RFID Journal, 22*(7), 97-114.

Atlam, H. F., Alenezi, A., Alassafi, M. O., & Wills, G. (2018). Blockchain with Internet of Things: Benefits, challenges, and future directions. *International Journal of Intelligent Systems and Applications, 10*(6), 40–48. doi:10.5815/ijisa.2018.06.05

Atzori, L., Iera, A., & Morabito, G. (2010). The Internet of Things: A Survey. *Computer Networks, 54*(15), 2787–2805. doi:10.1016/j.comnet.2010.05.010

Bahga, A., & Madisetti, V. K. (2016). Blockchain platform for industrial internet of things. *Journal of Software Engineering and Applications, 9*(10), 533–546. doi:10.4236/jsea.2016.910036

Banerjee, M., Lee, J., & Choo, K.-K. R. (2017). *A blockchain future to Internet of Things security: A position paper.* Digital Communications and Networks. doi:10.1016/j.dcan.2017.10.006

Banker, S. (2016). *Will blockchain technology revolutionize supply chain applications?* https://logisticsviewpoints.com/2016/06/20/will-block-chain-technology-revolutionize-supply-chain-applications/

Barenji, A. V., Guo, H., Tian, Z., Li, Z., Wang, W. M., & Huang, G. Q. (2019). Blockchain-Based Cloud Manufacturing: Decentralization. *Transdisciplinary Engineering Methods for Social Innovation of Industry 4.0.,* 1003 – 1011. doi:10.3233/978-1-61499-898-3-1003

Barreto, L., Amaral, A., & Pereira, T. (2017). Industry 4.0 implications in logistics: An overview. *Procedia Manufacturing, 2017*(13), 1245–1252. doi:10.1016/j.promfg.2017.09.045

Bassi, A., Bauer, M., Fiedler, M., & Kranenburg, R. V. (2013). *Enabling things to talk.* Springer-Verlag GmbH. doi:10.1007/978-3-642-40403-0

Bastos, D., Shackleton, M., & El-Moussa, F. (2018). *Internet of Things: A survey of technologies and security risks in smart home and city environments.* Academic Press.

Bauerle, N. (2017). *What is Blockchain Technology? Blockchain 101.* https://www.coindesk.com/learn/blockchain-101/what-is-blockchain-technology

Bauk, S., Dlabač, T., & Škurić, M. (2018, February). Internet of Things, high resolution management and new business models. In *2018 23rd International Scientific-Professional Conference on Information Technology (IT)* (pp. 1-4). IEEE. 10.1109/SPIT.2018.8350850

Belin, O. (n.d.). *The Difference Between Blockchain & Distributed Ledger Technology.* https://tradeix.com/distributed-ledger-technology/

Belluz, J., & Hoffman, S. (2015). *The One Chart You Need to Understand Any Health Study.* Vox. Available online at: https://www.vox.com/2015/1/5/7482871/types-of-study-design

Benchoufi, M., & Ravaud, P. (2017). Blockchain technology for improving clinical research quality. *Trials, 18*(1), 335. doi:10.118613063-017-2035-z PMID:28724395

Bendiab, K., Kolokotronis, N., Shiaeles, S., & Boucherkha, S. (2018). WiP: A novel blockchain-based trust model for cloud identity management. In *2018 IEEE 16th Intl Conf on Dependable, Autonomic and Secure Computing, 16th Intl Conf on Pervasive Intelligence and Computing, 4th Intl Conf on Big Data Intelligence and Computing and Cyber Science and Technology Congress (DASC/PiCom/DataCom/CyberSciTech)* (pp. 724-729). IEEE. 10.1109/DASC/PiCom/DataCom/CyberSciTec.2018.00126

Bernstein, A. J. (1966). Analysis of programs for parallel processing. *IEEE Transactions on Electronic Computers, EC-15*(5), 757–763. doi:10.1109/PGEC.1966.264565

Bistarelli, S., Mercanti, I., Santancini, P., & Santini, F. (2019). *End-to-End Voting with Non-Permissioned and Permissioned Ledgers.* Springer Nature B.V. doi:10.100710723-019-09478-y

Biswas, R., Das, S. K., Harvey, D., & Oliker, L. (1999). Portable parallel programming for the dynamic load balancing of unstructured grid applications. In *Proceedings 13th International Parallel Processing Symposium and 10th Symposium on Parallel and Distributed Processing. IPPS/SPDP 1999* (pp. 338-342). IEEE. 10.1109/IPPS.1999.760497

Blockchain & Distributed Ledger Technology (DLT). (2018). The World Bank. https://www.worldbank.org/en/topic/financialsector/brief/blockchain-dlt

Bodkhe, U., Mehta, D., Tanwar, S., Bhattacharya, P., Singh, P. K., & Hong, W. C. (2020). A Survey on Decentralized Consensus Mechanisms for Cyber Physical Systems. *IEEE Access: Practical Innovations, Open Solutions, 8*, 54371–54401. doi:10.1109/ACCESS.2020.2981415

Brown, R. G., Carlyle, J., Grigg, I., & Hearn, M. (2016). Corda: an introduction. *R3 CEV, 1*, 15.

Cam-Winget, N., Sadeghi, A.-R., & Jin, Y. (2016). INVITED: Can IoT be Secured: Emerging Challenges in Connecting the Unconnected. *Proceedings of the 53rd Annual Design Automation Conference (DAC '16)*. 10.1145/2744769.2905004

Chanti, S., Anwar, T., Chithralekha, T., & Uma, V. (2020). Global Naming and Storage System Using Blockchain. In Transforming Businesses With Bitcoin Mining and Blockchain Applications (pp. 146–165). IGI Global. doi:10.4018/978-1-7998-0186-3.ch008

Chanti, S., Anwar, T., Chithralekha, T., & Uma, V. (2020). Global Naming and Storage System Using Blockchain. In *Transforming Businesses With Bitcoin Mining and Blockchain Applications* (pp. 146–165). IGI Global. doi:10.4018/978-1-7998-0186-3.ch008

Chen, G., Xu, B., Lu, M., & Chen, N.-S. (2018). Exploring blockchain technology and its potential applications for education. *Smart Learning Environments, 5*(1), 1–10. doi:10.118640561-017-0050-x

Chen, R., Guo, J., & Bao, F. (2014). Trust management for service composition in SOA-based IoT systems. *Proceedings of the 2014 IEEE Wireless Communications and Networking Conference (WCNC)*, 3444–3449. 10.1109/WCNC.2014.6953138

Choi, S. S., Burm, J. W., Sung, W., Jang, J. W., & Reo, Y. J. (2018). A blockchain-based secure Iot control scheme. In *2018 International Conference on Advances in Computing and Communication Engineering (ICACCE)* (pp. 74-78). IEEE. 10.1109/ICACCE.2018.8441717

Chollet, Castiaux, Bruneton, & Sainlez. (2013). *Continuous interconnected supply chain using blockchain and internet of things supply chain traceability*. Deloitte Blockchain.

Christidis, K., & Devetsikiotis, M. (2016). Blockchains and Smart Contracts for the Internet of Things. *IEEE Access: Practical Innovations, Open Solutions, 4*, 2292–2303. doi:10.1109/ACCESS.2016.2566339

Čolaković, A., & Hadžialić, M. (2018). Internet of Things (IoT): A review of enabling technologies, challenges, and open research issues. *Computer Networks, 144*, 17–39. doi:10.1016/j.comnet.2018.07.017

Conoscenti, M., Torino, D., Vetr, A., Torino, D., & De Martin, J. C. (2016). Blockchain for the Internet of Things: a Systematic Literature Review. *IEEE/ACS 13th International Conference of Computer Systems and Applications (AICCSA)*. 10.1109/AICCSA.2016.7945805

Conti, M., Kumar, E. S., Lal, C., & Ruj, S. (2018). A survey on security and privacy issues of bitcoin. *IEEE Communications Surveys and Tutorials, 20*(4), 3416–3452. doi:10.1109/COMST.2018.2842460

Crosby, M., Nachiappan, Pattanayak, P., Verma, S., & Kalyanaraman, V. (2016). Blockchain technology: Beyond bitcoin. *Applied Innovation Review, 2*(6-10), 71.

Cui, Y. (2018). Supply Chain Innovation with IoT. In Multi-Criteria Methods and Techniques Applied to Supply Chain Management. Intech Open. doi:10.5772/intechopen.74155

Dagher, T. G. G., & Adhikari, C. L. (2018). *Iotex: A decentralized network for internet of things powered by a privacy-centric blockchain*. White Paper: https://whitepaper. io/document/131/ iotexwhitepaper

Daghmehchi Firoozjaei, M., Ghorbani, A., Kim, H., & Song, J. (2020). Hy-Bridge: A hybrid blockchain for privacy-preserving and trustful energy transactions in Internet-of-Things platforms. *Sensors (Basel)*, 20(3), 928. doi:10.339020030928 PMID:32050570

Dai, W. (1998). *B-money*. http://www.weidai.com/bmoney.txt

Dai, H. N., Zheng, Z., & Zhang, Y. (2019). Blockchain for internet of things: A survey. *IEEE Internet of Things Journal*, 6(5), 8076–8094. doi:10.1109/JIOT.2019.2920987

Daley, S. (2019). *Blockchain and IoT: 8 examples making our future smarter*. Retrieved from https://builtin.com/blockchain/blockchain-iot-examples

Datafloq. (n.d.). https://datafloq.com/read/securing-internet-of-things-iot-with-blockchain/2228

Deloitte. (2017). *Digital Procurement: New Capabilities from Disruptive Technologies*. Deloitte Development LLC.

Dhillon, V. (2016). *Blockchain-Enabled Open Science Framework*. O'Reilly Media. Available online at: https://www.oreilly.com/ideas/blockchain-enabled-open-science-framework

Dhillon, V. (2016). *Blockchain-Enabled Open Science Framework*. O'Reilly Media. https://www. oreilly.com/ideas/blockchain-enabled-open-science-framework

Dhillon, V., Metcalf, D., & Hooper, M. (2017). *Blockchain in science. Blockchain Enabled Applications* (1st ed.). Apress. doi:10.1007/978-1-4842-3081-7

Dhote, S. (2017). *Internet of Things (IoT)*. Market in India.

Díaz, M., Martín, C., & Rubio, B. (2016). State-of-the-art, challenges, and open issues in the integration of Internet of things and cloud computing. *Journal of Network and Computer Applications*, 67, 99–117. doi:10.1016/j.jnca.2016.01.010

Do, H. G., & Ng, W. K. (2017). Blockchain-based system for secure data storage with private keyword search. In *2017 IEEE World Congress on Services (SERVICES)* (pp. 90-93). IEEE. 10.1109/SERVICES.2017.23

Dorri, A., Kanhere, S. S., Jurdak, R., & Gauravaram, P. (2017). Blockchain for IoT security and privacy: The case study of a smart home. *Proceedings of the 2017 IEEE International Conference on Pervasive Computing and Communications Workshops (PerCom Workshops)*.

Dorri, A., Kanhere, S., & Jurdak, R. (2016). *Blockchain in internet of things: challenges and solutions*. arXiv: 1608.05187

Dorri, A., Kanhere, S. S., Jurdak, R., & Gauravaram, P. (2017, March). *Blockchain for IoT security and privacy: The case study of a smart home. In 2017 IEEE international conference on pervasive computing and communications workshops (PerCom workshops).* IEEE.

Draskovic, D., & Saleh, G. (2017). *Datapace - Decentralized Data Marketplace Based on Blockchain.* Available online at: https://www.datapace.io/datapace_whitepaper.pdf

Eldredge, M., Hughes, T. J., Ferencz, R. M., Rifai, S. M., Raefsky, A., & Herndon, B. (1997). High-performance parallel computing in industry. *Parallel Computing, 23*(9), 1217–1233. doi:10.1016/S0167-8191(97)00049-5

Ellervee, A., Matulevicius, R., & Mayer, N. (2017). A Comprehensive Reference Model for Blockchain-based Distributed Ledger Technology. In *ER Forum/Demos* (pp. 306-319). Academic Press.

Elrawy, M. F., Awad, A. I., & Hamed, H. F. (2018). Intrusion detection systems for IoT-based smart environments: A survey. *Journal of Cloud Computing, 7*(1), 21. doi:10.118613677-018-0123-6

Elsts, Mitskas, & Oikonomou. (2018). Distributed Ledger Technology and the Internet of Things: A Feasibility Study. In BlockSys, Shenzhen, China.

Evangelos A, K., Nikolaos D, T., & Anthony C, B. (2011). Integrating RFIDs and smart objects into a Unified Internet of Things architecture. *Advances in Internet of Things*.

Evans, D. (2011). The internet of things: How the next evolution of the internet is changing everything. *CISCO White Paper, 1*(2011), 1-11.

Evans, D. (2011). *The Internet of Things: How the Next Evolution of the Internet Is Changing Everything.* Cisco. www.cisco.com/web/about/ac79/docs/innov/IoT_IBSG_0411FINAL.pdf

Fan, P. F., Wang, L. L., Zhang, S. Y., & Lin, T. T. (2014). The Research on the Internet of Things Industry Chain for Barriers and Solutions. *Applied Mechanics and Materials, 441,* 1030–1035. doi:10.4028/www.scientific.net/AMM.441.1030

Fernández-Caramés, T. M., & Fraga-Lamas, P. (2018). A Review on the Use of Blockchain for the Internet of Things. *IEEE Access: Practical Innovations, Open Solutions, 6,* 32979–33001. doi:10.1109/ACCESS.2018.2842685

Ferrag, M. A., Derdour, M., Mukherjee, M., Derhab, A., Maglaras, L., & Janicke, H. (2018). Blockchain technologies for the internet of things: Research issues and challenges. *IEEE Internet of Things Journal, 6*(2), 2188–2204. doi:10.1109/JIOT.2018.2882794

Filament. (2018). *Blocklet USB Enclave Data Sheet.* Academic Press.

Finextra. (2016). *Everledger secures the first bottle of wine on the blockchain.* https://www.finextra.com/pressaritcle/67381/everledger-secures-the-first-bottle-of-wine-on-the-blockchain

Finney, H. (2004). *Reusable proofs of work (rpow).* http://web. archive. org/web/20071222072154/ http://rpow.net/

Fleisch, E. (2010). What is the internet of things? An economic perspective. *Economics, Management, and Financial Markets, 5*(2), 125-157.

Fruhlinger, J. (2018). *The Mirai botnet explained: How teen scammers and CCTV cameras almost brought down the internet.* Retrieved from https://www.csoonline.com/article/3258748/the-mirai-botnet-explained-how-teen-scammers-and-cctv-cameras-almost-brought-down-the-internet.html

Galvez, J. F., Mejuto, J. C., & Gandara, J. S. (2018). Future challenges on the use of blockchain for food traceability analysis. *Trends in Analytical Chemistry, 107,* 222–232. doi:10.1016/j.trac.2018.08.011

Garg, S., Gentry, C., Halevi, S., Sahai, A., & Waters, W. (2013). *Attribute-Based Encryption for Circuits from Multilinear Maps.* Academic Press. doi:10.1007/978-3-642-40084-1_27

Gartner Research. (n.d.). https://www.gartner.com/it-glossary/internet-of-things/

Gaurav, A. B., Kumar, P., Kumar, V., & Thakur, R. S. (2020). Conceptual Insights in Blockchain Technology: Security and Applications. In Transforming Businesses with Bitcoin Mining and Blockchain Applications (pp. 221-233). IGI Global.

Gaurav, A. B., Kumar, P., Kumar, V., & Thakur, R. S. (2020). Conceptual Insights in Blockchain Technology: Security and Applications. In Transforming Businesses With Bitcoin Mining and Blockchain Applications (pp. 221-233). IGI Global.

Giusto, D., Iera, A., Morabito, G., & Atzori, L. (2014). The Internet of Things. In *20th Tyrrhenian Workshop on Digital Communication.* Springer Publishing Company, Incorporated.

Golem. (2016). *The Golem Project - Global Market for Idle Computer Power.* Available online at: https://golem.network/crowdfunding

Gord, M. (2016). *Smart Contracts Described by Nick Szabo 20 Years ago now becoming Reality.* Bitcoin Magazine.

GSMAs Internet of Things Programme. (2018). *Opportunities and Use Cases for Distributed Ledger Technologies in IoT.* Academic Press.

Gubbi, J., Buyya, R., Marusic, S., & Palaniswami, M. (2013). Internet of Things (IoT): A vision, architectural elements, and future directions. *Future Generation Computer Systems, 29*(7), 1645-1660.

Gubbi, J., Buyya, R., Marusic, S., & Palaniswami, M. (2013). Internet of Things (IoT): A vision, architectural elements, and future directions. *Future Generation Computer Systems, 29*(7), 1645–1660. doi:10.1016/j.future.2013.01.010

Gu, J., Sum, B., Du, X., Wang, J., Zhuang, Y., & Wang, Z. (2018). Consortium Blockchain-Based Malware Detection in Mobile Devices. *IEEE Access: Practical Innovations, Open Solutions, 6,* 12118–12128. doi:10.1109/ACCESS.2018.2805783

Gundersen, T. (2011). *An introduction to the concept of exergy and energy quality*. Department of Energy and Process Engineering Norwegian University of Science and Technology, Version, 4.

Gupta, S., & Sadoghi, M. (2018). Blockchain transaction processing. In Encyclopedia of big data technologies, (pp. 1–11). doi:10.1007/978-3-319-63962-8_333-1

Haber, S., & Stometta, W. S. (1991). How to time stamp a digital documents. Journal of Cryptography, 3(2), 99-111. doi:10.1007/3-540-38424-3_32

Hamida, E. B., Brousmiche, K. L., Levard, H., & Thea, E. (2017, July). Blockchain for enterprise: overview, opportunities and challenges. Academic Press.

Hanada, Y., Hsiao, L., & Levis, P. (2018, November). Smart contracts for machine-to-machine communication: Possibilities and limitations. In *2018 IEEE International Conference on Internet of Things and Intelligence System (IOTAIS)* (pp. 130-136). IEEE. 10.1109/IOTAIS.2018.8600854

Hang, L., & Kim, D. H. (2019). Design and implementation of an integrated IoT blockchain platform for sensing data integrity. *Sensors (Basel)*, *19*(10), 2228. doi:10.339019102228 PMID:31091799

Hao, Z., Ji, R., & Li, Q. (2018, October). FastPay: A Secure Fast Payment Method for Edge-IoT Platforms using Blockchain. In *2018 IEEE/ACM Symposium on Edge Computing (SEC)* (pp. 410-415). IEEE. 10.1109/SEC.2018.00055

He, Y., Li, H., Cheng, X., Liu, Y., Yang, C., & Sun, L. (2018). A Blockchain based Truthful Incentive Mechanism for Distributed P2P Applications. *IEEE Access: Practical Innovations, Open Solutions*, *6*, 1–1. doi:10.1109/ACCESS.2018.2821705

Hîrțan, L. A., Dobre, C., & González-Vélez, H. (2020). Blockchain-based reputation for intelligent transportation systems. *Sensors (Basel)*, *20*(3), 791. doi:10.339020030791 PMID:32023997

Howells, R. (2015). *The Business Case for IoT*. SAP. http://scn.sap.com /community/business-trends/blog/2015/06/18/the-business-case-for-iot

Hua, J., Wang, X., Kang, M., Wang, H., & Wang, F. (2018). Blockchain based Provenance for Agricultural Products: A Distributed Platform with Duplicated and Shared Bookkeeping. *Proceedings of the IEEE Intelligent Vehicles Symposium (IV)*. 10.1109/IVS.2018.8500647

Huang, X., Xu, C., Wang, P., & Liu, H. (2018). LNSC: A security model for electric vehicle and charging pile management based on blockchain ecosystem. *IEEE Access: Practical Innovations, Open Solutions*, *6*, 13565–13574. doi:10.1109/ACCESS.2018.2812176

Huh & Seo. (2018). *Blockchain-based mobile fingerprint verification and automatic log-in platform for future computing*. Springer Science+Business Media, LLC.

Huh, Cho, & Kim. (2017). Managing IoT Devices using Blockchain Platform. *ICACT2017*.

Hulse Apple, C. (2015). *Block Verify uses blockchains to end counterfeiting and making world more honest*. https://cointelegraph.com/news/block-verify-uses-blockchains-to-end-counterfeiting-and-make-world-more-honest

Hur, J., & Noh, D. K. (2011). Attribute-based access control with efficient revocation in data outsourcing systems. *IEEE Transactions on Parallel and Distributed Systems*, 22(7), 1214–1221. doi:10.1109/TPDS.2010.203

Hyperledger Architecture Working Group. (2017). *Hyperledger Architecture* (Vol. 1). Introduction to Hyperledger Business Blockchain Design Philosophy and Consensus.

Internet of things beyond-bitcoin. (n.d.). https://www.cio.com/article/3027522/internet-of-things/beyond-bitcoin-can-the-blockchain-power-industrial-iot.html

Jankowski, S., Covello, J., Bellini, H., Ritchie, J., & Costa, D. (2014). *The Internet of Things: Making sense of the next mega-trend*. Goldman Sachs.

Janowicz, K., Regalia, B., Hitzler, P., Mai, G., Delbecque, S., Fröhlich, M., Martinent, P., & Lazarus, T. (2018). On the prospects of blockchain and distributed ledger technologies for open science and academic publishing. *Semantic Web*, 9(5), 545–555. doi:10.3233/SW-180322

Jemel, M., & Serhrouchni, A. (2017). Decentralized access control mechanism with temporal dimension based on blockchain. In *2017 IEEE 14th International Conference on e-Business Engineering (ICEBE)*. IEEE.

Jesus, E. F., Chicarino, V. R., de Albuquerque, C. V., & Rocha, A. A. D. A. (2018). A survey of how to use blockchain to secure internet of things and the stalker attack. *Security and Communication Networks*, 2018, 2018. doi:10.1155/2018/9675050

Kamilaris, A., Fonts, A., & Prenafeta-Boldv, F. X. (2019). The rise of blockchain technology in agriculture and food supply chain. *Trends in Food Science & Technology*, 91, 640–652. doi:10.1016/j.tifs.2019.07.034

Karaarslan & Adiguzel. (n.d.). Blockchain Based DNS and PKI Solutions. In *Standards for Major Internet Disrutors: Blockchain, Intents and Related Paradigm*. Academic Press.

Karimi, K., & Atkinson, G. (2013). *What the Internet of Things (IoT) needs to become a reality*. White Paper, FreeScale and ARM.

Katz, J., & Lindell, Y. (2007). *Digital Signature Schemes. In Introduction to Modern Cryptography*. Chapman & Hall/ CBC Press. doi:10.1201/9781420010756

Keenan, T. P. (2017). Alice in Blockchains: Surprising Security Pitfalls in PoW and PoSBlockchain Systems. In *2017 15th Annual Conference on Privacy, Security and Trust (PST)* (pp. 400-4002). IEEE.

Keertikumar, M., Shubham, M., & Banakar, R. M. (2015). Evolution of IoT in smart vehicles: An overview. *Proceedings of the International Conference on Green Computing and Internet of Things (ICGCIoT)*, 804–809. 10.1109/ICGCIoT.2015.7380573

Khadilkar, V., Kantarcioglu, M., Thuraisingham, B., & Mehrotra, S. (2011). *Secure data processing in a hybrid cloud*. arXiv preprint arXiv:1105-1982

Khan & Salah. (2017). IoT security: Review, blockchain solutions, and open challenges. *Future Generation Computer Systems*.

Kim, N. (2016, July). IBM pushes blockchain into the supply chain. *Wall Street Journal*.

Kirkman, S. (2018). A data movement policy framework for improving trust in the cloud using smart contracts and blockchains. In *2018 IEEE International Conference on Cloud Engineering (IC2E)* (pp. 270-273). IEEE. 10.1109/IC2E.2018.00054

Kombe, C., Manyilizu, M., & Mvuma, A. (2017). Design of land administration and title registration model based on blockchain technology. *Journal of Information Engineering and Applications*, 7, 8–15.

Kouicem, D. E., Bouabdallah, A., & Lakhlef, H. (2018). Internet of things security: A top-down survey. *Computer Networks*, *141*, 199–221. doi:10.1016/j.comnet.2018.03.012

Kranz, M., Holleis, P., & Schmidt, A. (2009). Embedded interaction: Interacting with the internet of things. *IEEE Internet Computing*, *14*(2), 46–53. doi:10.1109/MIC.2009.141

Kshetri & Voas. (2018). Blockchain-Enabled E-Voting. *IEEE Software*, 95-99.

Kshetri, N. (2017). Can Blockchain Strengthen the Internet of Things? *IEEE IT Professional*, *19*(4), 68–72. doi:10.1109/MITP.2017.3051335

Kumanduri, R., & Romero, C. (1998). *Number Theory with Computer Applications*. Prentice Hall.

Kumar & Thakur. (2017). A brief Investigation on Data Security Tools and Techniques for Big Data. *International Journal of Engineering Science Invention*, *6*(9), 20–27.

Kumar, M., Singh, A. K., & Kumar, T. S. (2018). Secure Log Storage Using Blockchain and Cloud Infrastructure. In *2018 9th International Conference on Computing, Communication and Networking Technologies (ICCCNT)* (pp. 1-4). IEEE. 10.1109/ICCCNT.2018.8494085

Kumaran, V. (2015). *IoT-Challenges and Opportunities in Indian Market*. IESA COMSNETS.

Kumar, M. V., & Iyengar, N. C. S. N. (2017). A Framework for blockchain technology in rice supply chain management. *Advanced Science and Technology Letters*, *146*, 125–130. doi:10.14257/astl.2017.146.22

Kumar, V., & Thakur, R. S. (2017). Jaccard Similarity based Mining for High Utility Webpage Sets from Weblog Database. *International Journal of Intelligent Engineering and Systems*, *10*(6), 211–220. doi:10.22266/ijies2017.1231.23

Lamichhane, Sadov, & Zaslavsky. (2017). *Smart Waste Management: An IoT and Blockchain based approach*. Academic Press.

Lansky, J. (2018). Possible state approaches to cryptocurrencies. *Journal of Systems Integration*, *9*(1), 19–31. doi:10.20470/jsi.v9i1.335

Lawrence, C. (2020). *The Convergence of IoT and Blockchain is Transforming Industries.* Retrieved from https://www.codemotion.com/magazine/dev-hub/blockchain-dev/blockchain-and-iot-in-industry-use-cases/

Lee, B., & Lee, J.-H. (2017). Blockchain-based secure firmware update for embedded devices in an Internet of Things environment. *The Journal of Supercomputing, 73*(3), pp1152–pp1167. doi:10.100711227-016-1870-0

Lee, I., & Lee, K. (2015). The Internet of Things (IoT): Applications, investments, and challenges for enterprises. *Business Horizons, 58*(4), 431–440. doi:10.1016/j.bushor.2015.03.008

Leiding, B., Memarmoshrefi, P., & Hogrefe, D. (2016, September). Self-managed and blockchain-based vehicular ad-hoc networks. In *Proceedings of the 2016 ACM International Joint Conference on Pervasive and Ubiquitous Computing: Adjunct* (pp. 137-140). ACM.

Lemieux, V. L. (2016). *Blockchain technology for recordkeeping: Help or hype.* Unpublished report. Available: https://www.researchgate.net/profile/Victoria_Lemieux

Liang, G., Weller, S. R., Luo, F., Zhao, J., & Dong, Z. Y. (2018). Distributed Blockchain-Based Data Protection Framework for Modern Power Systems against Cyber Attacks. *IEEE Transactions on Smart Grid*, 1–1.

Liang, X., Shetty, S., Tosh, D., Kamhoua, C., Kwiat, K., & Njilla, L. (2017). Provchain: A blockchain-based data provenance architecture in cloud environment with enhanced privacy and availability. In *Proceedings of the 17th IEEE/ACM international symposium on cluster, cloud and grid computing* (pp. 468-477). IEEE Press. 10.1109/CCGRID.2017.8

Liang, X., Zhao, J., Shetty, S., & Li, D. (2017). Towards data assurance and resilience in IoT using blockchain. *Conference Paper.* 10.1109/MILCOM.2017.8170858

Li, C., & Hains, G. (2011). A simple bridging model for high-performance computing. In *2011 International Conference on High Performance Computing & Simulation* (pp. 249-256). IEEE. 10.1109/HPCSim.2011.5999831

Li, H., Tian, H., Zhang, F., & He, J. (2019). Blockchain-based searchable symmetric encryption scheme. *Computers & Electrical Engineering, 73,* 32–45. doi:10.1016/j.compeleceng.2018.10.015

Li, J., Liu, Z., Chen, L., Chen, P., & Wu, J. (2017). Blockchain-based security architecture for distributed cloud storage. In *2017 IEEE International Symposium on Parallel and Distributed Processing with Applications and 2017 IEEE International Conference on Ubiquitous Computing and Communications (ISPA/IUCC)* (pp. 408-411). IEEE. 10.1109/ISPA/IUCC.2017.00065

Li, L., Liu, J., Cheng, L., Qiu, S., Wang, W., Zhang, X., & Zhang, Z. (2018). Creditcoin: A privacy-preserving blockchain-based incentive announcement network for communications of smart vehicles. *IEEE Transactions on Intelligent Transportation Systems, 19*(7), 2204–2220. doi:10.1109/TITS.2017.2777990

Lin, C., He, D., Huang, X., Choo, K. K. R., & Vasilakos, A. V. (2018). Bsein: A blockchain-based secure mutual authentication with fine-grained access control system for industry 4.0. *Journal of Network and Computer Applications*, *116*, 42–52. doi:10.1016/j.jnca.2018.05.005

Lin, I. C., Shin, H., Liu, J. C., & Jie, Y. X. (2017). Food traceability system using blockchain. *Proceedings of the 79th IASTEM International Conference*.

Lin, J., Shen, Z., Zhang, A., & Chai, Y. (2018). Blockchain and IoT based Food Traceability System. *International Journal of Information Technology*, *24*(1), 1–16.

Liu, D., Alahmadi, A., Ni, J., Lin, X., & Shen, X. (2019). Anonymous reputation system for iiot-enabled retail marketing atop pos blockchain. *IEEE Transactions on Industrial Informatics*, *15*(6), 3527–3537. doi:10.1109/TII.2019.2898900

Liu, J., Jager, T., Kakvi, S. A., & Warinschi, B. (2018). How to build time-lock encryption. *Designs, Codes and Cryptography*, *86*(11), 2549–2586. doi:10.100710623-018-0461-x

Liu, Y., Liu, X., Tang, C., Wang, J., & Zhang, L. (2018). Unlinkable Coin Mixing Scheme for Transaction Privacy Enhancement of Bitcoin. *IEEE Access: Practical Innovations, Open Solutions*, *6*, 23261–23270. doi:10.1109/ACCESS.2018.2827163

Li, Z., Kang, J., Yu, R., Ye, D., Deng, Q., & Zhang, Y. (2017). Consortium blockchain for secure energy trading in industrial internet of things. *IEEE Transactions on Industrial Informatics*, *14*(8), 3690–3700. doi:10.1109/TII.2017.2786307

Lonshakov, S., Krupenkin, A., Kapitonov, A., Radchenko, E., Khassanov, A., & Starostin, A. (2018). *Robonomics: platform for integration of cyber physical systems into human economy*. White Paper.

Lu, Y. (2018). Blockchain: A survey on functions, applications and open issues. *Journal of Industrial Integration and Management*, *3*(04), 1850015. doi:10.1142/S242486221850015X

Lu, Z., Liu, W., Wang, Q., Qu, G., & Liu, Z. (2018). A privacy-preserving trust model based on blockchain for VANETs. *IEEE Access: Practical Innovations, Open Solutions*, *6*, 45655–45664. doi:10.1109/ACCESS.2018.2864189

Macleod, M. R., Michie, S., Roberts, I., Dirnagl, U., Chalmers, I., Ioannidis, J. P., Salman, R. A.-S., Chan, A.-W., & Glasziou, P. (2014). Biomedical research: Increasing value, reducing waste. *Lancet*, *383*(9912), 101–104. doi:10.1016/S0140-6736(13)62329-6 PMID:24411643

Maggs, B. M., Matheson, L. R., & Tarjan, R. E. (1995). Models of parallel computation: A survey and synthesis. In *Proceedings of the Twenty-Eighth Annual Hawaii International Conference on System Sciences* (Vol. 2, pp. 61-70). IEEE. 10.1109/HICSS.1995.375476

Mahjabin, T., Xiao, Y., Sun, G., & Jiang, W. (2017). A survey of distributed denial-of-service attack, prevention, and mitigation techniques. *International Journal of Distributed Sensor Networks*, *13*(12), 155014771774146. doi:10.1177/1550147717741463

Makhdoom, I., Abolhasan, M., Abbas, H., & Ni, W. (2018). Blockchain's adoption in IoT: The challenges, and a way forward. *Journal of Network and Computer Applications*.

Maroufi, M., Abdolee, R., & Tazekand, B. M. (2019). *On the convergence of blockchain and internet of things (iot) technologies.* arXiv preprint arXiv:1904.01936

Mazhanda, F. (2019). *How Blockchain and IoT Are Opening New Capabilities in the Construction Industry.* Retrieved from https://www.iotforall.com/iot-in-construction/

Mettler, M. (2016, September). Blockchain technology in healthcare: The revolution starts here. In 2016 IEEE 18th International Conference on e-Health Networking, Applications and Services (Healthcom) (pp. 1-3). IEEE.

Minoli, D., & Occhiogrosso, B. (2018). Blockchain mechanisms for IoT security. Internet of Things, 1-2, 1–13. doi:10.1016/j.iot.2018.05.002

Minoli, D., & Occhiogrosso, B. (2018). Blockchain mechanisms for IoT security. *Internet of Things, 1,* 1–13. doi:10.1016/j.iot.2018.05.002

Miorandi, D., Sicari, S., De Pellegrini, F., & Chlamtac, I. (2012). Internet of things: Vision, applications and research challenges. *Ad Hoc Networks, 10*(7), 1497–1516. doi:10.1016/j.adhoc.2012.02.016

Miraz, M. H. (2019). *Blockchain of Things (BCoT): The Fusion of Blockchain and IoT Technologies.* Cuhk Law.

Moubarak, J., Filiol, E., & Chamoun, M. (2018, April). On blockchain security and relevant attacks. In 2018 IEEE Middle East and North Africa Communications Conference (MENACOMM) (pp. 1-6). IEEE. doi:10.1109/MENACOMM.2018.8371010

Muhammad, S., Aziz, M., Charles, K., Kevin, H., & Laurent, N. (2018). Countering double spending in next-generation blockchains. IEEE ICC 2018.

Murthy, D. N., & Kumar, B. V. (2015). Internet of things (IoT): Is IoT a disruptive technology or a disruptive business model? *Indian Journal of Marketing, 45*(8), 18–27. doi:10.17010/ijom/2015/v45/i8/79915

Myllylahti, M. (2014). Newspaper paywalls–the hype and the reality. *Digit. Journal., 2*(2), 179–194. doi:10.1080/21670811.2013.813214

Nadeem, S., Rizwan, M., Ahmad, F., & Manzoor, J. (2019). Securing Cognitive Radio Vehicular Ad Hoc Network with Fog Node based Distributed Blockchain Cloud Architecture. *International Journal of Advanced Computer Science and Applications, 10*(1), 288–295. doi:10.14569/IJACSA.2019.0100138

Nagaraj, K., & Maguire, E. (2017). *Securing the Chain.* KPMG International. https://assets.kpmg.com/content/dam/kpmg/xx/pdf/2017/05/securing-the-chain.pdf

Nagothu, D., Xu, R., Nikouei, S. Y., & Chen, Y. (2018, September). A microservice-enabled architecture for smart surveillance using blockchain technology. In *2018 IEEE International Smart Cities Conference (ISC2)* (pp. 1-4). IEEE. 10.1109/ISC2.2018.8656968

Nakamoto, S. (2008). *Bitcoin: A Peer to Peer electronic cash system*. https://bitcoin.org/bitcoin.pdf

Nakamoto, S. (2008). Bitcoin: A peer-to-peer electronic cash system. Retrieved from https://bitcoin.org/bitcoin.pdf

Nakamoto, S. (2008). Bitcoin: A Peer-to-Peer Electronoic Cash Aystem, 2008.

Nakamoto, S. (2008). *Bitcoin: A. Peer to Peer. Electronic cash system*. https://bitcoin.org/bitcoin.pdf

Nakamoto, S. (2019). *Bitcoin: A peer-to-peer electronic cash system*. Manubot.

Nikouei, S. Y., Xu, R., Nagothu, D., Chen, Y., Aved, A., & Blasch, E. (2018, September). Real-time index authentication for event-oriented surveillance video query using blockchain. In *2018 IEEE International Smart Cities Conference (ISC2)* (pp. 1-8). IEEE. 10.1109/ISC2.2018.8656668

Ning, H., & Hu, S. (2012). Technology classification, industry, and education for Future Internet of Things. *International Journal of Communication Systems*, *25*(9), 1230–1241. doi:10.1002/dac.2373

Niranjanamurthy, M., Nithya, B. N., & Jagannatha, S. (2018). Analysis of Blockchain technology: Pros, cons and SWOT. *Cluster Computing*, ●●●, 1–15.

Nunberg, G. (2012). *The advent of the internet*. Academic Press.

Ocheja, P., Flanagan, B., Ueda, H., & Ogata, H. (2019). *Managing lifelong learning records through blockchain*. Research and Practice in Technology Enhanced Learning. doi:10.118641039-019-0097-0

Osgood, R. (2016). The future of democracy: Blockchain voting. COMP116: Information Security, 1-21.

Otte, P., de Vos, M., & Pouwelse, J. (2017, Sept.). TrustChain: A Sybil-resistant scalable blockchain. *Future Generation Computer Systems*.

Paillisse, J., Subira, J., Lopez, L., Rodriguez-Natal, A., Ermagan, V., Maino, F., & Cabellos, A. (2019). *Distributed Access Control with Blockchain*. Academic Press.

Pal, K. (2019). Algorithmic Solutions for RFID Tag Anti-Collision Problem in Supply Chain Management. *Procedia Computer Science*, 929-934.

Pal, K. (2020). Information Sharing for Manufacturing Supply Chain Management Based on Blockchain Technology. In Cross-industry Use of Blockchain Technology and Opportunities for the Future. IGI Global.

Pal, K. (2020a). Ontology-Assisted Enterprise Information Systems Integration in Manufacturing Supply Chain. In Handbook of Research on Developments and Trends in Industrial and Material Engineering. IGI Global.

Pal, K., & Ul-Haque, A. (2020). Internet of Things and Blockchain Technology in Apparel Manufacturing Supply Chain Data Management. *Proceeding of 11th International Conference on Ambient Systems, Networks and Technologies (ANT-2020).*

Pal, K. (2017). Supply Chain Coordination Based on Web Services. In H. K. Chan, N. Subramanian, & M. D. Abdulrahman (Eds.), *Supply Chain Management in the Big Data Era* (pp. 137–171). IGI Global Publication. doi:10.4018/978-1-5225-0956-1.ch009

Panarello, A., Tapas, N., Merlino, G., Longo, F., & Puliafito, A. (2018). Blockchain and iot integration: A systematic survey. *Sensors (Basel), 18*(8), 2575.

Pappalardo, G., Di Matteo, T., Caldarelli, G., & Aste, T. (2018). Blockchain inefficiency in the bitcoin peers network. *EPJ Data Science, 7*(1), 30. doi:10.1140/epjds13688-018-0159-3

Park, S. J. (2009). An Analysis of GPU Parallel Computing. In *2009 DoD High Performance Computing Modernization Program Users Group Conference,* (pp. 365-369). IEEE. doi: 10.1109/HPCMP-UGC.2009.59

Perugini, S. (2018). The design of an emerging/multi-paradigm programming languages course. *Journal of Computing Sciences in Colleges, 34*(1), 52–59.

Pieroni, A., Scarpato, N., Di Nunzio, L., Fallucchi, F., & Raso, M. (2018). Smarter city: Smart energy grid based on blockchain technology. *Int. J. Adv. Sci. Eng. Inf. Technol, 8*(1), 298–306. doi:10.18517/ijaseit.8.1.4954

Pilkington. (2016). Blockchain technology: Principle and applications. *Research Handbook on Digital Transformations.*

Pilkington, M. (2016). *Blockchain technology: Principle and applications.* Research Handbook on Digital Transformations.

Pongle, P., & Chavan, G. (2015, January). A survey: Attacks on RPL and 6LoWPAN in IoT. In *2015 International conference on pervasive computing (ICPC)* (pp. 1-6). IEEE. 10.1109/PERVASIVE.2015.7087034

Poon, J., & Dryja, T. (2016). *The bitcoin lightning network: Scalable off-chain instant payments.* Academic Press.

Porter, M. E., & Heppelmann, J. E. (2014). How smart, connected products are transforming competition. *Harvard Business Review, 92*(11), 64–88.

Pustišeka. (2018). Approaches to Front-End IoT Application Development for the Ethereum Blockchain. *Procedia Computer Science, 129*, 410–419.

Queiroz, M. M., & Wamba, S. F. (2019). Blockchain adoption challenges in supply chain: An empirical investigation of the main drivers in India and the USA. *International Journal of Information Management*, *46*, 70–82. doi:10.1016/j.ijinfomgt.2018.11.021

Rampton, J. (n.d.). *5 applications for blockchain in your business*. The Economist. https://execed.economist.com/blog/industry-trends/5-applications-blockchain-your-business

Rathee, G., Sharma, A., Kumar, R., & Iqbal, R. (2019). A Secure Communicating Things Network Framework for Industrial IoT using Blockchain Technology. *Ad Hoc Networks*, *94*, 94. doi:10.1016/j.adhoc.2019.101933

Ray, P. P., Dash, D., Salah, K., & Kumar, N. (2020). Blockchain for IoT-Based Healthcare: Background, Consensus, Platforms, and Use Cases. *IEEE Systems Journal*, 1–10. doi:10.1109/JSYST.2020.2963840

Reiff, N. (2020). Blockchain Explained. *Investopedia*. https://www.investopedia.com/terms/b/blockchain.asp

Rejeb, A. (2018). Blockchain Potential in Tilapia Supply Chain in Ghana. *Acta Tech. Jaurinensis*, *11*(2), 104–118. doi:10.14513/actatechjaur.v11.n2.462

Rejeb, A., Keogh, J. G., & Treiblmaier, H. (2019). Leveraging the Internet of Things and Blockchain Technology in Supply Chain Management. *Future Internet*, *11*(7), 161. doi:10.3390/fi11070161

Report, S. (2015). *Reference Architecture Model Industrie 4.0 (RAMI4.0), VDI/VDE Society Measurement and Automatic Control*. www.vdi.de/fileadmin/vdi_de/redakteur_dateien/gma_dateien/5305_Publikation_GMA_Status_Report_ZVEI_Reference_Architecture_Model.pdf

Reyna, A., Martín, C., Chen, J., Soler, E., & Díaz, M. (2018). On blockchain and its integration with IoT. Challenges and opportunities. *Future Generation Computer Systems*, *88*, 173–190. doi:10.1016/j.future.2018.05.046

Rifi, N., Agoulmine, N., Chendeb Taher, N., & Rachkidi, E. (2018). Blockchain technology: Is it a good candidate for securing iot sensitive medical data? *Wireless Communications and Mobile Computing*, *2018*, 2018. doi:10.1155/2018/9763937

Rivera, J., & van der Meulen, R. (2014). *Forecast alert: Internet of things—endpoints and associated services*. Technical Rreport.

Romero-Laorden, D., Villazón-Terrazas, J., Martinez-Graullera, O., Ibanez, A., Parrilla, M., & Penas, M. S. (2016). Analysis of parallel computing strategies to accelerate ultrasound imaging processes. *IEEE Transactions on Parallel and Distributed Systems*, *27*(12), 3429–3440. doi:10.1109/TPDS.2016.2544312

Rosic, A. (2017). *17 Blockchain Applications That Are Transforming Society*. Blockgeeks. https://blockgeeks.com/guides/blockchain-applications/

Ryu, Sharma, Jo, & Park. (2019). *A blockchain-based decentralized efcient investigation framework for IoT digital forensics*. Springer Science+Business Media, LLC.

Sahai, A., & Waters, B. (2005). Fuzzy identity-based encryption. In *Annual International Conference on the Theory and Applications of Cryptographic Techniques*. Springer.

Schiltz, M. (2018). Science without publication paywalls: cOAlition S for the realisation of full and immediate open access. *PLoS Medicine, 15*(9), e1002663. doi:10.1371/journal.pmed.1002663 PMID:30178782

Security, X. (2019). *Next-Generation Industrial Cybersecurity Introduces Hierarchical-Tree and Conditional Consensus in Blockchain for the First Time.* https://www. globenewswire.com/news-release/2019/10/10/1928089/0/ en/Xage-Security-Reveals-New-Blockchain-Innovation-to-Protect-Trillions-of-Industrial-Devices-and-Interactions.html

Shahzad. (2019). Trustworthy Electronic Voting Using Adjusted Blockchain Technology. *IEEE Access: Practical Innovations, Open Solutions, 7*, 24477–24488.

Sharma, P. K., Singh, S., Jeong, Y. S., & Park, J. H. (2017). DistBlockNet: A Distributed Blockchains-Based Secure SDN Architecture for IoT Networks. *IEEE Communication Management, 55*(9), 78–85. doi:10.1109/MCOM.2017.1700041

Shen, B., Guo, J., & Yang, Y. (2019). MedChain: Efficient healthcare data sharing via blockchain. *Applied Sciences (Basel, Switzerland), 9*(6), 1207. doi:10.3390/app9061207

Shih, W. C., Tseng, S. S., & Yang, C. T. (2010). Performance study of parallel programming on cloud computing environments using mapreduce. In *2010 International Conference on Information Science and Applications* (pp. 1-8). IEEE. 10.1109/ICISA.2010.5480515

Shrestha, R., & Kim, S. (2019). Integration of IoT with blockchain and homomorphic encryption: Challenging issues and opportunities. Role of Blockchain Technology in IoT Applications, 115, 293–331. doi:10.1016/bs.adcom.2019.06.002

Shrouf, F., Ordieres, J., & Miragliotta, G. (2014). Smart factories in Industry 4.0: A review of the concept and of energy management approached in production based on the Internet of Things paradigm. *Proceedings of the IEEE International Conference on Industrial Engineering and Engineering Management*, 679–701. 10.1109/IEEM.2014.7058728

Singh, M., & Kim, S. (2017). *Intelligent vehicle-trust point: Reward based intelligent vehicle communication using blockchain.* arXiv preprint arXiv:1707.07442

Singh, S., & Singh, N. (2016). Blockchain: Future of financial and cyber security. In *2016 2nd International Conference on Contemporary Computing and Informatics (IC3I)* (pp. 463-467). IEEE.

Stahel, P. F., & Moore, E. E. (2014). Peer review for biomedical publications: We can improve the system. *BMC Medicine, 12*(1), 179. doi:10.118612916-014-0179-1 PMID:25270270

Sukhodolskiy, I., & Zapechnikov, S. (2018). A blockchain-based access control system for cloud storage. In *2018 IEEE Conference of Russian Young Researchers in Electrical and Electronic Engineering (EIConRus)* (pp. 1575-1578). IEEE. 10.1109/EIConRus.2018.8317400

Swan. (2015). *Blockchain Blue Print for a new economy.* O'Reilly Media.

Szabo, N. (1994). *Smart Contracts*. Available online: https://archive.is/zQ1p8

Tan, L., & Wang, N. (2010, August). Future internet: The internet of things. In *2010 3rd international conference on advanced computer theory and engineering (ICACTE)* (Vol. 5, pp. V5-376). IEEE.

Tapscott & Tapscott. (2016). *Blockchain Revolution: How the Technology Behind Bitcoin Is Changing Money, Business, and the World*. Penguin Random House.

Teplitskiy, M., Lu, G., & Duede, E. (2017). Amplifying the impact of open access: Wikipedia and the diffusion of science. *Journal of the Association for Information Science and Technology*, *68*(9), 2116–2127. doi:10.1002/asi.23687

Tse, D., Zhang, B., Yang, Y., Cheng, C., & My, H. (2017). Blockchain application in food supply information security. *Proceedings of the IEEE International Conference on Industrial Engineering and Engineering Management (IEEM 2017)*, 1357–1361. 10.1109/IEEM.2017.8290114

Tssandor (.2019). Retrieved 24 July 2019, from https://steemit.com/blockchain/@tssandor/a-gentle-introduction-to-blockchain-scalability-part-i

Turkanovic. (2018, January 5). EduCTX: A Blockchain-Based Higher Education Credit Platform. *IEEE Access: Practical Innovations, Open Solutions*, 5112–5127.

Tzounis, A., Katsoulas, N., Bartzanas, T., & Kittas, C. (2017). Internet of things in agriculture, recent advances and future challenges. *Biosystems Engineering*, *164*, 31–48. doi:10.1016/j.biosystemseng.2017.09.007

Uddin, M. A., Stranieri, A., Gondal, I., & Balasubramanian, V. (2020). Blockchain Leveraged Decentralized IoT eHealth Framework. *Internet of Things*.

van Rossum, J. (2017). *Blockchain for Research - Perspectives on a New Paradigm for Scholarly Communication. Technical report*. Digital Science. doi:10.6084/m9.figshare.5607778

Vujičić, D., Jagodić, D., & Ranđić, S. (2018). *Blockchain technology, bitcoin, and Ethereum: A brief overview. In 2018 17th International Symposium Infoteh-Jahorina (INFOTEH)*. IEEE., doi:10.1109/INFOTEH.2018.8345547.

Waller, M. A., & Fawcett, S. E. (2013). Data science, predictive analytics, and big data: A revolution that will transform supply chain design and management. *Journal of Business Logistics*, *34*(2), 77–84. doi:10.1111/jbl.12010

Wang, Q., Qin, B., Hu, J., & Xiao, F. (2017, Sept.). Preserving transaction privacy in bitcoin. *Future Generation Computer Systems*.

Wang, B., Sun, J., He, Y., Pang, D., & Lu, N. (2018). Large-scale Election Based On Blockchain. *Procedia Computer Science*, *129*, 234–237. doi:10.1016/j.procs.2018.03.063

Wang, K., Kulkarni, A., Lang, M., Arnold, D., & Raicu, I. (2015). Exploring the design tradeoffs for extreme-scale high-performance computing system software. *IEEE Transactions on Parallel and Distributed Systems*, *27*(4), 1070–1084. doi:10.1109/TPDS.2015.2430852

Wang, S. J., Liu, S. F., & Wang, W. L. (2008). The simulated impact of RFID-enabled supply chain on pull-based inventory replenishment in TFT-LCD industry. *International Journal of Production Economics*, *112*(2), 570–586. doi:10.1016/j.ijpe.2007.05.002

Wang, S., Zhang, Y., & Zhang, Y. (2018). A blockchain-based framework for data sharing with fine-grained access control in decentralized storage systems. *IEEE Access: Practical Innovations, Open Solutions*, *6*, 38437–38450. doi:10.1109/ACCESS.2018.2851611

Wan, J., Li, J., Imran, M., Li, D., & Fazal-e-Amin. (2019). A blockchain-based solution for enhancing security and privacy in smart factory. *IEEE Transactions on Industrial Informatics*, *15*(6), 3652–3660. doi:10.1109/TII.2019.2894573

Washington, L. C. (2008). *Elliptic Curves: Number Theory and Cryptography* (2nd ed.). Chapman & Hall/CRC. doi:10.1201/9781420071474

Weyrich, M., & Ebert, C. (2015). Reference architectures for the internet of things. *IEEE Software*, *33*(1), 112–116. doi:10.1109/MS.2016.20

Witkowski, K. (2017). Internet of Things, Big Data, Industry 4.0 - Innovative Solutions in Logistics and Supply Chains Management. *Procedia Engineering*, *2017*(182), 763–769. doi:10.1016/j.proeng.2017.03.197

Wolf, M., Wiegand, M., & Drichel, A. (2016). *PEvO (Publish and Evaluate Onchain)*. Available online at: https://pevo.science/files/pevo_whitepaper.pdf

Wortner, P., Schubotz, M., Breitinger, C., Leible, S., & Gipp, B. (2019). Securing the integrity of time series data in open science projects using blockchain-based trusted timestamping. *Proceedings of the Workshop on Web Archiving and Digital Libraries (WADL '19)*, 1–3.

Wuille, P. (2019). Segregated-witness-and-its-impact-on-scalability. Retrieved 24 July 2019, from https://diyhpl.us/wiki/transcripts/scalingbitcoin/hong-kong/segregated-witness-and-its-impact-on-scalability/

Wüst, K., & Gervais, A. (2018, June). Do you need a blockchain? In *2018 Crypto Valley Conference on Blockchain Technology (CVCBT)* (pp. 45-54). IEEE. 10.1109/CVCBT.2018.00011

Xu, R., Chen, Y., Blasch, E., & Chen, G. (2018). Blendcac: A blockchain-enabled decentralized capability-based access control for iots. In *2018 IEEE International Conference on Internet of Things (iThings) and IEEE Green Computing and Communications (GreenCom) and IEEE Cyber, Physical and Social Computing (CPSCom) and IEEE Smart Data (SmartData)* (pp. 1027-1034). IEEE. 10.1109/Cybermatics_2018.2018.00191

Xu, R., Nikouei, S. Y., Chen, Y., Blasch, E., & Aved, A. (2019, July). Blendmas: A blockchain-enabled decentralized microservices architecture for smart public safety. In *2019 IEEE International Conference on Blockchain (Blockchain)* (pp. 564-571). IEEE. 10.1109/Blockchain.2019.00082

Xu, Y., Ren, J., Wang, G., Zhang, C., Yang, J., & Zhang, Y. (2019). A blockchain-based nonrepudiation network computing service scheme for industrial IoT. *IEEE Transactions on Industrial Informatics*, *15*(6), 3632–3641. doi:10.1109/TII.2019.2897133

Yan-e, D. (2011). Design of intelligent agriculture management information system based on IoT. *Proceedings of the 2011 Fourth International Conference on Intelligent Computation Technology and Automation*, 1, 1045–1049. 10.1109/ICICTA.2011.262

Yin, W., Wen, Q., Li, W., Zhang, H., & Jin, Z. (2018). An Anti-Quantum Transaction Authentication Approach in Blockchain. *IEEE Access: Practical Innovations, Open Solutions*, 6, 5393–5401. doi:10.1109/ACCESS.2017.2788411

Yli-Huumo, J., Ko, D., Choi, S., Park, S., & Smolander, K. (2016). Where is current research on blockchain technology?—A systematic review. *PLoS One*, 11(10), e0163477. doi:10.1371/journal.pone.0163477 PubMed

Yuan, Y., & Wang, F. Y. (2016, November). Towards blockchain-based intelligent transportation systems. In *2016 IEEE 19th International Conference on Intelligent Transportation Systems (ITSC)* (pp. 2663-2668). IEEE. 10.1109/ITSC.2016.7795984

Yu, Y., Li, Y., Tian, J., & Liu, J. (2018). Blockchain-based solutions to security and privacy issues in the Internet of Things. *IEEE Wireless Communications*, 25(6), 12–18. doi:10.1109/MWC.2017.1800116

Zhang, Y., Wu, S., Jin, B., & Du, J. (2017). A blockchain-based process provenance for cloud forensics. In *2017 3rd IEEE International Conference on Computer and Communications (ICCC)* (pp. 2470-2473). IEEE. 10.1109/CompComm.2017.8322979

Zhang, Y., & Wen, J. (2015). *An IoT electric business model based on the protocol of bitcoin. In ICIN*. IEEE.

Zhao, S., Li, S., & Yao, Y. (2019). Blockchain enabled industrial Internet of Things technology. *IEEE Transactions on Computational Social Systems*, 6(6), 1442–1453. doi:10.1109/TCSS.2019.2924054

Zheng, Z., Xie, S., Dai, H., Chen, X., & Wang, H. (2017). An overview of blockchain technology: Architecture, consensus and future trends. *IEEE International Congress on Big Data (Big Data Congress)*.

Zheng, Z., Xie, S., Dai, H., Chen, X., & Wang, H. (2017). An Overview of Blockchain Technology: Architecture, Consensus, and Future Trends. *2017 IEEE International Congress on Big Data (BigData Congress)*, 557–564.

Zheng, Z., Xie, S., Dai, H., Chen, X., & Wang, H. (2017, June). An overview of blockchain technology: Architecture, consensus, and future trends. In 2017 IEEE International Congress on Big Data (BigData Congress) (pp. 557-564). IEEE. doi:10.1109/BigDataCongress.2017.85

Zheng, Z., Xie, S., Dai, H., Chen, X., & Wang, H. (2017). An overview of blockchain technology: Architecture, consensus, and future trends. In *2017 IEEE International Congress on Big Data (BigData Congress)* (pp. 557-564). IEEE. 10.1109/BigDataCongress.2017.85

Zheng, Z., Xie, S., Dai, H., Chen, X., & Wang, H. (2017). *An overview of blockchain technology: Architecture, consensus, and future trends. In Big Data (Big DataCongress)*. IEEE International.

Zhou, Z. (2012). Applying RFID to reduce bullwhip effect in a FMCG supply chain. In *Proceedings of the Advances in Computational Environment Science* (pp. 193-199). Springer.

Zhou, L., Wang, L., Sun, Y., & Lv, P. (2018). BeeKeeper: A Blockchain-Based IoT System With Secure Storage and Homomorphic Computation. *IEEE Access: Practical Innovations, Open Solutions*, 6, 43472–43488. doi:10.1109/ACCESS.2018.2847632

Zhou, Y., Han, M., Liu, L., Wang, Y., Liang, Y., & Tian, L. (2018). Improving IoT Services in Smart-Home Using Blockchain Smart Contract. *IEEE International Conference on Internet of Things (iThings) and IEEE Green Computing and Communications (GreenCom) and IEEE Cyber, Physical and Social Computing (CPSCom) and IEEE Smart Data (SmartData)*, 81-87. 10.1109/Cybermatics_2018.2018.00047

Ziegeldorf, J. H., Matzutt, R., Henze, M., Grossmann, F., & Wehrle, K. (2018). Secure and anonymous decentralized Bitcoin mixing. *Future Generation Computer Systems*, 80, 448–466. doi:10.1016/j.future.2016.05.018

Related References

To continue our tradition of advancing information science and technology research, we have compiled a list of recommended IGI Global readings. These references will provide additional information and guidance to further enrich your knowledge and assist you with your own research and future publications.

Aasi, P., Rusu, L., & Vieru, D. (2017). The Role of Culture in IT Governance Five Focus Areas: A Literature Review. *International Journal of IT/Business Alignment and Governance, 8*(2), 42-61. doi:10.4018/IJITBAG.2017070103

Abdrabo, A. A. (2018). Egypt's Knowledge-Based Development: Opportunities, Challenges, and Future Possibilities. In A. Alraouf (Ed.), *Knowledge-Based Urban Development in the Middle East* (pp. 80–101). Hershey, PA: IGI Global. doi:10.4018/978-1-5225-3734-2.ch005

Abu Doush, I., & Alhami, I. (2018). Evaluating the Accessibility of Computer Laboratories, Libraries, and Websites in Jordanian Universities and Colleges. *International Journal of Information Systems and Social Change, 9*(2), 44–60. doi:10.4018/IJISSC.2018040104

Adeboye, A. (2016). Perceived Use and Acceptance of Cloud Enterprise Resource Planning (ERP) Implementation in the Manufacturing Industries. *International Journal of Strategic Information Technology and Applications, 7*(3), 24–40. doi:10.4018/IJSITA.2016070102

Adegbore, A. M., Quadri, M. O., & Oyewo, O. R. (2018). A Theoretical Approach to the Adoption of Electronic Resource Management Systems (ERMS) in Nigerian University Libraries. In A. Tella & T. Kwanya (Eds.), *Handbook of Research on Managing Intellectual Property in Digital Libraries* (pp. 292–311). Hershey, PA: IGI Global. doi:10.4018/978-1-5225-3093-0.ch015

Adhikari, M., & Roy, D. (2016). Green Computing. In G. Deka, G. Siddesh, K. Srinivasa, & L. Patnaik (Eds.), *Emerging Research Surrounding Power Consumption and Performance Issues in Utility Computing* (pp. 84–108). Hershey, PA: IGI Global. doi:10.4018/978-1-4666-8853-7.ch005

Afolabi, O. A. (2018). Myths and Challenges of Building an Effective Digital Library in Developing Nations: An African Perspective. In A. Tella & T. Kwanya (Eds.), *Handbook of Research on Managing Intellectual Property in Digital Libraries* (pp. 51–79). Hershey, PA: IGI Global. doi:10.4018/978-1-5225-3093-0.ch004

Agarwal, R., Singh, A., & Sen, S. (2016). Role of Molecular Docking in Computer-Aided Drug Design and Development. In S. Dastmalchi, M. Hamzeh-Mivehroud, & B. Sokouti (Eds.), *Applied Case Studies and Solutions in Molecular Docking-Based Drug Design* (pp. 1–28). Hershey, PA: IGI Global. doi:10.4018/978-1-5225-0362-0.ch001

Ali, O., & Soar, J. (2016). Technology Innovation Adoption Theories. In L. Al-Hakim, X. Wu, A. Koronios, & Y. Shou (Eds.), *Handbook of Research on Driving Competitive Advantage through Sustainable, Lean, and Disruptive Innovation* (pp. 1–38). Hershey, PA: IGI Global. doi:10.4018/978-1-5225-0135-0.ch001

Alsharo, M. (2017). Attitudes Towards Cloud Computing Adoption in Emerging Economies. *International Journal of Cloud Applications and Computing*, 7(3), 44–58. doi:10.4018/IJCAC.2017070102

Amer, T. S., & Johnson, T. L. (2016). Information Technology Progress Indicators: Temporal Expectancy, User Preference, and the Perception of Process Duration. *International Journal of Technology and Human Interaction*, 12(4), 1–14. doi:10.4018/IJTHI.2016100101

Amer, T. S., & Johnson, T. L. (2017). Information Technology Progress Indicators: Research Employing Psychological Frameworks. In A. Mesquita (Ed.), *Research Paradigms and Contemporary Perspectives on Human-Technology Interaction* (pp. 168–186). Hershey, PA: IGI Global. doi:10.4018/978-1-5225-1868-6.ch008

Anchugam, C. V., & Thangadurai, K. (2016). Introduction to Network Security. In D. G., M. Singh, & M. Jayanthi (Eds.), *Network Security Attacks and Countermeasures* (pp. 1-48). Hershey, PA: IGI Global. doi:10.4018/978-1-4666-8761-5.ch001

Anchugam, C. V., & Thangadurai, K. (2016). Classification of Network Attacks and Countermeasures of Different Attacks. In D. G., M. Singh, & M. Jayanthi (Eds.), *Network Security Attacks and Countermeasures* (pp. 115-156). Hershey, PA: IGI Global. doi:10.4018/978-1-4666-8761-5.ch004

Anohah, E. (2016). Pedagogy and Design of Online Learning Environment in Computer Science Education for High Schools. *International Journal of Online Pedagogy and Course Design*, *6*(3), 39–51. doi:10.4018/IJOPCD.2016070104

Anohah, E. (2017). Paradigm and Architecture of Computing Augmented Learning Management System for Computer Science Education. *International Journal of Online Pedagogy and Course Design*, *7*(2), 60–70. doi:10.4018/IJOPCD.2017040105

Anohah, E., & Suhonen, J. (2017). Trends of Mobile Learning in Computing Education from 2006 to 2014: A Systematic Review of Research Publications. *International Journal of Mobile and Blended Learning*, *9*(1), 16–33. doi:10.4018/IJMBL.2017010102

Assis-Hassid, S., Heart, T., Reychav, I., & Pliskin, J. S. (2016). Modelling Factors Affecting Patient-Doctor-Computer Communication in Primary Care. *International Journal of Reliable and Quality E-Healthcare*, *5*(1), 1–17. doi:10.4018/IJRQEH.2016010101

Bailey, E. K. (2017). Applying Learning Theories to Computer Technology Supported Instruction. In M. Grassetti & S. Brookby (Eds.), *Advancing Next-Generation Teacher Education through Digital Tools and Applications* (pp. 61–81). Hershey, PA: IGI Global. doi:10.4018/978-1-5225-0965-3.ch004

Balasubramanian, K. (2016). Attacks on Online Banking and Commerce. In K. Balasubramanian, K. Mala, & M. Rajakani (Eds.), *Cryptographic Solutions for Secure Online Banking and Commerce* (pp. 1–19). Hershey, PA: IGI Global. doi:10.4018/978-1-5225-0273-9.ch001

Baldwin, S., Opoku-Agyemang, K., & Roy, D. (2016). Games People Play: A Trilateral Collaboration Researching Computer Gaming across Cultures. In K. Valentine & L. Jensen (Eds.), *Examining the Evolution of Gaming and Its Impact on Social, Cultural, and Political Perspectives* (pp. 364–376). Hershey, PA: IGI Global. doi:10.4018/978-1-5225-0261-6.ch017

Banerjee, S., Sing, T. Y., Chowdhury, A. R., & Anwar, H. (2018). Let's Go Green: Towards a Taxonomy of Green Computing Enablers for Business Sustainability. In M. Khosrow-Pour (Ed.), *Green Computing Strategies for Competitive Advantage and Business Sustainability* (pp. 89–109). Hershey, PA: IGI Global. doi:10.4018/978-1-5225-5017-4.ch005

Basham, R. (2018). Information Science and Technology in Crisis Response and Management. In M. Khosrow-Pour, D.B.A. (Ed.), Encyclopedia of Information Science and Technology, Fourth Edition (pp. 1407-1418). Hershey, PA: IGI Global. doi:10.4018/978-1-5225-2255-3.ch121

Batyashe, T., & Iyamu, T. (2018). Architectural Framework for the Implementation of Information Technology Governance in Organisations. In M. Khosrow-Pour, D.B.A. (Ed.), Encyclopedia of Information Science and Technology, Fourth Edition (pp. 810-819). Hershey, PA: IGI Global. doi:10.4018/978-1-5225-2255-3.ch070

Bekleyen, N., & Çelik, S. (2017). Attitudes of Adult EFL Learners towards Preparing for a Language Test via CALL. In D. Tafazoli & M. Romero (Eds.), *Multiculturalism and Technology-Enhanced Language Learning* (pp. 214–229). Hershey, PA: IGI Global. doi:10.4018/978-1-5225-1882-2.ch013

Bennett, A., Eglash, R., Lachney, M., & Babbitt, W. (2016). Design Agency: Diversifying Computer Science at the Intersections of Creativity and Culture. In M. Raisinghani (Ed.), *Revolutionizing Education through Web-Based Instruction* (pp. 35–56). Hershey, PA: IGI Global. doi:10.4018/978-1-4666-9932-8.ch003

Bergeron, F., Croteau, A., Uwizeyemungu, S., & Raymond, L. (2017). A Framework for Research on Information Technology Governance in SMEs. In S. De Haes & W. Van Grembergen (Eds.), *Strategic IT Governance and Alignment in Business Settings* (pp. 53–81). Hershey, PA: IGI Global. doi:10.4018/978-1-5225-0861-8.ch003

Bhatt, G. D., Wang, Z., & Rodger, J. A. (2017). Information Systems Capabilities and Their Effects on Competitive Advantages: A Study of Chinese Companies. *Information Resources Management Journal*, 30(3), 41–57. doi:10.4018/IRMJ.2017070103

Bogdanoski, M., Stoilkovski, M., & Risteski, A. (2016). Novel First Responder Digital Forensics Tool as a Support to Law Enforcement. In M. Hadji-Janev & M. Bogdanoski (Eds.), *Handbook of Research on Civil Society and National Security in the Era of Cyber Warfare* (pp. 352–376). Hershey, PA: IGI Global. doi:10.4018/978-1-4666-8793-6.ch016

Boontarig, W., Papasratorn, B., & Chutimaskul, W. (2016). The Unified Model for Acceptance and Use of Health Information on Online Social Networks: Evidence from Thailand. *International Journal of E-Health and Medical Communications*, 7(1), 31–47. doi:10.4018/IJEHMC.2016010102

Brown, S., & Yuan, X. (2016). Techniques for Retaining Computer Science Students at Historical Black Colleges and Universities. In C. Prince & R. Ford (Eds.), *Setting a New Agenda for Student Engagement and Retention in Historically Black Colleges and Universities* (pp. 251–268). Hershey, PA: IGI Global. doi:10.4018/978-1-5225-0308-8.ch014

Burcoff, A., & Shamir, L. (2017). Computer Analysis of Pablo Picasso's Artistic Style. *International Journal of Art, Culture and Design Technologies*, 6(1), 1–18. doi:10.4018/IJACDT.2017010101

Byker, E. J. (2017). I Play I Learn: Introducing Technological Play Theory. In C. Martin & D. Polly (Eds.), *Handbook of Research on Teacher Education and Professional Development* (pp. 297–306). Hershey, PA: IGI Global. doi:10.4018/978-1-5225-1067-3.ch016

Calongne, C. M., Stricker, A. G., Truman, B., & Arenas, F. J. (2017). Cognitive Apprenticeship and Computer Science Education in Cyberspace: Reimagining the Past. In A. Stricker, C. Calongne, B. Truman, & F. Arenas (Eds.), *Integrating an Awareness of Selfhood and Society into Virtual Learning* (pp. 180–197). Hershey, PA: IGI Global. doi:10.4018/978-1-5225-2182-2.ch013

Carlton, E. L., Holsinger, J. W. Jr, & Anunobi, N. (2016). Physician Engagement with Health Information Technology: Implications for Practice and Professionalism. *International Journal of Computers in Clinical Practice, 1*(2), 51–73. doi:10.4018/IJCCP.2016070103

Carneiro, A. D. (2017). Defending Information Networks in Cyberspace: Some Notes on Security Needs. In M. Dawson, D. Kisku, P. Gupta, J. Sing, & W. Li (Eds.), *Developing Next-Generation Countermeasures for Homeland Security Threat Prevention* (pp. 354-375). Hershey, PA: IGI Global. doi:10.4018/978-1-5225-0703-1.ch016

Cavalcanti, J. C. (2016). The New "ABC" of ICTs (Analytics + Big Data + Cloud Computing): A Complex Trade-Off between IT and CT Costs. In J. Martins & A. Molnar (Eds.), *Handbook of Research on Innovations in Information Retrieval, Analysis, and Management* (pp. 152–186). Hershey, PA: IGI Global. doi:10.4018/978-1-4666-8833-9.ch006

Chase, J. P., & Yan, Z. (2017). Affect in Statistics Cognition. In *Assessing and Measuring Statistics Cognition in Higher Education Online Environments: Emerging Research and Opportunities* (pp. 144–187). Hershey, PA: IGI Global. doi:10.4018/978-1-5225-2420-5.ch005

Chen, C. (2016). Effective Learning Strategies for the 21st Century: Implications for the E-Learning. In M. Anderson & C. Gavan (Eds.), *Developing Effective Educational Experiences through Learning Analytics* (pp. 143–169). Hershey, PA: IGI Global. doi:10.4018/978-1-4666-9983-0.ch006

Chen, E. T. (2016). Examining the Influence of Information Technology on Modern Health Care. In P. Manolitzas, E. Grigoroudis, N. Matsatsinis, & D. Yannacopoulos (Eds.), *Effective Methods for Modern Healthcare Service Quality and Evaluation* (pp. 110–136). Hershey, PA: IGI Global. doi:10.4018/978-1-4666-9961-8.ch006

Cimermanova, I. (2017). Computer-Assisted Learning in Slovakia. In D. Tafazoli & M. Romero (Eds.), *Multiculturalism and Technology-Enhanced Language Learning* (pp. 252–270). Hershey, PA: IGI Global. doi:10.4018/978-1-5225-1882-2.ch015

Cipolla-Ficarra, F. V., & Cipolla-Ficarra, M. (2018). Computer Animation for Ingenious Revival. In F. Cipolla-Ficarra, M. Ficarra, M. Cipolla-Ficarra, A. Quiroga, J. Alma, & J. Carré (Eds.), *Technology-Enhanced Human Interaction in Modern Society* (pp. 159–181). Hershey, PA: IGI Global. doi:10.4018/978-1-5225-3437-2.ch008

Cockrell, S., Damron, T. S., Melton, A. M., & Smith, A. D. (2018). Offshoring IT. In M. Khosrow-Pour, D.B.A. (Ed.), Encyclopedia of Information Science and Technology, Fourth Edition (pp. 5476-5489). Hershey, PA: IGI Global. doi:10.4018/978-1-5225-2255-3.ch476

Coffey, J. W. (2018). Logic and Proof in Computer Science: Categories and Limits of Proof Techniques. In J. Horne (Ed.), *Philosophical Perceptions on Logic and Order* (pp. 218–240). Hershey, PA: IGI Global. doi:10.4018/978-1-5225-2443-4.ch007

Dale, M. (2017). Re-Thinking the Challenges of Enterprise Architecture Implementation. In M. Tavana (Ed.), *Enterprise Information Systems and the Digitalization of Business Functions* (pp. 205–221). Hershey, PA: IGI Global. doi:10.4018/978-1-5225-2382-6.ch009

Das, A., Dasgupta, R., & Bagchi, A. (2016). Overview of Cellular Computing-Basic Principles and Applications. In J. Mandal, S. Mukhopadhyay, & T. Pal (Eds.), *Handbook of Research on Natural Computing for Optimization Problems* (pp. 637–662). Hershey, PA: IGI Global. doi:10.4018/978-1-5225-0058-2.ch026

De Maere, K., De Haes, S., & von Kutzschenbach, M. (2017). CIO Perspectives on Organizational Learning within the Context of IT Governance. *International Journal of IT/Business Alignment and Governance, 8*(1), 32-47. doi:10.4018/IJITBAG.2017010103

Demir, K., Çaka, C., Yaman, N. D., İslamoğlu, H., & Kuzu, A. (2018). Examining the Current Definitions of Computational Thinking. In H. Ozcinar, G. Wong, & H. Ozturk (Eds.), *Teaching Computational Thinking in Primary Education* (pp. 36–64). Hershey, PA: IGI Global. doi:10.4018/978-1-5225-3200-2.ch003

Deng, X., Hung, Y., & Lin, C. D. (2017). Design and Analysis of Computer Experiments. In S. Saha, A. Mandal, A. Narasimhamurthy, S. V, & S. Sangam (Eds.), Handbook of Research on Applied Cybernetics and Systems Science (pp. 264-279). Hershey, PA: IGI Global. doi:10.4018/978-1-5225-2498-4.ch013

Denner, J., Martinez, J., & Thiry, H. (2017). Strategies for Engaging Hispanic/Latino Youth in the US in Computer Science. In Y. Rankin & J. Thomas (Eds.), *Moving Students of Color from Consumers to Producers of Technology* (pp. 24–48). Hershey, PA: IGI Global. doi:10.4018/978-1-5225-2005-4.ch002

Devi, A. (2017). Cyber Crime and Cyber Security: A Quick Glance. In R. Kumar, P. Pattnaik, & P. Pandey (Eds.), *Detecting and Mitigating Robotic Cyber Security Risks* (pp. 160–171). Hershey, PA: IGI Global. doi:10.4018/978-1-5225-2154-9.ch011

Dores, A. R., Barbosa, F., Guerreiro, S., Almeida, I., & Carvalho, I. P. (2016). Computer-Based Neuropsychological Rehabilitation: Virtual Reality and Serious Games. In M. Cruz-Cunha, I. Miranda, R. Martinho, & R. Rijo (Eds.), *Encyclopedia of E-Health and Telemedicine* (pp. 473–485). Hershey, PA: IGI Global. doi:10.4018/978-1-4666-9978-6.ch037

Doshi, N., & Schaefer, G. (2016). Computer-Aided Analysis of Nailfold Capillaroscopy Images. In D. Fotiadis (Ed.), *Handbook of Research on Trends in the Diagnosis and Treatment of Chronic Conditions* (pp. 146–158). Hershey, PA: IGI Global. doi:10.4018/978-1-4666-8828-5.ch007

Doyle, D. J., & Fahy, P. J. (2018). Interactivity in Distance Education and Computer-Aided Learning, With Medical Education Examples. In M. Khosrow-Pour, D.B.A. (Ed.), Encyclopedia of Information Science and Technology, Fourth Edition (pp. 5829-5840). Hershey, PA: IGI Global. doi:10.4018/978-1-5225-2255-3.ch507

Elias, N. I., & Walker, T. W. (2017). Factors that Contribute to Continued Use of E-Training among Healthcare Professionals. In F. Topor (Ed.), *Handbook of Research on Individualism and Identity in the Globalized Digital Age* (pp. 403–429). Hershey, PA: IGI Global. doi:10.4018/978-1-5225-0522-8.ch018

Eloy, S., Dias, M. S., Lopes, P. F., & Vilar, E. (2016). Digital Technologies in Architecture and Engineering: Exploring an Engaged Interaction within Curricula. In D. Fonseca & E. Redondo (Eds.), *Handbook of Research on Applied E-Learning in Engineering and Architecture Education* (pp. 368–402). Hershey, PA: IGI Global. doi:10.4018/978-1-4666-8803-2.ch017

Estrela, V. V., Magalhães, H. A., & Saotome, O. (2016). Total Variation Applications in Computer Vision. In N. Kamila (Ed.), *Handbook of Research on Emerging Perspectives in Intelligent Pattern Recognition, Analysis, and Image Processing* (pp. 41–64). Hershey, PA: IGI Global. doi:10.4018/978-1-4666-8654-0.ch002

Filipovic, N., Radovic, M., Nikolic, D. D., Saveljic, I., Milosevic, Z., Exarchos, T. P., ... Parodi, O. (2016). Computer Predictive Model for Plaque Formation and Progression in the Artery. In D. Fotiadis (Ed.), *Handbook of Research on Trends in the Diagnosis and Treatment of Chronic Conditions* (pp. 279–300). Hershey, PA: IGI Global. doi:10.4018/978-1-4666-8828-5.ch013

Fisher, R. L. (2018). Computer-Assisted Indian Matrimonial Services. In M. Khosrow-Pour, D.B.A. (Ed.), Encyclopedia of Information Science and Technology, Fourth Edition (pp. 4136-4145). Hershey, PA: IGI Global. doi:10.4018/978-1-5225-2255-3.ch358

Fleenor, H. G., & Hodhod, R. (2016). Assessment of Learning and Technology: Computer Science Education. In V. Wang (Ed.), *Handbook of Research on Learning Outcomes and Opportunities in the Digital Age* (pp. 51–78). Hershey, PA: IGI Global. doi:10.4018/978-1-4666-9577-1.ch003

García-Valcárcel, A., & Mena, J. (2016). Information Technology as a Way To Support Collaborative Learning: What In-Service Teachers Think, Know and Do. *Journal of Information Technology Research*, 9(1), 1–17. doi:10.4018/JITR.2016010101

Gardner-McCune, C., & Jimenez, Y. (2017). Historical App Developers: Integrating CS into K-12 through Cross-Disciplinary Projects. In Y. Rankin & J. Thomas (Eds.), *Moving Students of Color from Consumers to Producers of Technology* (pp. 85–112). Hershey, PA: IGI Global. doi:10.4018/978-1-5225-2005-4.ch005

Garvey, G. P. (2016). Exploring Perception, Cognition, and Neural Pathways of Stereo Vision and the Split–Brain Human Computer Interface. In A. Ursyn (Ed.), *Knowledge Visualization and Visual Literacy in Science Education* (pp. 28–76). Hershey, PA: IGI Global. doi:10.4018/978-1-5225-0480-1.ch002

Ghafele, R., & Gibert, B. (2018). Open Growth: The Economic Impact of Open Source Software in the USA. In M. Khosrow-Pour (Ed.), *Optimizing Contemporary Application and Processes in Open Source Software* (pp. 164–197). Hershey, PA: IGI Global. doi:10.4018/978-1-5225-5314-4.ch007

Ghobakhloo, M., & Azar, A. (2018). Information Technology Resources, the Organizational Capability of Lean-Agile Manufacturing, and Business Performance. *Information Resources Management Journal*, 31(2), 47–74. doi:10.4018/IRMJ.2018040103

Gianni, M., & Gotzamani, K. (2016). Integrated Management Systems and Information Management Systems: Common Threads. In P. Papajorgji, F. Pinet, A. Guimarães, & J. Papathanasiou (Eds.), *Automated Enterprise Systems for Maximizing Business Performance* (pp. 195–214). Hershey, PA: IGI Global. doi:10.4018/978-1-4666-8841-4.ch011

Gikandi, J. W. (2017). Computer-Supported Collaborative Learning and Assessment: A Strategy for Developing Online Learning Communities in Continuing Education. In J. Keengwe & G. Onchwari (Eds.), *Handbook of Research on Learner-Centered Pedagogy in Teacher Education and Professional Development* (pp. 309–333). Hershey, PA: IGI Global. doi:10.4018/978-1-5225-0892-2.ch017

Gokhale, A. A., & Machina, K. F. (2017). Development of a Scale to Measure Attitudes toward Information Technology. In L. Tomei (Ed.), *Exploring the New Era of Technology-Infused Education* (pp. 49–64). Hershey, PA: IGI Global. doi:10.4018/978-1-5225-1709-2.ch004

Grace, A., O'Donoghue, J., Mahony, C., Heffernan, T., Molony, D., & Carroll, T. (2016). Computerized Decision Support Systems for Multimorbidity Care: An Urgent Call for Research and Development. In M. Cruz-Cunha, I. Miranda, R. Martinho, & R. Rijo (Eds.), *Encyclopedia of E-Health and Telemedicine* (pp. 486–494). Hershey, PA: IGI Global. doi:10.4018/978-1-4666-9978-6.ch038

Gupta, A., & Singh, O. (2016). Computer Aided Modeling and Finite Element Analysis of Human Elbow. *International Journal of Biomedical and Clinical Engineering*, *5*(1), 31–38. doi:10.4018/IJBCE.2016010104

H., S. K. (2016). Classification of Cybercrimes and Punishments under the Information Technology Act, 2000. In S. Geetha, & A. Phamila (Eds.), *Combating Security Breaches and Criminal Activity in the Digital Sphere* (pp. 57-66). Hershey, PA: IGI Global. doi:10.4018/978-1-5225-0193-0.ch004

Hafeez-Baig, A., Gururajan, R., & Wickramasinghe, N. (2017). Readiness as a Novel Construct of Readiness Acceptance Model (RAM) for the Wireless Handheld Technology. In N. Wickramasinghe (Ed.), *Handbook of Research on Healthcare Administration and Management* (pp. 578–595). Hershey, PA: IGI Global. doi:10.4018/978-1-5225-0920-2.ch035

Hanafizadeh, P., Ghandchi, S., & Asgarimehr, M. (2017). Impact of Information Technology on Lifestyle: A Literature Review and Classification. *International Journal of Virtual Communities and Social Networking*, *9*(2), 1–23. doi:10.4018/IJVCSN.2017040101

Harlow, D. B., Dwyer, H., Hansen, A. K., Hill, C., Iveland, A., Leak, A. E., & Franklin, D. M. (2016). Computer Programming in Elementary and Middle School: Connections across Content. In M. Urban & D. Falvo (Eds.), *Improving K-12 STEM Education Outcomes through Technological Integration* (pp. 337–361). Hershey, PA: IGI Global. doi:10.4018/978-1-4666-9616-7.ch015

Haseski, H. İ., Ilic, U., & Tuğtekin, U. (2018). Computational Thinking in Educational Digital Games: An Assessment Tool Proposal. In H. Ozcinar, G. Wong, & H. Ozturk (Eds.), *Teaching Computational Thinking in Primary Education* (pp. 256–287). Hershey, PA: IGI Global. doi:10.4018/978-1-5225-3200-2.ch013

Hee, W. J., Jalleh, G., Lai, H., & Lin, C. (2017). E-Commerce and IT Projects: Evaluation and Management Issues in Australian and Taiwanese Hospitals. *International Journal of Public Health Management and Ethics*, 2(1), 69–90. doi:10.4018/IJPHME.2017010104

Hernandez, A. A. (2017). Green Information Technology Usage: Awareness and Practices of Philippine IT Professionals. *International Journal of Enterprise Information Systems*, 13(4), 90–103. doi:10.4018/IJEIS.2017100106

Hernandez, A. A., & Ona, S. E. (2016). Green IT Adoption: Lessons from the Philippines Business Process Outsourcing Industry. *International Journal of Social Ecology and Sustainable Development*, 7(1), 1–34. doi:10.4018/IJSESD.2016010101

Hernandez, M. A., Marin, E. C., Garcia-Rodriguez, J., Azorin-Lopez, J., & Cazorla, M. (2017). Automatic Learning Improves Human-Robot Interaction in Productive Environments: A Review. *International Journal of Computer Vision and Image Processing*, 7(3), 65–75. doi:10.4018/IJCVIP.2017070106

Horne-Popp, L. M., Tessone, E. B., & Welker, J. (2018). If You Build It, They Will Come: Creating a Library Statistics Dashboard for Decision-Making. In L. Costello & M. Powers (Eds.), *Developing In-House Digital Tools in Library Spaces* (pp. 177–203). Hershey, PA: IGI Global. doi:10.4018/978-1-5225-2676-6.ch009

Hossan, C. G., & Ryan, J. C. (2016). Factors Affecting e-Government Technology Adoption Behaviour in a Voluntary Environment. *International Journal of Electronic Government Research*, 12(1), 24–49. doi:10.4018/IJEGR.2016010102

Hu, H., Hu, P. J., & Al-Gahtani, S. S. (2017). User Acceptance of Computer Technology at Work in Arabian Culture: A Model Comparison Approach. In M. Khosrow-Pour (Ed.), *Handbook of Research on Technology Adoption, Social Policy, and Global Integration* (pp. 205–228). Hershey, PA: IGI Global. doi:10.4018/978-1-5225-2668-1.ch011

Huie, C. P. (2016). Perceptions of Business Intelligence Professionals about Factors Related to Business Intelligence input in Decision Making. *International Journal of Business Analytics*, *3*(3), 1–24. doi:10.4018/IJBAN.2016070101

Hung, S., Huang, W., Yen, D. C., Chang, S., & Lu, C. (2016). Effect of Information Service Competence and Contextual Factors on the Effectiveness of Strategic Information Systems Planning in Hospitals. *Journal of Global Information Management*, *24*(1), 14–36. doi:10.4018/JGIM.2016010102

Ifinedo, P. (2017). Using an Extended Theory of Planned Behavior to Study Nurses' Adoption of Healthcare Information Systems in Nova Scotia. *International Journal of Technology Diffusion*, *8*(1), 1–17. doi:10.4018/IJTD.2017010101

Ilie, V., & Sneha, S. (2018). A Three Country Study for Understanding Physicians' Engagement With Electronic Information Resources Pre and Post System Implementation. *Journal of Global Information Management*, *26*(2), 48–73. doi:10.4018/JGIM.2018040103

Inoue-Smith, Y. (2017). Perceived Ease in Using Technology Predicts Teacher Candidates' Preferences for Online Resources. *International Journal of Online Pedagogy and Course Design*, *7*(3), 17–28. doi:10.4018/IJOPCD.2017070102

Islam, A. A. (2016). Development and Validation of the Technology Adoption and Gratification (TAG) Model in Higher Education: A Cross-Cultural Study Between Malaysia and China. *International Journal of Technology and Human Interaction*, *12*(3), 78–105. doi:10.4018/IJTHI.2016070106

Islam, A. Y. (2017). Technology Satisfaction in an Academic Context: Moderating Effect of Gender. In A. Mesquita (Ed.), *Research Paradigms and Contemporary Perspectives on Human-Technology Interaction* (pp. 187–211). Hershey, PA: IGI Global. doi:10.4018/978-1-5225-1868-6.ch009

Jamil, G. L., & Jamil, C. C. (2017). Information and Knowledge Management Perspective Contributions for Fashion Studies: Observing Logistics and Supply Chain Management Processes. In G. Jamil, A. Soares, & C. Pessoa (Eds.), *Handbook of Research on Information Management for Effective Logistics and Supply Chains* (pp. 199–221). Hershey, PA: IGI Global. doi:10.4018/978-1-5225-0973-8.ch011

Jamil, G. L., Jamil, L. C., Vieira, A. A., & Xavier, A. J. (2016). Challenges in Modelling Healthcare Services: A Study Case of Information Architecture Perspectives. In G. Jamil, J. Poças Rascão, F. Ribeiro, & A. Malheiro da Silva (Eds.), *Handbook of Research on Information Architecture and Management in Modern Organizations* (pp. 1–23). Hershey, PA: IGI Global. doi:10.4018/978-1-4666-8637-3.ch001

Janakova, M. (2018). Big Data and Simulations for the Solution of Controversies in Small Businesses. In M. Khosrow-Pour, D.B.A. (Ed.), Encyclopedia of Information Science and Technology, Fourth Edition (pp. 6907-6915). Hershey, PA: IGI Global. doi:10.4018/978-1-5225-2255-3.ch598

Jha, D. G. (2016). Preparing for Information Technology Driven Changes. In S. Tiwari & L. Nafees (Eds.), *Innovative Management Education Pedagogies for Preparing Next-Generation Leaders* (pp. 258–274). Hershey, PA: IGI Global. doi:10.4018/978-1-4666-9691-4.ch015

Jhawar, A., & Garg, S. K. (2018). Logistics Improvement by Investment in Information Technology Using System Dynamics. In A. Azar & S. Vaidyanathan (Eds.), *Advances in System Dynamics and Control* (pp. 528–567). Hershey, PA: IGI Global. doi:10.4018/978-1-5225-4077-9.ch017

Kalelioğlu, F., Gülbahar, Y., & Doğan, D. (2018). Teaching How to Think Like a Programmer: Emerging Insights. In H. Ozcinar, G. Wong, & H. Ozturk (Eds.), *Teaching Computational Thinking in Primary Education* (pp. 18–35). Hershey, PA: IGI Global. doi:10.4018/978-1-5225-3200-2.ch002

Kamberi, S. (2017). A Girls-Only Online Virtual World Environment and its Implications for Game-Based Learning. In A. Stricker, C. Calongne, B. Truman, & F. Arenas (Eds.), *Integrating an Awareness of Selfhood and Society into Virtual Learning* (pp. 74–95). Hershey, PA: IGI Global. doi:10.4018/978-1-5225-2182-2.ch006

Kamel, S., & Rizk, N. (2017). ICT Strategy Development: From Design to Implementation – Case of Egypt. In C. Howard & K. Hargiss (Eds.), *Strategic Information Systems and Technologies in Modern Organizations* (pp. 239–257). Hershey, PA: IGI Global. doi:10.4018/978-1-5225-1680-4.ch010

Kamel, S. H. (2018). The Potential Role of the Software Industry in Supporting Economic Development. In M. Khosrow-Pour, D.B.A. (Ed.), Encyclopedia of Information Science and Technology, Fourth Edition (pp. 7259-7269). Hershey, PA: IGI Global. doi:10.4018/978-1-5225-2255-3.ch631

Karon, R. (2016). Utilisation of Health Information Systems for Service Delivery in the Namibian Environment. In T. Iyamu & A. Tatnall (Eds.), *Maximizing Healthcare Delivery and Management through Technology Integration* (pp. 169–183). Hershey, PA: IGI Global. doi:10.4018/978-1-4666-9446-0.ch011

Kawata, S. (2018). Computer-Assisted Parallel Program Generation. In M. Khosrow-Pour, D.B.A. (Ed.), Encyclopedia of Information Science and Technology, Fourth Edition (pp. 4583-4593). Hershey, PA: IGI Global. doi:10.4018/978-1-5225-2255-3. ch398

Khanam, S., Siddiqui, J., & Talib, F. (2016). A DEMATEL Approach for Prioritizing the TQM Enablers and IT Resources in the Indian ICT Industry. *International Journal of Applied Management Sciences and Engineering, 3*(1), 11–29. doi:10.4018/IJAMSE.2016010102

Khari, M., Shrivastava, G., Gupta, S., & Gupta, R. (2017). Role of Cyber Security in Today's Scenario. In R. Kumar, P. Pattnaik, & P. Pandey (Eds.), *Detecting and Mitigating Robotic Cyber Security Risks* (pp. 177–191). Hershey, PA: IGI Global. doi:10.4018/978-1-5225-2154-9.ch013

Khouja, M., Rodriguez, I. B., Ben Halima, Y., & Moalla, S. (2018). IT Governance in Higher Education Institutions: A Systematic Literature Review. *International Journal of Human Capital and Information Technology Professionals, 9*(2), 52–67. doi:10.4018/IJHCITP.2018040104

Kim, S., Chang, M., Choi, N., Park, J., & Kim, H. (2016). The Direct and Indirect Effects of Computer Uses on Student Success in Math. *International Journal of Cyber Behavior, Psychology and Learning, 6*(3), 48–64. doi:10.4018/IJCBPL.2016070104

Kiourt, C., Pavlidis, G., Koutsoudis, A., & Kalles, D. (2017). Realistic Simulation of Cultural Heritage. *International Journal of Computational Methods in Heritage Science, 1*(1), 10–40. doi:10.4018/IJCMHS.2017010102

Korikov, A., & Krivtsov, O. (2016). System of People-Computer: On the Way of Creation of Human-Oriented Interface. In V. Mkrttchian, A. Bershadsky, A. Bozhday, M. Kataev, & S. Kataev (Eds.), *Handbook of Research on Estimation and Control Techniques in E-Learning Systems* (pp. 458–470). Hershey, PA: IGI Global. doi:10.4018/978-1-4666-9489-7.ch032

Köse, U. (2017). An Augmented-Reality-Based Intelligent Mobile Application for Open Computer Education. In G. Kurubacak & H. Altinpulluk (Eds.), *Mobile Technologies and Augmented Reality in Open Education* (pp. 154–174). Hershey, PA: IGI Global. doi:10.4018/978-1-5225-2110-5.ch008

Lahmiri, S. (2018). Information Technology Outsourcing Risk Factors and Provider Selection. In M. Gupta, R. Sharman, J. Walp, & P. Mulgund (Eds.), *Information Technology Risk Management and Compliance in Modern Organizations* (pp. 214–228). Hershey, PA: IGI Global. doi:10.4018/978-1-5225-2604-9.ch008

Landriscina, F. (2017). Computer-Supported Imagination: The Interplay Between Computer and Mental Simulation in Understanding Scientific Concepts. In I. Levin & D. Tsybulsky (Eds.), *Digital Tools and Solutions for Inquiry-Based STEM Learning* (pp. 33–60). Hershey, PA: IGI Global. doi:10.4018/978-1-5225-2525-7.ch002

Lau, S. K., Winley, G. K., Leung, N. K., Tsang, N., & Lau, S. Y. (2016). An Exploratory Study of Expectation in IT Skills in a Developing Nation: Vietnam. *Journal of Global Information Management*, *24*(1), 1–13. doi:10.4018/JGIM.2016010101

Lavranos, C., Kostagiolas, P., & Papadatos, J. (2016). Information Retrieval Technologies and the "Realities" of Music Information Seeking. In I. Deliyannis, P. Kostagiolas, & C. Banou (Eds.), *Experimental Multimedia Systems for Interactivity and Strategic Innovation* (pp. 102–121). Hershey, PA: IGI Global. doi:10.4018/978-1-4666-8659-5.ch005

Lee, W. W. (2018). Ethical Computing Continues From Problem to Solution. In M. Khosrow-Pour, D.B.A. (Ed.), Encyclopedia of Information Science and Technology, Fourth Edition (pp. 4884-4897). Hershey, PA: IGI Global. doi:10.4018/978-1-5225-2255-3.ch423

Lehto, M. (2016). Cyber Security Education and Research in the Finland's Universities and Universities of Applied Sciences. *International Journal of Cyber Warfare & Terrorism*, *6*(2), 15–31. doi:10.4018/IJCWT.2016040102

Lin, C., Jalleh, G., & Huang, Y. (2016). Evaluating and Managing Electronic Commerce and Outsourcing Projects in Hospitals. In A. Dwivedi (Ed.), *Reshaping Medical Practice and Care with Health Information Systems* (pp. 132–172). Hershey, PA: IGI Global. doi:10.4018/978-1-4666-9870-3.ch005

Lin, S., Chen, S., & Chuang, S. (2017). Perceived Innovation and Quick Response Codes in an Online-to-Offline E-Commerce Service Model. *International Journal of E-Adoption*, *9*(2), 1–16. doi:10.4018/IJEA.2017070101

Liu, M., Wang, Y., Xu, W., & Liu, L. (2017). Automated Scoring of Chinese Engineering Students' English Essays. *International Journal of Distance Education Technologies*, *15*(1), 52–68. doi:10.4018/IJDET.2017010104

Luciano, E. M., Wiedenhöft, G. C., Macadar, M. A., & Pinheiro dos Santos, F. (2016). Information Technology Governance Adoption: Understanding its Expectations Through the Lens of Organizational Citizenship. *International Journal of IT/Business Alignment and Governance, 7*(2), 22-32. doi:10.4018/IJITBAG.2016070102

Mabe, L. K., & Oladele, O. I. (2017). Application of Information Communication Technologies for Agricultural Development through Extension Services: A Review. In T. Tossy (Ed.), *Information Technology Integration for Socio-Economic Development* (pp. 52–101). Hershey, PA: IGI Global. doi:10.4018/978-1-5225-0539-6.ch003

Manogaran, G., Thota, C., & Lopez, D. (2018). Human-Computer Interaction With Big Data Analytics. In D. Lopez & M. Durai (Eds.), *HCI Challenges and Privacy Preservation in Big Data Security* (pp. 1–22). Hershey, PA: IGI Global. doi:10.4018/978-1-5225-2863-0.ch001

Margolis, J., Goode, J., & Flapan, J. (2017). A Critical Crossroads for Computer Science for All: "Identifying Talent" or "Building Talent," and What Difference Does It Make? In Y. Rankin & J. Thomas (Eds.), *Moving Students of Color from Consumers to Producers of Technology* (pp. 1–23). Hershey, PA: IGI Global. doi:10.4018/978-1-5225-2005-4.ch001

Mbale, J. (2018). Computer Centres Resource Cloud Elasticity-Scalability (CRECES): Copperbelt University Case Study. In S. Aljawarneh & M. Malhotra (Eds.), *Critical Research on Scalability and Security Issues in Virtual Cloud Environments* (pp. 48–70). Hershey, PA: IGI Global. doi:10.4018/978-1-5225-3029-9.ch003

McKee, J. (2018). The Right Information: The Key to Effective Business Planning. In *Business Architectures for Risk Assessment and Strategic Planning: Emerging Research and Opportunities* (pp. 38–52). Hershey, PA: IGI Global. doi:10.4018/978-1-5225-3392-4.ch003

Mensah, I. K., & Mi, J. (2018). Determinants of Intention to Use Local E-Government Services in Ghana: The Perspective of Local Government Workers. *International Journal of Technology Diffusion*, 9(2), 41–60. doi:10.4018/IJTD.2018040103

Mohamed, J. H. (2018). Scientograph-Based Visualization of Computer Forensics Research Literature. In J. Jeyasekar & P. Saravanan (Eds.), *Innovations in Measuring and Evaluating Scientific Information* (pp. 148–162). Hershey, PA: IGI Global. doi:10.4018/978-1-5225-3457-0.ch010

Moore, R. L., & Johnson, N. (2017). Earning a Seat at the Table: How IT Departments Can Partner in Organizational Change and Innovation. *International Journal of Knowledge-Based Organizations*, 7(2), 1–12. doi:10.4018/IJKBO.2017040101

Mtebe, J. S., & Kissaka, M. M. (2016). Enhancing the Quality of Computer Science Education with MOOCs in Sub-Saharan Africa. In J. Keengwe & G. Onchwari (Eds.), *Handbook of Research on Active Learning and the Flipped Classroom Model in the Digital Age* (pp. 366–377). Hershey, PA: IGI Global. doi:10.4018/978-1-4666-9680-8.ch019

Mukul, M. K., & Bhattaharyya, S. (2017). Brain-Machine Interface: Human-Computer Interaction. In E. Noughabi, B. Raahemi, A. Albadvi, & B. Far (Eds.), *Handbook of Research on Data Science for Effective Healthcare Practice and Administration* (pp. 417–443). Hershey, PA: IGI Global. doi:10.4018/978-1-5225-2515-8.ch018

Na, L. (2017). Library and Information Science Education and Graduate Programs in Academic Libraries. In L. Ruan, Q. Zhu, & Y. Ye (Eds.), *Academic Library Development and Administration in China* (pp. 218–229). Hershey, PA: IGI Global. doi:10.4018/978-1-5225-0550-1.ch013

Nabavi, A., Taghavi-Fard, M. T., Hanafizadeh, P., & Taghva, M. R. (2016). Information Technology Continuance Intention: A Systematic Literature Review. *International Journal of E-Business Research*, *12*(1), 58–95. doi:10.4018/IJEBR.2016010104

Nath, R., & Murthy, V. N. (2018). What Accounts for the Differences in Internet Diffusion Rates Around the World? In M. Khosrow-Pour, D.B.A. (Ed.), Encyclopedia of Information Science and Technology, Fourth Edition (pp. 8095-8104). Hershey, PA: IGI Global. doi:10.4018/978-1-5225-2255-3.ch705

Nedelko, Z., & Potocan, V. (2018). The Role of Emerging Information Technologies for Supporting Supply Chain Management. In M. Khosrow-Pour, D.B.A. (Ed.), Encyclopedia of Information Science and Technology, Fourth Edition (pp. 5559-5569). Hershey, PA: IGI Global. doi:10.4018/978-1-5225-2255-3.ch483

Ngafeeson, M. N. (2018). User Resistance to Health Information Technology. In M. Khosrow-Pour, D.B.A. (Ed.), Encyclopedia of Information Science and Technology, Fourth Edition (pp. 3816-3825). Hershey, PA: IGI Global. doi:10.4018/978-1-5225-2255-3.ch331

Nozari, H., Najafi, S. E., Jafari-Eskandari, M., & Aliahmadi, A. (2016). Providing a Model for Virtual Project Management with an Emphasis on IT Projects. In C. Graham (Ed.), *Strategic Management and Leadership for Systems Development in Virtual Spaces* (pp. 43–63). Hershey, PA: IGI Global. doi:10.4018/978-1-4666-9688-4.ch003

Nurdin, N., Stockdale, R., & Scheepers, H. (2016). Influence of Organizational Factors in the Sustainability of E-Government: A Case Study of Local E-Government in Indonesia. In I. Sodhi (Ed.), *Trends, Prospects, and Challenges in Asian E-Governance* (pp. 281–323). Hershey, PA: IGI Global. doi:10.4018/978-1-4666-9536-8.ch014

Odagiri, K. (2017). Introduction of Individual Technology to Constitute the Current Internet. In *Strategic Policy-Based Network Management in Contemporary Organizations* (pp. 20–96). Hershey, PA: IGI Global. doi:10.4018/978-1-68318-003-6.ch003

Okike, E. U. (2018). Computer Science and Prison Education. In I. Biao (Ed.), *Strategic Learning Ideologies in Prison Education Programs* (pp. 246–264). Hershey, PA: IGI Global. doi:10.4018/978-1-5225-2909-5.ch012

Olelewe, C. J., & Nwafor, I. P. (2017). Level of Computer Appreciation Skills Acquired for Sustainable Development by Secondary School Students in Nsukka LGA of Enugu State, Nigeria. In C. Ayo & V. Mbarika (Eds.), *Sustainable ICT Adoption and Integration for Socio-Economic Development* (pp. 214–233). Hershey, PA: IGI Global. doi:10.4018/978-1-5225-2565-3.ch010

Oliveira, M., Maçada, A. C., Curado, C., & Nodari, F. (2017). Infrastructure Profiles and Knowledge Sharing. *International Journal of Technology and Human Interaction*, *13*(3), 1–12. doi:10.4018/IJTHI.2017070101

Otarkhani, A., Shokouhyar, S., & Pour, S. S. (2017). Analyzing the Impact of Governance of Enterprise IT on Hospital Performance: Tehran's (Iran) Hospitals – A Case Study. *International Journal of Healthcare Information Systems and Informatics*, *12*(3), 1–20. doi:10.4018/IJHISI.2017070101

Otunla, A. O., & Amuda, C. O. (2018). Nigerian Undergraduate Students' Computer Competencies and Use of Information Technology Tools and Resources for Study Skills and Habits' Enhancement. In M. Khosrow-Pour, D.B.A. (Ed.), Encyclopedia of Information Science and Technology, Fourth Edition (pp. 2303-2313). Hershey, PA: IGI Global. doi:10.4018/978-1-5225-2255-3.ch200

Özçınar, H. (2018). A Brief Discussion on Incentives and Barriers to Computational Thinking Education. In H. Ozcinar, G. Wong, & H. Ozturk (Eds.), *Teaching Computational Thinking in Primary Education* (pp. 1–17). Hershey, PA: IGI Global. doi:10.4018/978-1-5225-3200-2.ch001

Pandey, J. M., Garg, S., Mishra, P., & Mishra, B. P. (2017). Computer Based Psychological Interventions: Subject to the Efficacy of Psychological Services. *International Journal of Computers in Clinical Practice*, *2*(1), 25–33. doi:10.4018/IJCCP.2017010102

Parry, V. K., & Lind, M. L. (2016). Alignment of Business Strategy and Information Technology Considering Information Technology Governance, Project Portfolio Control, and Risk Management. *International Journal of Information Technology Project Management*, *7*(4), 21–37. doi:10.4018/IJITPM.2016100102

Patro, C. (2017). Impulsion of Information Technology on Human Resource Practices. In P. Ordóñez de Pablos (Ed.), *Managerial Strategies and Solutions for Business Success in Asia* (pp. 231–254). Hershey, PA: IGI Global. doi:10.4018/978-1-5225-1886-0.ch013

Patro, C. S., & Raghunath, K. M. (2017). Information Technology Paraphernalia for Supply Chain Management Decisions. In M. Tavana (Ed.), *Enterprise Information Systems and the Digitalization of Business Functions* (pp. 294–320). Hershey, PA: IGI Global. doi:10.4018/978-1-5225-2382-6.ch014

Paul, P. K. (2016). Cloud Computing: An Agent of Promoting Interdisciplinary Sciences, Especially Information Science and I-Schools – Emerging Techno-Educational Scenario. In L. Chao (Ed.), *Handbook of Research on Cloud-Based STEM Education for Improved Learning Outcomes* (pp. 247–258). Hershey, PA: IGI Global. doi:10.4018/978-1-4666-9924-3.ch016

Paul, P. K. (2018). The Context of IST for Solid Information Retrieval and Infrastructure Building: Study of Developing Country. *International Journal of Information Retrieval Research*, 8(1), 86–100. doi:10.4018/IJIRR.2018010106

Paul, P. K., & Chatterjee, D. (2018). iSchools Promoting "Information Science and Technology" (IST) Domain Towards Community, Business, and Society With Contemporary Worldwide Trend and Emerging Potentialities in India. In M. Khosrow-Pour, D.B.A. (Ed.), Encyclopedia of Information Science and Technology, Fourth Edition (pp. 4723-4735). Hershey, PA: IGI Global. doi:10.4018/978-1-5225-2255-3.ch410

Pessoa, C. R., & Marques, M. E. (2017). Information Technology and Communication Management in Supply Chain Management. In G. Jamil, A. Soares, & C. Pessoa (Eds.), *Handbook of Research on Information Management for Effective Logistics and Supply Chains* (pp. 23–33). Hershey, PA: IGI Global. doi:10.4018/978-1-5225-0973-8.ch002

Pineda, R. G. (2016). Where the Interaction Is Not: Reflections on the Philosophy of Human-Computer Interaction. *International Journal of Art, Culture and Design Technologies*, 5(1), 1–12. doi:10.4018/IJACDT.2016010101

Pineda, R. G. (2018). Remediating Interaction: Towards a Philosophy of Human-Computer Relationship. In M. Khosrow-Pour (Ed.), *Enhancing Art, Culture, and Design With Technological Integration* (pp. 75–98). Hershey, PA: IGI Global. doi:10.4018/978-1-5225-5023-5.ch004

Poikela, P., & Vuojärvi, H. (2016). Learning ICT-Mediated Communication through Computer-Based Simulations. In M. Cruz-Cunha, I. Miranda, R. Martinho, & R. Rijo (Eds.), *Encyclopedia of E-Health and Telemedicine* (pp. 674–687). Hershey, PA: IGI Global. doi:10.4018/978-1-4666-9978-6.ch052

Qian, Y. (2017). Computer Simulation in Higher Education: Affordances, Opportunities, and Outcomes. In P. Vu, S. Fredrickson, & C. Moore (Eds.), *Handbook of Research on Innovative Pedagogies and Technologies for Online Learning in Higher Education* (pp. 236–262). Hershey, PA: IGI Global. doi:10.4018/978-1-5225-1851-8.ch011

Radant, O., Colomo-Palacios, R., & Stantchev, V. (2016). Factors for the Management of Scarce Human Resources and Highly Skilled Employees in IT-Departments: A Systematic Review. *Journal of Information Technology Research*, *9*(1), 65–82. doi:10.4018/JITR.2016010105

Rahman, N. (2016). Toward Achieving Environmental Sustainability in the Computer Industry. *International Journal of Green Computing*, *7*(1), 37–54. doi:10.4018/IJGC.2016010103

Rahman, N. (2017). Lessons from a Successful Data Warehousing Project Management. *International Journal of Information Technology Project Management*, *8*(4), 30–45. doi:10.4018/IJITPM.2017100103

Rahman, N. (2018). Environmental Sustainability in the Computer Industry for Competitive Advantage. In M. Khosrow-Pour (Ed.), *Green Computing Strategies for Competitive Advantage and Business Sustainability* (pp. 110–130). Hershey, PA: IGI Global. doi:10.4018/978-1-5225-5017-4.ch006

Rajh, A., & Pavetic, T. (2017). Computer Generated Description as the Required Digital Competence in Archival Profession. *International Journal of Digital Literacy and Digital Competence*, *8*(1), 36–49. doi:10.4018/IJDLDC.2017010103

Raman, A., & Goyal, D. P. (2017). Extending IMPLEMENT Framework for Enterprise Information Systems Implementation to Information System Innovation. In M. Tavana (Ed.), *Enterprise Information Systems and the Digitalization of Business Functions* (pp. 137–177). Hershey, PA: IGI Global. doi:10.4018/978-1-5225-2382-6.ch007

Rao, Y. S., Rauta, A. K., Saini, H., & Panda, T. C. (2017). Mathematical Model for Cyber Attack in Computer Network. *International Journal of Business Data Communications and Networking*, *13*(1), 58–65. doi:10.4018/IJBDCN.2017010105

Rapaport, W. J. (2018). Syntactic Semantics and the Proper Treatment of Computationalism. In M. Danesi (Ed.), *Empirical Research on Semiotics and Visual Rhetoric* (pp. 128–176). Hershey, PA: IGI Global. doi:10.4018/978-1-5225-5622-0.ch007

Raut, R., Priyadarshinee, P., & Jha, M. (2017). Understanding the Mediation Effect of Cloud Computing Adoption in Indian Organization: Integrating TAM-TOE- Risk Model. *International Journal of Service Science, Management, Engineering, and Technology*, 8(3), 40–59. doi:10.4018/IJSSMET.2017070103

Regan, E. A., & Wang, J. (2016). Realizing the Value of EHR Systems Critical Success Factors. *International Journal of Healthcare Information Systems and Informatics*, 11(3), 1–18. doi:10.4018/IJHISI.2016070101

Rezaie, S., Mirabedini, S. J., & Abtahi, A. (2018). Designing a Model for Implementation of Business Intelligence in the Banking Industry. *International Journal of Enterprise Information Systems*, 14(1), 77–103. doi:10.4018/IJEIS.2018010105

Rezende, D. A. (2016). Digital City Projects: Information and Public Services Offered by Chicago (USA) and Curitiba (Brazil). *International Journal of Knowledge Society Research*, 7(3), 16–30. doi:10.4018/IJKSR.2016070102

Rezende, D. A. (2018). Strategic Digital City Projects: Innovative Information and Public Services Offered by Chicago (USA) and Curitiba (Brazil). In M. Lytras, L. Daniela, & A. Visvizi (Eds.), *Enhancing Knowledge Discovery and Innovation in the Digital Era* (pp. 204–223). Hershey, PA: IGI Global. doi:10.4018/978-1-5225-4191-2.ch012

Riabov, V. V. (2016). Teaching Online Computer-Science Courses in LMS and Cloud Environment. *International Journal of Quality Assurance in Engineering and Technology Education*, 5(4), 12–41. doi:10.4018/IJQAETE.2016100102

Ricordel, V., Wang, J., Da Silva, M. P., & Le Callet, P. (2016). 2D and 3D Visual Attention for Computer Vision: Concepts, Measurement, and Modeling. In R. Pal (Ed.), *Innovative Research in Attention Modeling and Computer Vision Applications* (pp. 1–44). Hershey, PA: IGI Global. doi:10.4018/978-1-4666-8723-3.ch001

Rodriguez, A., Rico-Diaz, A. J., Rabuñal, J. R., & Gestal, M. (2017). Fish Tracking with Computer Vision Techniques: An Application to Vertical Slot Fishways. In M. S., & V. V. (Eds.), *Multi-Core Computer Vision and Image Processing for Intelligent Applications* (pp. 74-104). Hershey, PA: IGI Global. doi:10.4018/978-1-5225-0889-2.ch003

Romero, J. A. (2018). Sustainable Advantages of Business Value of Information Technology. In M. Khosrow-Pour, D.B.A. (Ed.), Encyclopedia of Information Science and Technology, Fourth Edition (pp. 923-929). Hershey, PA: IGI Global. doi:10.4018/978-1-5225-2255-3.ch079

Romero, J. A. (2018). The Always-On Business Model and Competitive Advantage. In N. Bajgoric (Ed.), *Always-On Enterprise Information Systems for Modern Organizations* (pp. 23–40). Hershey, PA: IGI Global. doi:10.4018/978-1-5225-3704-5.ch002

Rosen, Y. (2018). Computer Agent Technologies in Collaborative Learning and Assessment. In M. Khosrow-Pour, D.B.A. (Ed.), Encyclopedia of Information Science and Technology, Fourth Edition (pp. 2402-2410). Hershey, PA: IGI Global. doi:10.4018/978-1-5225-2255-3.ch209

Rosen, Y., & Mosharraf, M. (2016). Computer Agent Technologies in Collaborative Assessments. In Y. Rosen, S. Ferrara, & M. Mosharraf (Eds.), *Handbook of Research on Technology Tools for Real-World Skill Development* (pp. 319–343). Hershey, PA: IGI Global. doi:10.4018/978-1-4666-9441-5.ch012

Roy, D. (2018). Success Factors of Adoption of Mobile Applications in Rural India: Effect of Service Characteristics on Conceptual Model. In M. Khosrow-Pour (Ed.), *Green Computing Strategies for Competitive Advantage and Business Sustainability* (pp. 211–238). Hershey, PA: IGI Global. doi:10.4018/978-1-5225-5017-4.ch010

Ruffin, T. R. (2016). Health Information Technology and Change. In V. Wang (Ed.), *Handbook of Research on Advancing Health Education through Technology* (pp. 259–285). Hershey, PA: IGI Global. doi:10.4018/978-1-4666-9494-1.ch012

Ruffin, T. R. (2016). Health Information Technology and Quality Management. *International Journal of Information Communication Technologies and Human Development*, 8(4), 56–72. doi:10.4018/IJICTHD.2016100105

Ruffin, T. R., & Hawkins, D. P. (2018). Trends in Health Care Information Technology and Informatics. In M. Khosrow-Pour, D.B.A. (Ed.), Encyclopedia of Information Science and Technology, Fourth Edition (pp. 3805-3815). Hershey, PA: IGI Global. doi:10.4018/978-1-5225-2255-3.ch330

Safari, M. R., & Jiang, Q. (2018). The Theory and Practice of IT Governance Maturity and Strategies Alignment: Evidence From Banking Industry. *Journal of Global Information Management*, 26(2), 127–146. doi:10.4018/JGIM.2018040106

Sahin, H. B., & Anagun, S. S. (2018). Educational Computer Games in Math Teaching: A Learning Culture. In E. Toprak & E. Kumtepe (Eds.), *Supporting Multiculturalism in Open and Distance Learning Spaces* (pp. 249–280). Hershey, PA: IGI Global. doi:10.4018/978-1-5225-3076-3.ch013

Sanna, A., & Valpreda, F. (2017). An Assessment of the Impact of a Collaborative Didactic Approach and Students' Background in Teaching Computer Animation. *International Journal of Information and Communication Technology Education,* *13*(4), 1–16. doi:10.4018/IJICTE.2017100101

Savita, K., Dominic, P., & Ramayah, T. (2016). The Drivers, Practices and Outcomes of Green Supply Chain Management: Insights from ISO14001 Manufacturing Firms in Malaysia. *International Journal of Information Systems and Supply Chain Management, 9*(2), 35–60. doi:10.4018/IJISSCM.2016040103

Scott, A., Martin, A., & McAlear, F. (2017). Enhancing Participation in Computer Science among Girls of Color: An Examination of a Preparatory AP Computer Science Intervention. In Y. Rankin & J. Thomas (Eds.), *Moving Students of Color from Consumers to Producers of Technology* (pp. 62–84). Hershey, PA: IGI Global. doi:10.4018/978-1-5225-2005-4.ch004

Shahsavandi, E., Mayah, G., & Rahbari, H. (2016). Impact of E-Government on Transparency and Corruption in Iran. In I. Sodhi (Ed.), *Trends, Prospects, and Challenges in Asian E-Governance* (pp. 75–94). Hershey, PA: IGI Global. doi:10.4018/978-1-4666-9536-8.ch004

Siddoo, V., & Wongsai, N. (2017). Factors Influencing the Adoption of ISO/IEC 29110 in Thai Government Projects: A Case Study. *International Journal of Information Technologies and Systems Approach, 10*(1), 22–44. doi:10.4018/IJITSA.2017010102

Sidorkina, I., & Rybakov, A. (2016). Computer-Aided Design as Carrier of Set Development Changes System in E-Course Engineering. In V. Mkrttchian, A. Bershadsky, A. Bozhday, M. Kataev, & S. Kataev (Eds.), *Handbook of Research on Estimation and Control Techniques in E-Learning Systems* (pp. 500–515). Hershey, PA: IGI Global. doi:10.4018/978-1-4666-9489-7.ch035

Sidorkina, I., & Rybakov, A. (2016). Creating Model of E-Course: As an Object of Computer-Aided Design. In V. Mkrttchian, A. Bershadsky, A. Bozhday, M. Kataev, & S. Kataev (Eds.), *Handbook of Research on Estimation and Control Techniques in E-Learning Systems* (pp. 286–297). Hershey, PA: IGI Global. doi:10.4018/978-1-4666-9489-7.ch019

Simões, A. (2017). Using Game Frameworks to Teach Computer Programming. In R. Alexandre Peixoto de Queirós & M. Pinto (Eds.), *Gamification-Based E-Learning Strategies for Computer Programming Education* (pp. 221–236). Hershey, PA: IGI Global. doi:10.4018/978-1-5225-1034-5.ch010

Sllame, A. M. (2017). Integrating LAB Work With Classes in Computer Network Courses. In H. Alphin Jr, R. Chan, & J. Lavine (Eds.), *The Future of Accessibility in International Higher Education* (pp. 253–275). Hershey, PA: IGI Global. doi:10.4018/978-1-5225-2560-8.ch015

Smirnov, A., Ponomarev, A., Shilov, N., Kashevnik, A., & Teslya, N. (2018). Ontology-Based Human-Computer Cloud for Decision Support: Architecture and Applications in Tourism. *International Journal of Embedded and Real-Time Communication Systems*, *9*(1), 1–19. doi:10.4018/IJERTCS.2018010101

Smith-Ditizio, A. A., & Smith, A. D. (2018). Computer Fraud Challenges and Its Legal Implications. In M. Khosrow-Pour, D.B.A. (Ed.), Encyclopedia of Information Science and Technology, Fourth Edition (pp. 4837-4848). Hershey, PA: IGI Global. doi:10.4018/978-1-5225-2255-3.ch419

Sohani, S. S. (2016). Job Shadowing in Information Technology Projects: A Source of Competitive Advantage. *International Journal of Information Technology Project Management*, *7*(1), 47–57. doi:10.4018/IJITPM.2016010104

Sosnin, P. (2018). Figuratively Semantic Support of Human-Computer Interactions. In *Experience-Based Human-Computer Interactions: Emerging Research and Opportunities* (pp. 244–272). Hershey, PA: IGI Global. doi:10.4018/978-1-5225-2987-3.ch008

Spinelli, R., & Benevolo, C. (2016). From Healthcare Services to E-Health Applications: A Delivery System-Based Taxonomy. In A. Dwivedi (Ed.), *Reshaping Medical Practice and Care with Health Information Systems* (pp. 205–245). Hershey, PA: IGI Global. doi:10.4018/978-1-4666-9870-3.ch007

Srinivasan, S. (2016). Overview of Clinical Trial and Pharmacovigilance Process and Areas of Application of Computer System. In P. Chakraborty & A. Nagal (Eds.), *Software Innovations in Clinical Drug Development and Safety* (pp. 1–13). Hershey, PA: IGI Global. doi:10.4018/978-1-4666-8726-4.ch001

Srisawasdi, N. (2016). Motivating Inquiry-Based Learning Through a Combination of Physical and Virtual Computer-Based Laboratory Experiments in High School Science. In M. Urban & D. Falvo (Eds.), *Improving K-12 STEM Education Outcomes through Technological Integration* (pp. 108–134). Hershey, PA: IGI Global. doi:10.4018/978-1-4666-9616-7.ch006

Stavridi, S. V., & Hamada, D. R. (2016). Children and Youth Librarians: Competencies Required in Technology-Based Environment. In J. Yap, M. Perez, M. Ayson, & G. Entico (Eds.), *Special Library Administration, Standardization and Technological Integration* (pp. 25–50). Hershey, PA: IGI Global. doi:10.4018/978-1-4666-9542-9.ch002

Sung, W., Ahn, J., Kai, S. M., Choi, A., & Black, J. B. (2016). Incorporating Touch-Based Tablets into Classroom Activities: Fostering Children's Computational Thinking through iPad Integrated Instruction. In D. Mentor (Ed.), *Handbook of Research on Mobile Learning in Contemporary Classrooms* (pp. 378–406). Hershey, PA: IGI Global. doi:10.4018/978-1-5225-0251-7.ch019

Syväjärvi, A., Leinonen, J., Kivivirta, V., & Kesti, M. (2017). The Latitude of Information Management in Local Government: Views of Local Government Managers. *International Journal of Electronic Government Research, 13*(1), 69–85. doi:10.4018/IJEGR.2017010105

Tanque, M., & Foxwell, H. J. (2018). Big Data and Cloud Computing: A Review of Supply Chain Capabilities and Challenges. In A. Prasad (Ed.), *Exploring the Convergence of Big Data and the Internet of Things* (pp. 1–28). Hershey, PA: IGI Global. doi:10.4018/978-1-5225-2947-7.ch001

Teixeira, A., Gomes, A., & Orvalho, J. G. (2017). Auditory Feedback in a Computer Game for Blind People. In T. Issa, P. Kommers, T. Issa, P. Isaías, & T. Issa (Eds.), *Smart Technology Applications in Business Environments* (pp. 134–158). Hershey, PA: IGI Global. doi:10.4018/978-1-5225-2492-2.ch007

Thompson, N., McGill, T., & Murray, D. (2018). Affect-Sensitive Computer Systems. In M. Khosrow-Pour, D.B.A. (Ed.), Encyclopedia of Information Science and Technology, Fourth Edition (pp. 4124-4135). Hershey, PA: IGI Global. doi:10.4018/978-1-5225-2255-3.ch357

Trad, A., & Kalpić, D. (2016). The E-Business Transformation Framework for E-Commerce Control and Monitoring Pattern. In I. Lee (Ed.), *Encyclopedia of E-Commerce Development, Implementation, and Management* (pp. 754–777). Hershey, PA: IGI Global. doi:10.4018/978-1-4666-9787-4.ch053

Triberti, S., Brivio, E., & Galimberti, C. (2018). On Social Presence: Theories, Methodologies, and Guidelines for the Innovative Contexts of Computer-Mediated Learning. In M. Marmon (Ed.), *Enhancing Social Presence in Online Learning Environments* (pp. 20–41). Hershey, PA: IGI Global. doi:10.4018/978-1-5225-3229-3.ch002

Tripathy, B. K. T. R., S., & Mohanty, R. K. (2018). Memetic Algorithms and Their Applications in Computer Science. In S. Dash, B. Tripathy, & A. Rahman (Eds.), Handbook of Research on Modeling, Analysis, and Application of Nature-Inspired Metaheuristic Algorithms (pp. 73-93). Hershey, PA: IGI Global. doi:10.4018/978-1-5225-2857-9.ch004

Turulja, L., & Bajgoric, N. (2017). Human Resource Management IT and Global Economy Perspective: Global Human Resource Information Systems. In M. Khosrow-Pour (Ed.), *Handbook of Research on Technology Adoption, Social Policy, and Global Integration* (pp. 377–394). Hershey, PA: IGI Global. doi:10.4018/978-1-5225-2668-1.ch018

Unwin, D. W., Sanzogni, L., & Sandhu, K. (2017). Developing and Measuring the Business Case for Health Information Technology. In K. Moahi, K. Bwalya, & P. Sebina (Eds.), *Health Information Systems and the Advancement of Medical Practice in Developing Countries* (pp. 262–290). Hershey, PA: IGI Global. doi:10.4018/978-1-5225-2262-1.ch015

Vadhanam, B. R. S., M., Sugumaran, V., V., V., & Ramalingam, V. V. (2017). Computer Vision Based Classification on Commercial Videos. In M. S., & V. V. (Eds.), Multi-Core Computer Vision and Image Processing for Intelligent Applications (pp. 105-135). Hershey, PA: IGI Global. doi:10.4018/978-1-5225-0889-2.ch004

Valverde, R., Torres, B., & Motaghi, H. (2018). A Quantum NeuroIS Data Analytics Architecture for the Usability Evaluation of Learning Management Systems. In S. Bhattacharyya (Ed.), *Quantum-Inspired Intelligent Systems for Multimedia Data Analysis* (pp. 277–299). Hershey, PA: IGI Global. doi:10.4018/978-1-5225-5219-2.ch009

Vassilis, E. (2018). Learning and Teaching Methodology: "1:1 Educational Computing. In K. Koutsopoulos, K. Doukas, & Y. Kotsanis (Eds.), *Handbook of Research on Educational Design and Cloud Computing in Modern Classroom Settings* (pp. 122–155). Hershey, PA: IGI Global. doi:10.4018/978-1-5225-3053-4.ch007

Wadhwani, A. K., Wadhwani, S., & Singh, T. (2016). Computer Aided Diagnosis System for Breast Cancer Detection. In Y. Morsi, A. Shukla, & C. Rathore (Eds.), *Optimizing Assistive Technologies for Aging Populations* (pp. 378–395). Hershey, PA: IGI Global. doi:10.4018/978-1-4666-9530-6.ch015

Wang, L., Wu, Y., & Hu, C. (2016). English Teachers' Practice and Perspectives on Using Educational Computer Games in EIL Context. *International Journal of Technology and Human Interaction, 12*(3), 33–46. doi:10.4018/IJTHI.2016070103

Watfa, M. K., Majeed, H., & Salahuddin, T. (2016). Computer Based E-Healthcare Clinical Systems: A Comprehensive Survey. *International Journal of Privacy and Health Information Management, 4*(1), 50–69. doi:10.4018/IJPHIM.2016010104

Weeger, A., & Haase, U. (2016). Taking up Three Challenges to Business-IT Alignment Research by the Use of Activity Theory. *International Journal of IT/Business Alignment and Governance, 7*(2), 1-21. doi:10.4018/IJITBAG.2016070101

Wexler, B. E. (2017). Computer-Presented and Physical Brain-Training Exercises for School Children: Improving Executive Functions and Learning. In B. Dubbels (Ed.), *Transforming Gaming and Computer Simulation Technologies across Industries* (pp. 206–224). Hershey, PA: IGI Global. doi:10.4018/978-1-5225-1817-4.ch012

Williams, D. M., Gani, M. O., Addo, I. D., Majumder, A. J., Tamma, C. P., Wang, M., ... Chu, C. (2016). Challenges in Developing Applications for Aging Populations. In Y. Morsi, A. Shukla, & C. Rathore (Eds.), *Optimizing Assistive Technologies for Aging Populations* (pp. 1–21). Hershey, PA: IGI Global. doi:10.4018/978-1-4666-9530-6.ch001

Wimble, M., Singh, H., & Phillips, B. (2018). Understanding Cross-Level Interactions of Firm-Level Information Technology and Industry Environment: A Multilevel Model of Business Value. *Information Resources Management Journal, 31*(1), 1–20. doi:10.4018/IRMJ.2018010101

Wimmer, H., Powell, L., Kilgus, L., & Force, C. (2017). Improving Course Assessment via Web-based Homework. *International Journal of Online Pedagogy and Course Design, 7*(2), 1–19. doi:10.4018/IJOPCD.2017040101

Wong, Y. L., & Siu, K. W. (2018). Assessing Computer-Aided Design Skills. In M. Khosrow-Pour, D.B.A. (Ed.), Encyclopedia of Information Science and Technology, Fourth Edition (pp. 7382-7391). Hershey, PA: IGI Global. doi:10.4018/978-1-5225-2255-3.ch642

Wongsurawat, W., & Shrestha, V. (2018). Information Technology, Globalization, and Local Conditions: Implications for Entrepreneurs in Southeast Asia. In P. Ordóñez de Pablos (Ed.), *Management Strategies and Technology Fluidity in the Asian Business Sector* (pp. 163–176). Hershey, PA: IGI Global. doi:10.4018/978-1-5225-4056-4.ch010

Yang, Y., Zhu, X., Jin, C., & Li, J. J. (2018). Reforming Classroom Education Through a QQ Group: A Pilot Experiment at a Primary School in Shanghai. In H. Spires (Ed.), *Digital Transformation and Innovation in Chinese Education* (pp. 211–231). Hershey, PA: IGI Global. doi:10.4018/978-1-5225-2924-8.ch012

Yilmaz, R., Sezgin, A., Kurnaz, S., & Arslan, Y. Z. (2018). Object-Oriented Programming in Computer Science. In M. Khosrow-Pour, D.B.A. (Ed.), Encyclopedia of Information Science and Technology, Fourth Edition (pp. 7470-7480). Hershey, PA: IGI Global. doi:10.4018/978-1-5225-2255-3.ch650

Yu, L. (2018). From Teaching Software Engineering Locally and Globally to Devising an Internationalized Computer Science Curriculum. In S. Dikli, B. Etheridge, & R. Rawls (Eds.), *Curriculum Internationalization and the Future of Education* (pp. 293–320). Hershey, PA: IGI Global. doi:10.4018/978-1-5225-2791-6.ch016

Yuhua, F. (2018). Computer Information Library Clusters. In M. Khosrow-Pour, D.B.A. (Ed.), Encyclopedia of Information Science and Technology, Fourth Edition (pp. 4399-4403). Hershey, PA: IGI Global. doi:10.4018/978-1-5225-2255-3.ch382

Zare, M. A., Taghavi Fard, M. T., & Hanafizadeh, P. (2016). The Assessment of Outsourcing IT Services using DEA Technique: A Study of Application Outsourcing in Research Centers. *International Journal of Operations Research and Information Systems*, 7(1), 45–57. doi:10.4018/IJORIS.2016010104

Zhao, J., Wang, Q., Guo, J., Gao, L., & Yang, F. (2016). An Overview on Passive Image Forensics Technology for Automatic Computer Forgery. *International Journal of Digital Crime and Forensics*, 8(4), 14–25. doi:10.4018/IJDCF.2016100102

Zimeras, S. (2016). Computer Virus Models and Analysis in M-Health IT Systems: Computer Virus Models. In A. Moumtzoglou (Ed.), *M-Health Innovations for Patient-Centered Care* (pp. 284–297). Hershey, PA: IGI Global. doi:10.4018/978-1-4666-9861-1.ch014

Zlatanovska, K. (2016). Hacking and Hacktivism as an Information Communication System Threat. In M. Hadji-Janev & M. Bogdanoski (Eds.), *Handbook of Research on Civil Society and National Security in the Era of Cyber Warfare* (pp. 68–101). Hershey, PA: IGI Global. doi:10.4018/978-1-4666-8793-6.ch004

About the Contributors

Harshita Patel had a Ph.D. awarded entitled 'Efficient Computational Models for Classification of Imbalanced Data' in Dept. of Computer Applications, Maulana Azad National Institute of Technology Bhopal (M.P.) in November 2017. Self-motivated learner gives emphasis on conceptual teaching and fundamentals. Generates subject interest in students through motivation, creative thinking, positive thinking with CAN DO approach and good verbal & communication skills. Impart theoretical knowledge with emphasis on application knowledge associated with lab learning, experimental and innovative approach in teaching with success records.

* * *

Ankit Agrawal received his B.Tech. degree in Computer Science & Engineering from Uttar Pradesh Technical University, Lucknow, India, in 2009. From 2010-2013 he worked as an IT Programmer in NGOs. He received his M.E. degree in Information Security from Thapar University, Patiala, Punjab, India, in 2016. From 2016-2019, he worked as an Assistant Professor in an engineering college (PSIT kanpur) affiliated to AKTU. He is pursuing Ph.D. as a full time scholar at BITS, Pilani under the guidance of Dr. Ashutosh Bhatia, Assistant Professor, Department of Computer Science & Information Systems, BITS, Pialni. His major areas of interest are Computer Networks, Information Security, Cryptography and IOT security.

Taushif Anwar is a Ph.D. scholar in the Department computer science at Pondicherry University, Pondicherry, India. He received MCA degree from, Punjab Technical University and B.C.A degree from Jamia Hamdard University, New Delhi, India. His research interests include the area of Machine Learning, Data Mining and Recommender System.

Amit Bhagat has received his B.C.A and MCA degree in Computer Applications from Makhanlal Chaturvedi National University of Journal- ism, Madhya Pradesh in the year 2000 and 2003. He has done PhD from MANIT Bhopal in the year 2013. He is currently working as Assistant Professor in the Department of Mathematics and Computer Applications, Maulana Azad National Institute of Technology, Bhopal, Madhya Pradesh, India. His research interests include Data Mining, Neural Networks, Sentiment Analysis, Web Mining and Big Data.

Ashutosh Bhatia received his B.E. degree in Computer Science from Barkatullah University, Bhopal, India, in 2000. From 2001-2005 he worked as a scientist in Defence Research and Development Organization (DRDO), India. He received his M.E. degree in Computer Science from Indian Institute of Science (IISc), Bangalore, India, in 2007. From 2007-2010, he worked as a research engineer in Samsung India Software Operations (SISO). He received the Ph.D. degree in Computer Science from Indian Institute of Science, Bangalore, India, in 2016. Currently, he is working as an Assistant Professor in the Department of Computer Science and Information Systems, BITS, Pilani, India. His research interests include building new designs, protocols, algorithms, and theories that improve the robustness and performance of computer networks.

Manjula Bollarapu has completed her B.Tech. in Computer Science & Engineering in 2013 and she has received her M.Tech. degree in Computer Science & Technology in 2016 from JNTU, Kakinada. Currently she is working as an Assistant Professor in Computer Science & Engineering, K. L University, Guntur, India. She has published her post graduation thesis papers in the area of Networks and Cloud Computing. Her area of interest also include Machine Learning and Data Mining.

Dipti Chauhan is working as Associate Professor in the Department of Computer Science & Engineering at Prestige Institute of Engineering Management & Research, Indore. She completed her Ph.D. from Maulana Azad National Institute of Technology, Bhopal in 2016. She is having teaching & Research experience of 14.5 years. She is active researcher in the field of next generation networks & IPv6, Internet of Things & many more. She is IPv6 Certified Gold and Silver Network Engineer from IPv6 forum, University Sains Malaysia.

Mohd Azeem Faizi Noor is a research scholar in the computer science department at Jamia Millia Islamia, New Delhi, India. He completed dual degree M.C.A. and M.Tech. (NIE) from Pondicherry Central University, Puducherry, India. He received B.Sc degree in PCM from Shibli National PG College, Azamgarh, India. He cleared JRF-NET and UGC-NET (3 times). His research interests include Blockchain and steganography.

Thippa Reddy Gadekallu has received his B-Tech in Computer Science and Engineering from Nagarjuna University, India in the year 2003, M-Tech in Computer Science and Engineering from Anna University, India in the Year 2010, and Ph.D from VIT University, India in the year 2017. He is working as an Assistant professor (Senior) in VIT University, India. His research interests are Data Mining in Healthcare, Natural Language Processing, Knowledge Mining, Big Data Analytics, Internet of Things.

Jay Kumar Jain is working as an Associate Professor in the Department of Information of Technology at Sagar Institute of Research & Technology, Bhopal, India. He did his Ph. D. from Maulana Azad National Institute of Technology Bhopal in 2015. He is having a research as well as teaching experience of about 13 years. He has published many research papers in International/National Journal and Conferences. His research interests include Wireless Sensor Networks, Internet of Things and MANETs.

Sreelakshmi K. K. received her B.Tech degree in Computer Science and Engineering from Cochin University of Science and Technology (CUSAT), Kerala, India, in 2017. Currently doing her Masters in Computer Science and Engineering at BITS Pilani. Her research domains include Artificial Intelligence and Deep Learning, IoT and Network Security.

Rama Rao K. V. S. N. is working as a Professor in Koneru Lakshmaiah Education Foundation in Dept.of CSE. Had 20+ years of experience in academics and industry. International research experience at Australian university. His research interests include cyber security, machine learning and bioacoustics.

Ruth Ramya Kalangi is an Assistant Professor in department of Computer Science and Engineering, Koneru Lakshmaiah Education Founadtion, Guntur, Andhra Pradesh, India. Her Teaching experience is 15 years. She published 22 research papers in the areas of cyber security & cloud computing. Her research interests are Cloud Computing, Cyber Security, Biometrics, Network Security and Wireless Sensor Networks.

Rajesh Kaluri obtained B.Tech (2008) in CSE from St. Johns College of Engineering and Technology, JNTU, Hyderabad and completed M.Tech (2010) in CSE from ANU, Guntur. He received Ph.D (2017) from VIT University, Tamil Nadu. He has 8+ years of experience in teaching and currently, he is working as an Assistant Professor (senior) in School of Information Technology and Engineering, Vellore Institute of Technology. He works on Computer Vision, Human Computer Interaction and Visualization. His focus is on investigating how cognitive design principles can be used to improve the effectiveness of Indian sign language. The goals of this work are to discover the design principles and then instantiate them in both interactive and automated design tools. He was a Visiting Professor in Guangdong University of Technology, China. He is a reviewer for various international journals and his current research is in the area of computer vision and IoT.

Pushpendra Kumar is an Assistant Professor in the Department of Computer Science and Technology at Central University of Jharkhand, Ranchi, India. He received the Bachelor and Master degree in Computer Applications from B.N.M.U Madhepura (Bihar) in 2011 and R.G.P.V Bhopal (MP) in 2014 respectively. His area of interest includes Data Mining and Machine Learning.

Vinod Kumar has received the degree Bachelor of Science (PCM) from University of Allahabad, Uttar Pradesh-India in 2008, Master of Computer Applications in 2011 and Master of Technology (IT) in 2013. He has Qualified UGC-NET(Computer Science and Applications) in 2013. He has worked as a Project Fellow on Project "Network Simulation Testbed at MCTE, MHOW(MP)" in Indian Institute of Information Technology-Allahabad(U.P.) in Collaboration with Military College of Telecommunication Engineering(MCTE), Mhow (MP) funded by Army Technology Board. He joined as Assistant professor in Department School of Information Technology, MATS University, Raipur (C.G) in 2013 and served for two years. He is PhD in Computer Applications from Department of Computer Application,Maulana Azad National Institute of Technology(MANIT),Bhopal (MP).Currently, He is Working as assistant Professor in Department of Computer Applications, Madanapalle Institute of Technology & Science. He is active researcher in the field of Web Usage Mining, Machine Learning, Internet of Things, Big Data Analytics.

Kuruva Lakshmanna has received his Ph.D. in the year 2017 from VIT Vellore, India, B-Tech in Computer Science and Engineering from Sri Venkateswara University College of Engineering -Tirupathi, India in the year 2006, M-Tech in Computer Science and Engineering(Information Security) from National Institute of Technology Calicut, Kerala, India in the Year 2009. He is working as an Assistant professor - senior in VIT University, India. His research interests are Data Mining in DNA sequences, algorithms, Knowledge Mining, etc.

Kamalendu Pal is with the Department of Computer Science, School of Mathematics, Computer Science and Engineering, City University London. Kamalendu received his BSc (Hons) degree in Physics from Calcutta University, India, Postgraduate Diploma in Computer Science from Pune, India; MSc degree in Software Systems Technology from Sheffield University, Postgraduate Diploma in Artificial Intelligence from Kingston University, MPhil degree in Computer Science from University College London, and MBA degree from University of Hull, United Kingdom. He has published dozens of research papers in international journals and conferences. His research interests include knowledge-based systems, decision support systems, computer integrated design, software engineering, and service oriented computing. He is on the editorial board of international computer science journals. He is a member of the British Computer Society, the Institution of Engineering and Technology, and the IEEE Computer Society.

Harsha Patil is working as a Head of the computer science department of Ashoka center for business and computer studies, Her area of research is distributed database, Data Science, Machine learning.

Narendran Rajagopalan received the Masters degree from Sri Jayachamarajendra College of Engineering, Mysore, India in 2007. He completed Ph.D degree in the Department of Computer Science and Engineering at National Institute of Technology, Trichy, India in 2013 and is currently working as assistant professor in the department of computer science and engineering, National Institute of Technology, Puducherry. His research interests include Wireless Networking, Security, Quality of Service and Soft Computing.

Praveen Kumar Reddy M. is a Professor at School of Information Technology and Engineering, VIT University. He obtained his BTech in CSE from JNT University, A.P and MTech. in C.S.E. from VIT University, Vellore, Tamil Nadu, India. He produced more than 15 international/national publications Currently, Praveen Kumar Reddy is working in the area of energy aware applications for Internet of Things (IoT) and high-performance applications for Multi-Core Architectures.

Puneeta Rosmin has received her B.Sc. degree in Computer Science from Jiwaji University, Gwalior, Madhya Pradesh in 2005. She has received M.Sc. degree in 2007 from Jiwaji University, Gwalior, Madhya Pradesh and M.Phil. Degree from Jiwaji University, Gwalior, Madhya Pradesh.

Suvarna Sharma has received her B.Sc. degree in Computer Science from Jiwaji University, Gwalior, Madhya Pradesh in 2005. She has received M.Sc. degree in 2007 from Jiwaji University, Gwalior, Madhya Pradesh and M.Tech. Degree from Davv, Indore, Madhya Pradesh in year 2013. She is currently pursuing her Ph. D. degree from the Department of Mathematics and Computer Applications, Maulana Azad National Institute of Technology, Bhopal, Madhya Pradesh, India. Her research interests include Web Mining, Web Structure Mining and Web Crawling from Web Data.

Gotam Singh Lalotra is working as Assistant Professor in Govt. Degree College for Women affiliated to University of Jammu. He is active researcher in the field of Data Mining.

Padmavathi U. completed her Bachelors in Engineering in 2009 and Master in Engineering in 2011, both in Computer Science and Engineering from Annamalai University. Currently she is pursuing Ph.D in the department of Computer Science and Engineering at National Institute of Technology Puducherry. Her research interest include security, cloud computing, and blockchain technologies.

Index

A

B

C

D

Ensure Quality Research is Introduced to the Academic Community

Become an IGI Global Reviewer for Authored Book Projects

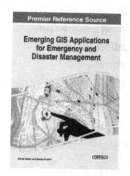

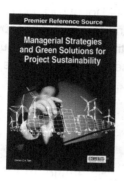

The overall success of an authored book project is dependent on quality and timely reviews.

In this competitive age of scholarly publishing, constructive and timely feedback significantly expedites the turnaround time of manuscripts from submission to acceptance, allowing the publication and discovery of forward-thinking research at a much more expeditious rate. Several IGI Global authored book projects are currently seeking highly-qualified experts in the field to fill vacancies on their respective editorial review boards:

Applications and Inquiries may be sent to:
development@igi-global.com

Applicants must have a doctorate (or an equivalent degree) as well as publishing and reviewing experience. Reviewers are asked to complete the open-ended evaluation questions with as much detail as possible in a timely, collegial, and constructive manner. All reviewers' tenures run for one-year terms on the editorial review boards and are expected to complete at least three reviews per term. Upon successful completion of this term, reviewers can be considered for an additional term.

If you have a colleague that may be interested in this opportunity, we encourage you to share this information with them.

IGI Global Proudly Partners With eContent Pro International

Receive a 25% Discount on all Editorial Services

Editorial Services

IGI Global expects all final manuscripts submitted for publication to be in their final form. This means they must be reviewed, revised, and professionally copy edited prior to their final submission. Not only does this support with accelerating the publication process, but it also ensures that the highest quality scholarly work can be disseminated.

English Language Copy Editing

Let eContent Pro International's expert copy editors perform edits on your manuscript to resolve spelling, punctuaion, grammar, syntax, flow, formatting issues and more.

Scientific and Scholarly Editing

Allow colleagues in your research area to examine the content of your manuscript and provide you with valuable feedback and suggestions before submission.

Figure, Table, Chart & Equation Conversions

Do you have poor quality figures? Do you need visual elements in your manuscript created or converted? A design expert can help!

Translation

Need your documjent translated into English? eContent Pro International's expert translators are fluent in English and more than 40 different languages.

Hear What Your Colleagues are Saying About Editorial Services Supported by IGI Global

"The service was very fast, very thorough, and very helpful in ensuring our chapter meets the criteria and requirements of the book's editors. I was quite impressed and happy with your service."

– Prof. Tom Brinthaupt,
Middle Tennessee State University, USA

"I found the work actually spectacular. The editing, formatting, and other checks were very thorough. The turnaround time was great as well. I will definitely use eContent Pro in the future."

– Nickanor Amwata, Lecturer,
University of Kurdistan Hawler, Iraq

"I was impressed that it was done timely, and wherever the content was not clear for the reader, the paper was improved with better readability for the audience."

– Prof. James Chilembwe,
Mzuzu University, Malawi

Email: customerservice@econtentpro.com   **www.igi-global.com/editorial-service-partners**

Printed in the United States
By Bookmasters